TEEN TITANS

YEAR ONE

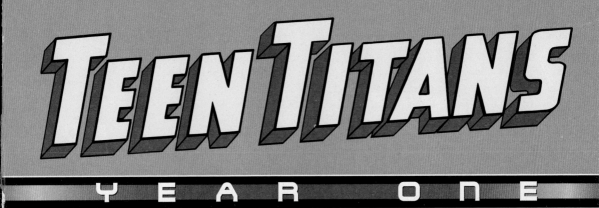

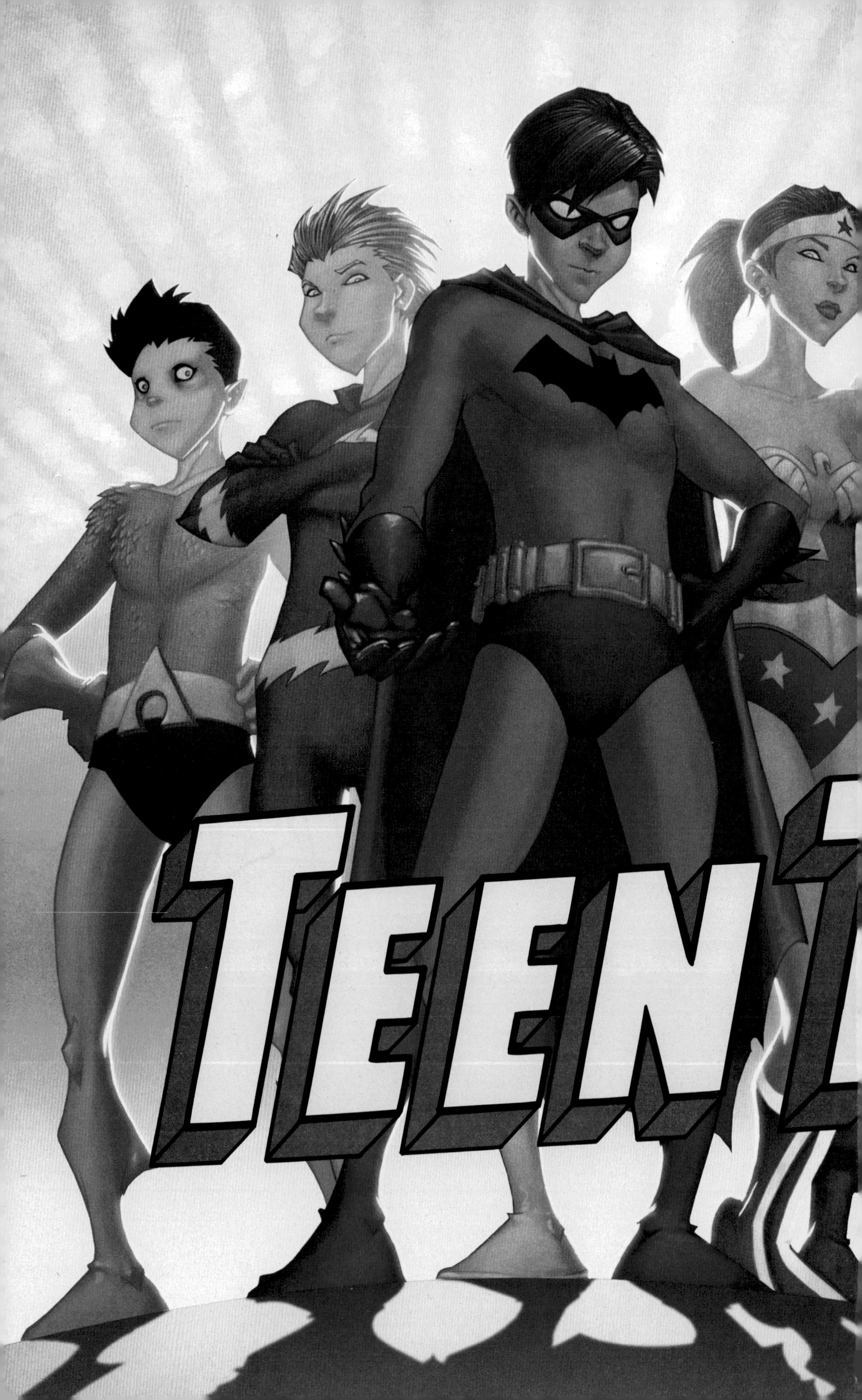
TEEN

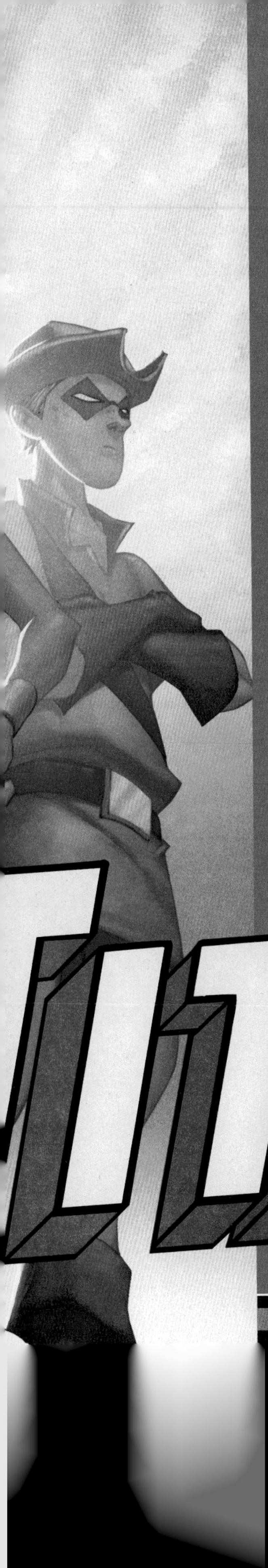

Written by
AMY WOLFRAM

Pencilled by
KARL KERSCHL

Inked by
SERGE LAPOINTE

Colored by
STEPH PERU
JOHN RAUCH

Lettered by
NICK J. NAPOLITANO

Original covers by
KARL KERSHL &
SERGE LAPOINTE

TITANS
YEAR ONE

In memory of Stephane Peru

[1981 – 2008]

Receiving the latest pages from Steph was always a bit like Christmas. *—Amy Wolfram*

Of all the work I've ever done, these pages are the ones I'm most proud of. *—Karl Kerschl*

We miss you... Je t'aime mon frere. *—Serge LaPointe*

Dan DiDio Senior VP-Executive Editor

Eddie Berganza Editor-original series

Adam Schlagman Assistant Editor-original series

Anton Kawasaki Editor-collected edition

Robbin Brosterman Senior Art Director

Paul Levitz President & Publisher

Georg Brewer VP-Design & DC Direct Creative

Richard Bruning Senior VP-Creative Director

Patrick Caldon Executive VP-Finance & Operations

Chris Caramalis VP-Finance

John Cunningham VP-Marketing

Terri Cunningham VP-Managing Editor

Amy Genkins Senior VP-Business & Legal Affairs

Alison Gill VP-Manufacturing

David Hyde VP-Publicity

Hank Kanalz VP-General Manager, WildStorm

Jim Lee Editorial Director-WildStorm

Gregory Noveck Senior VP-Creative Affairs

Sue Pohja VP-Book Trade Sales

Steve Rotterdam Senior VP-Sales & Marketing

Cheryl Rubin Senior VP-Brand Management

Alysse Soll VP-Advertising & Custom Publishing

Jeff Trojan VP-Business Development, DC Direct

Bob Wayne VP-Sales

Cover by Karl Kerschl & Serge LaPointe

TEEN TITANS: YEAR ONE

Published by DC Comics. Cover and compilation Copyright © 2008 DC Comics.
All Rights Reserved.

Originally published in single magazine form in TEEN TITANS: YEAR ONE #1-6.
Copyright © 2008 DC Comics. All Rights Reserved.
All characters, their distinctive likenesses and related elements featured in
this publication are trademarks of DC Comics.
The stories, characters and incidents featured in this publication are entirely fictional.
DC Comics does not read or accept unsolicited submissions of ideas, stories or artwork.

DC Comics, 1700 Broadway, New York, NY 10019
A Warner Bros. Entertainment Company
Printed in Canada. First Printing.
ISBN: 978-1-4012-1927-7

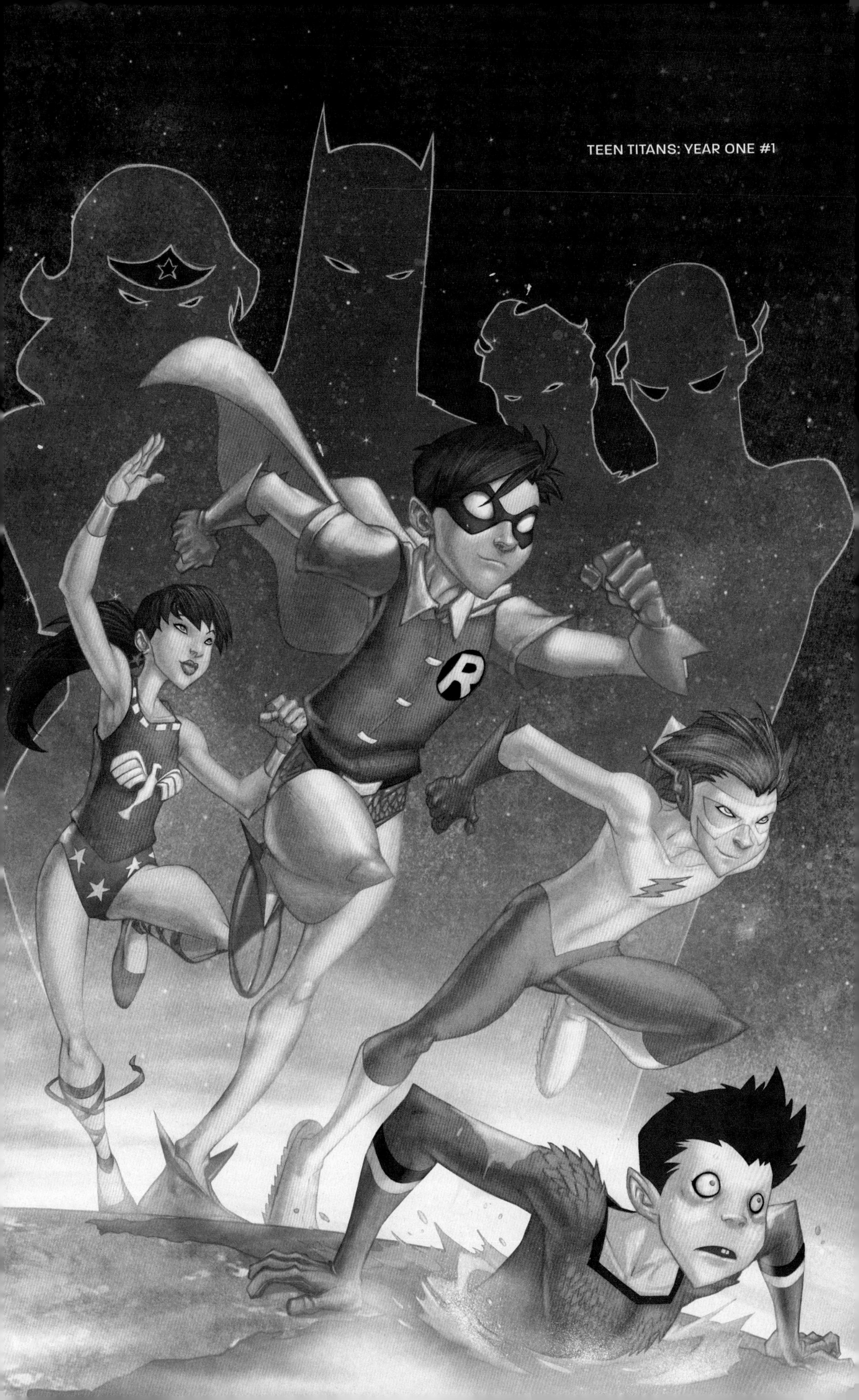
TEEN TITANS: YEAR ONE #1

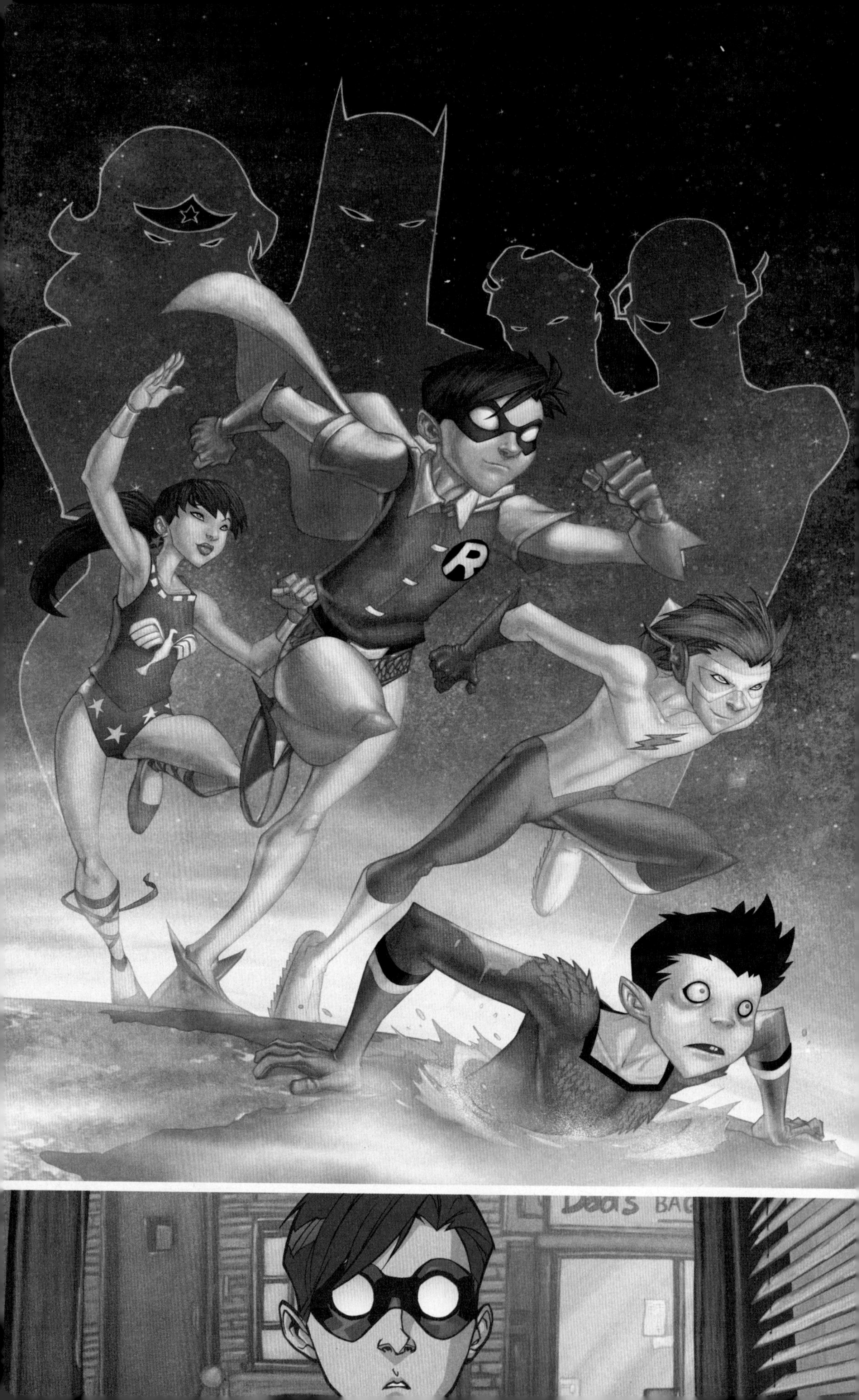

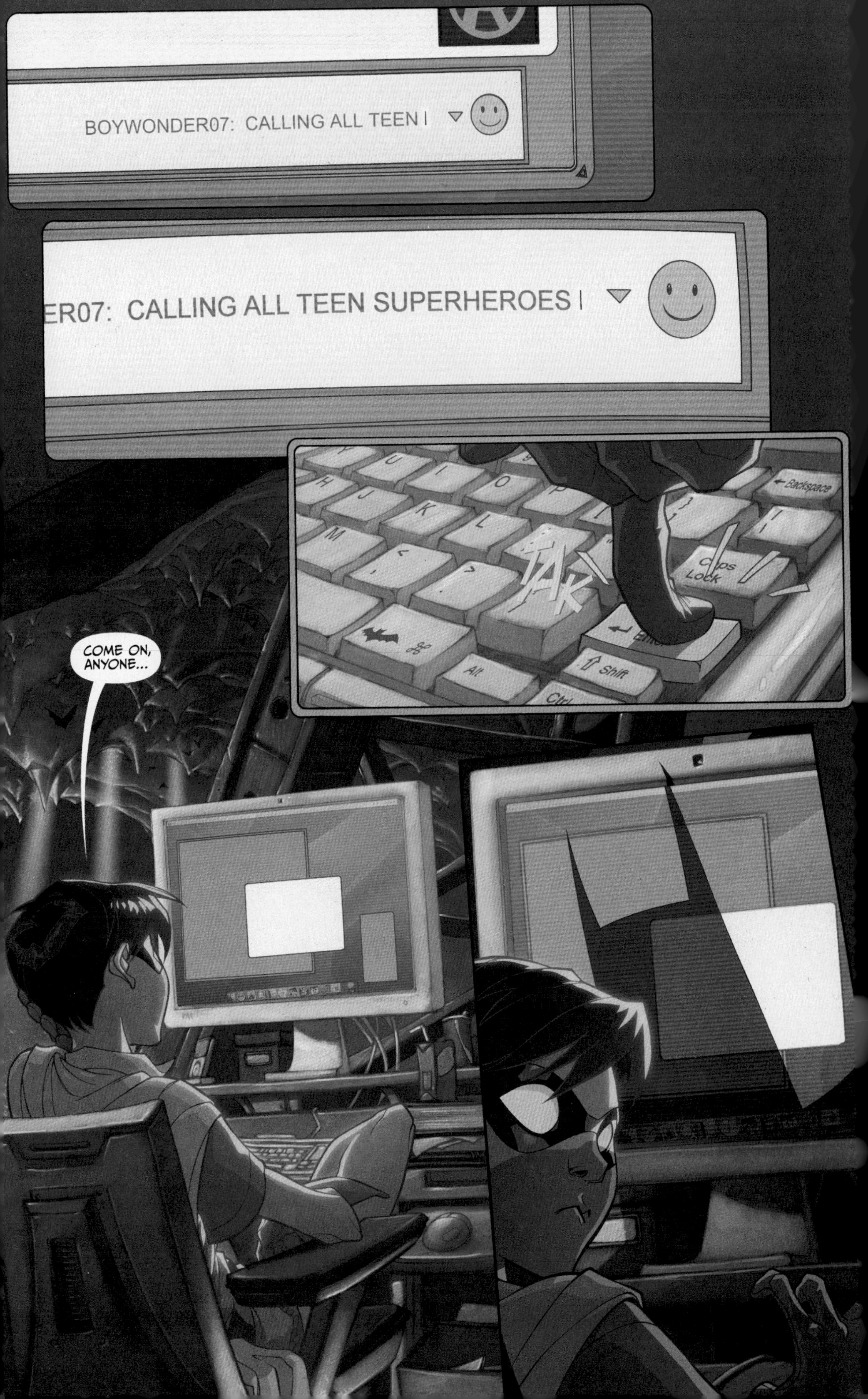
BOYWONDER07: CALLING ALL TEEN
ER07: CALLING ALL TEEN SUPERHEROES
TAK
COME ON, ANYONE...

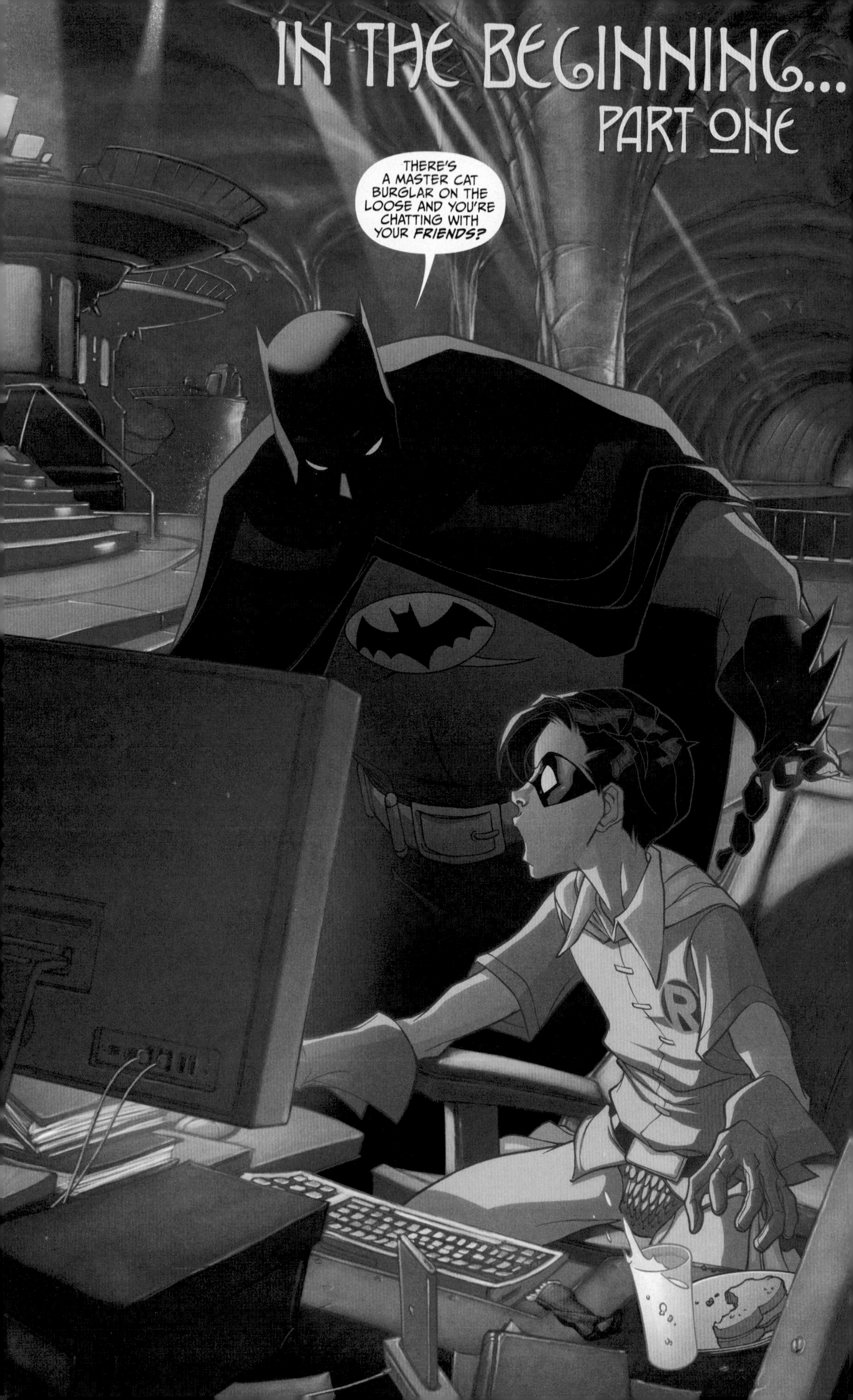
IN THE BEGINNING...
PART ONE
THERE'S A MASTER CAT BURGLAR ON THE LOOSE AND YOU'RE CHATTING WITH YOUR FRIENDS?

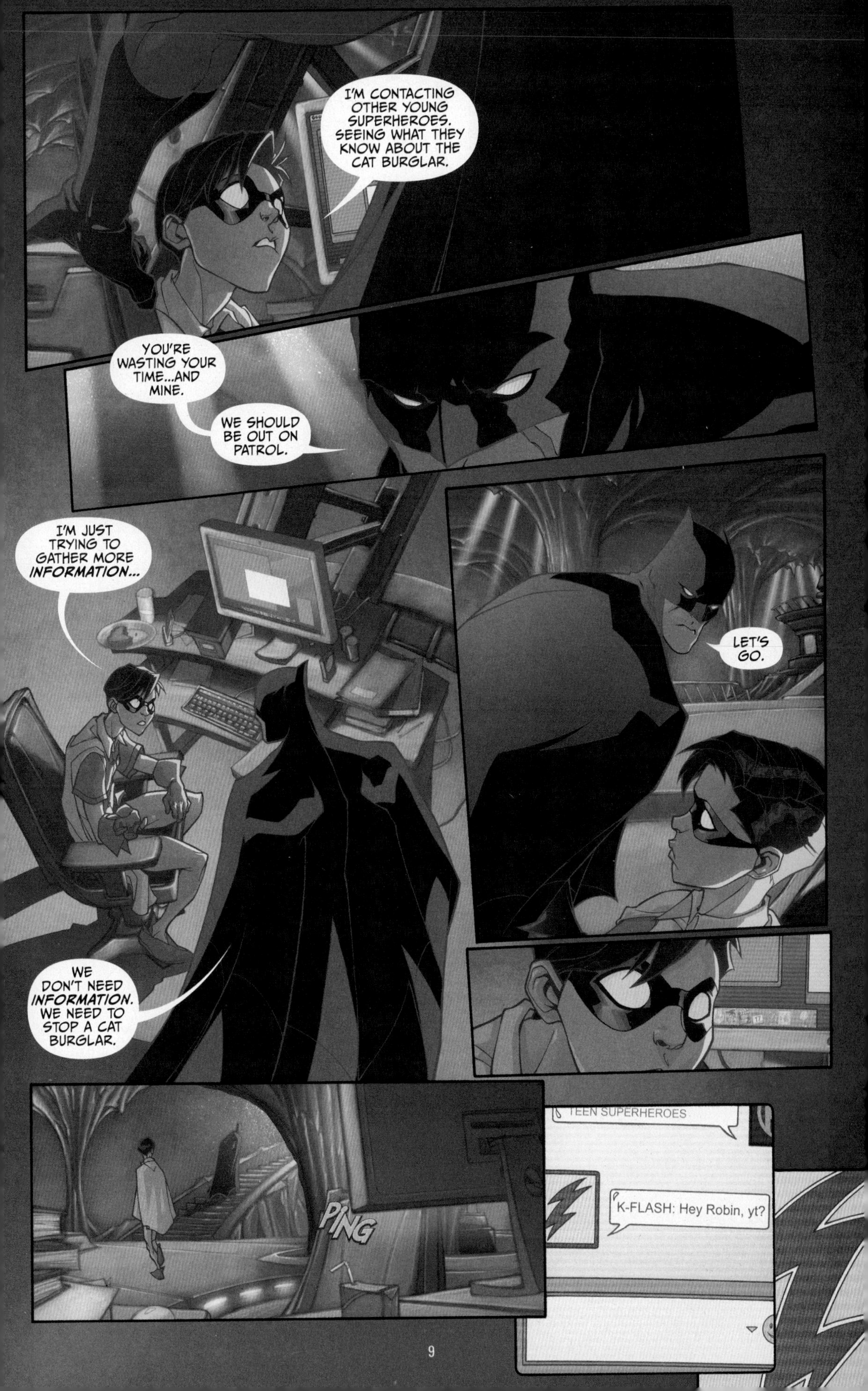
I'M CONTACTING OTHER YOUNG SUPERHEROES. SEEING WHAT THEY KNOW ABOUT THE CAT BURGLAR.
YOU'RE WASTING YOUR TIME...AND MINE.
WE SHOULD BE OUT ON PATROL.
I'M JUST TRYING TO GATHER MORE *INFORMATION*...
WE DON'T NEED *INFORMATION*. WE NEED TO STOP A CAT BURGLAR.
LET'S GO.
PING
TEEN SUPERHEROES
K-FLASH: Hey Robin, yt?

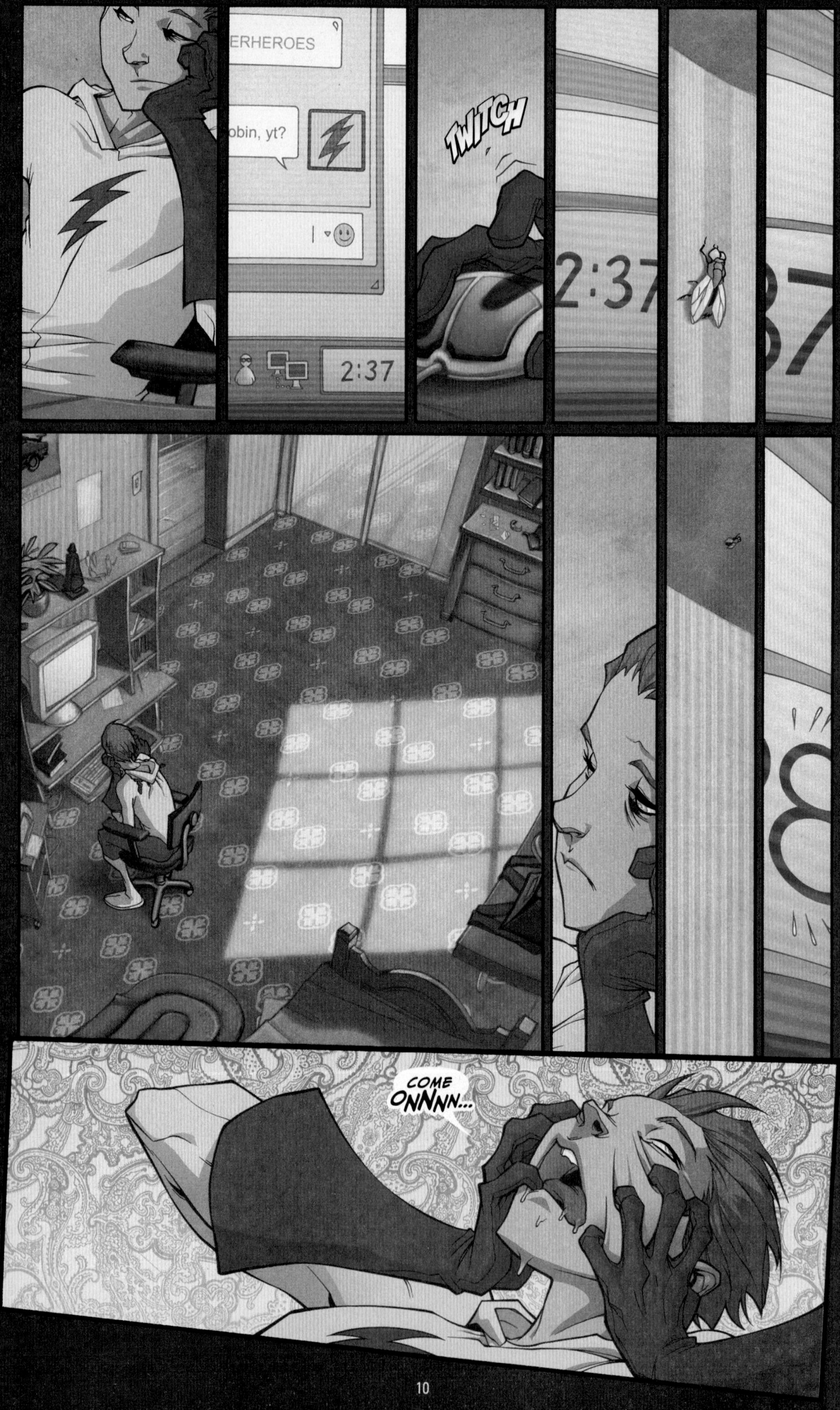
ERHEROES
obin, yt?
2:37
TWITCH
2:37
COME ONNNN...

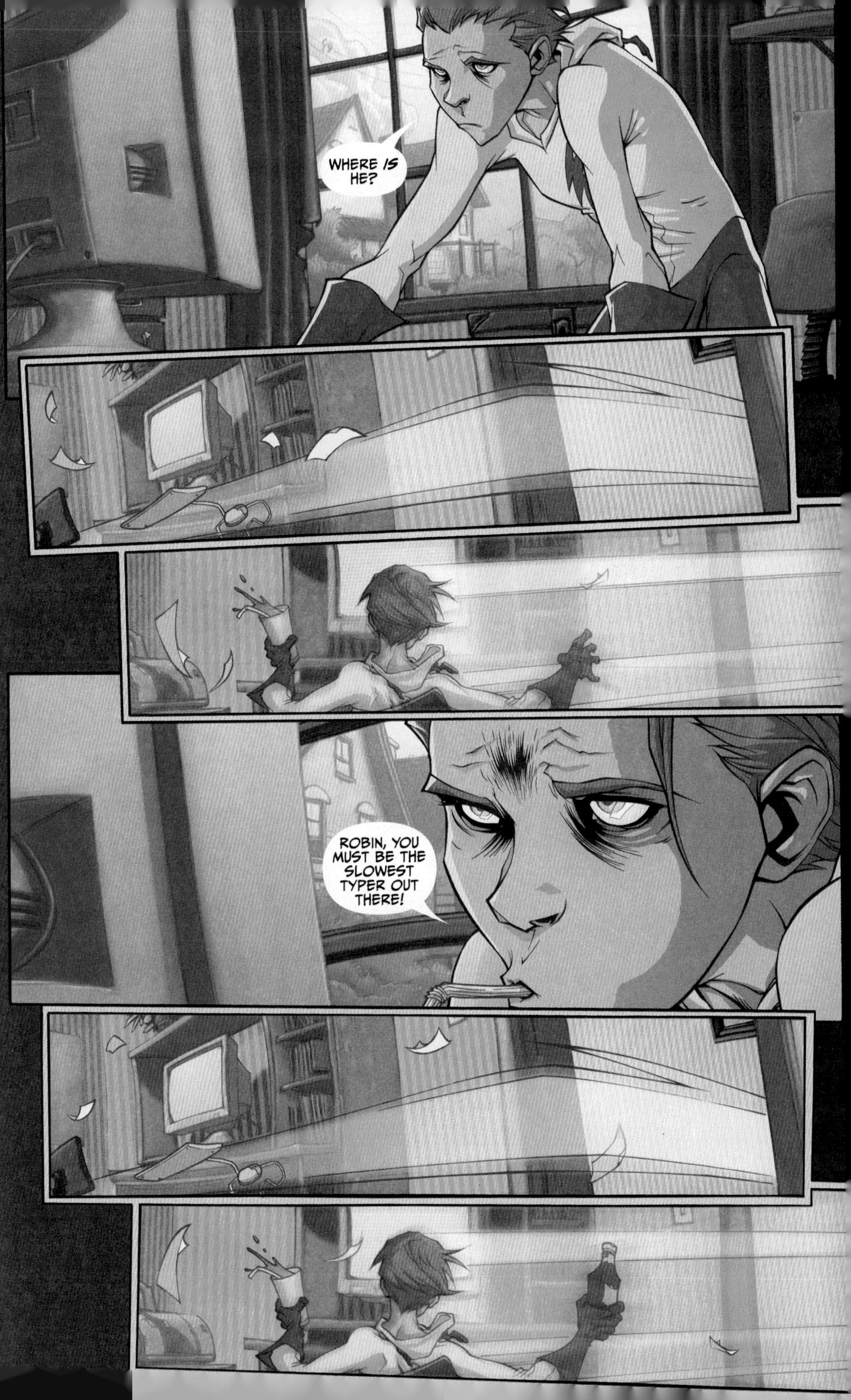
WHERE IS HE?
ROBIN, YOU MUST BE THE SLOWEST TYPER OUT THERE!

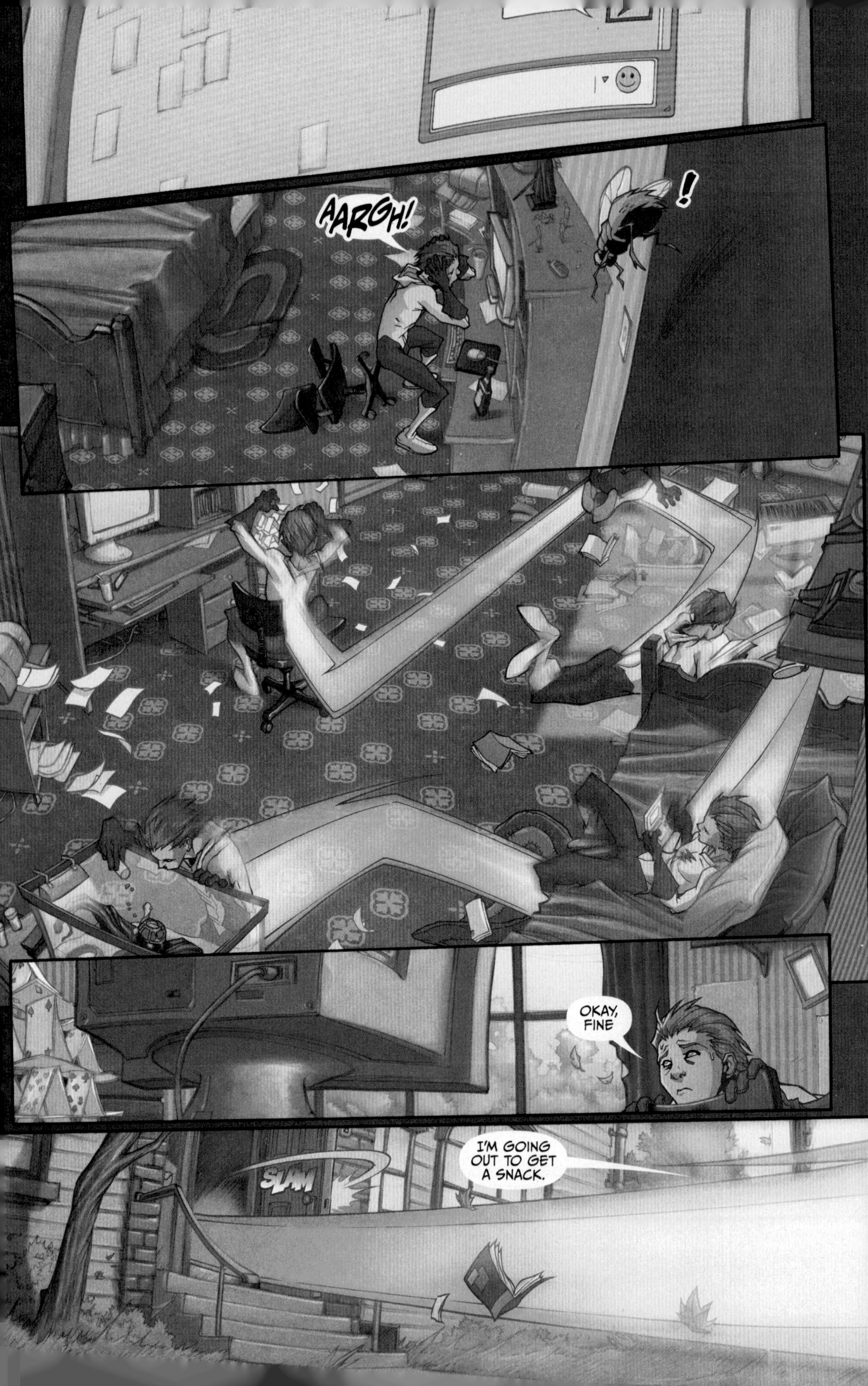
AARGH!
!
OKAY, FINE
SLAM
I'M GOING OUT TO GET A SNACK.

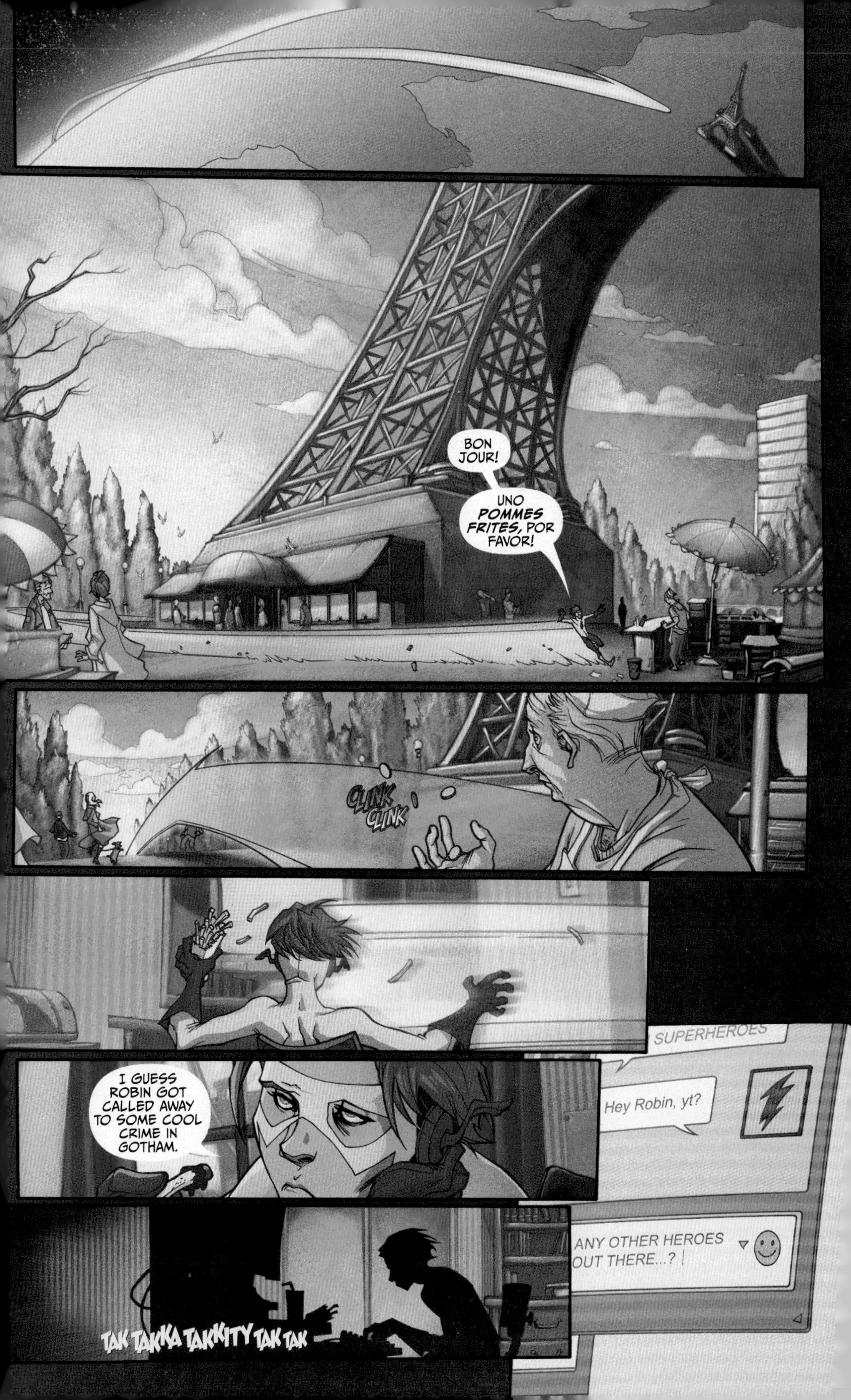
BON JOUR!
UNO POMMES FRITES, POR FAVOR!
CLINK CLINK
SUPERHEROES
Hey Robin, yt?
I GUESS ROBIN GOT CALLED AWAY TO SOME COOL CRIME IN GOTHAM.
ANY OTHER HEROES OUT THERE...?
TAK TAKKA TAKKITY TAK TAK

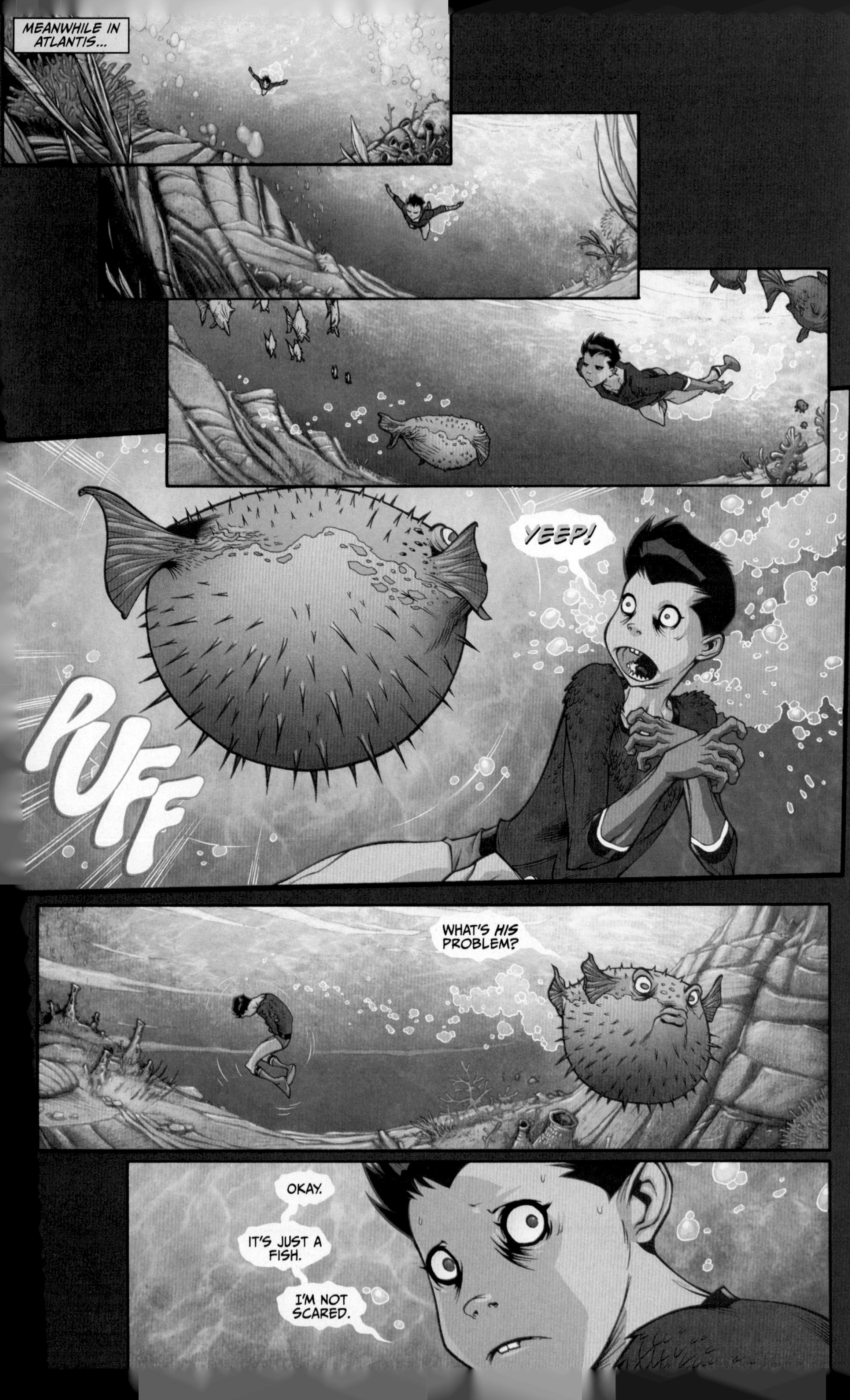
MEANWHILE IN ATLANTIS...
YEEP!
PUFF
WHAT'S HIS PROBLEM?
OKAY.
IT'S JUST A FISH.
I'M NOT SCARED.

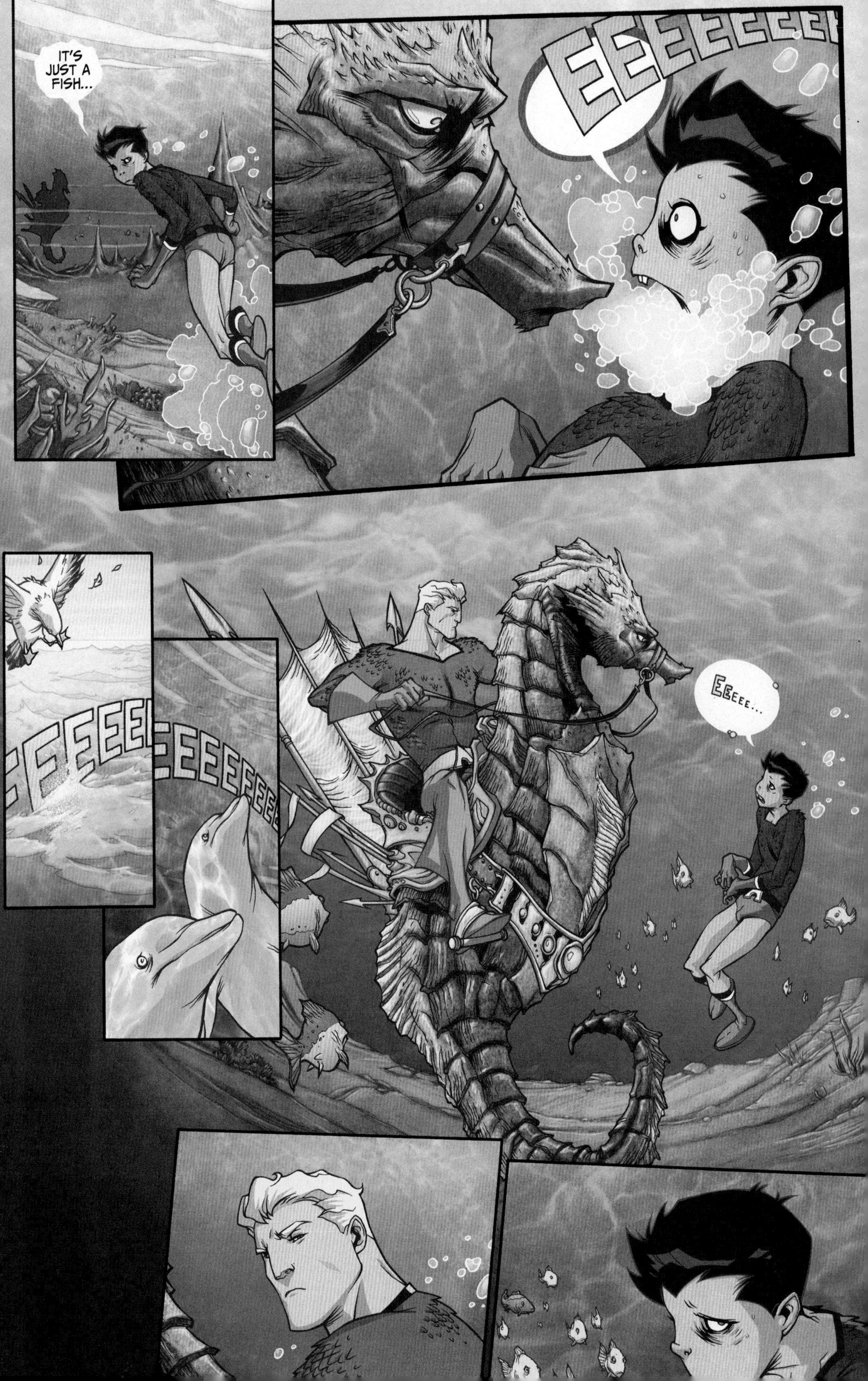
IT'S JUST A FISH...
EEEEEEEE
EEEEE
EEEEEEEEEE
Eeeee...

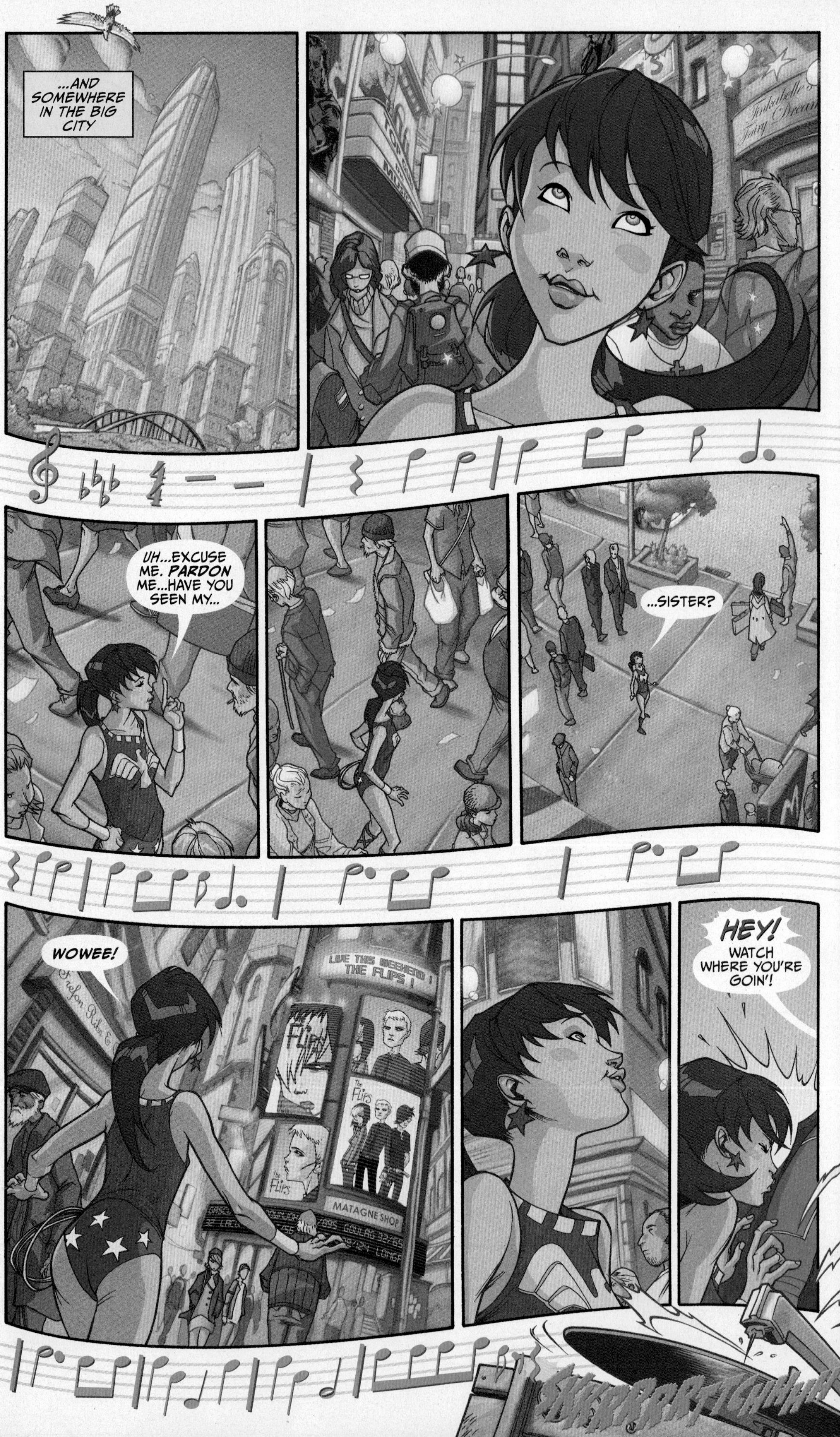
...AND SOMEWHERE IN THE BIG CITY
UH...EXCUSE ME. PARDON ME...HAVE YOU SEEN MY...
...SISTER?
WOWEE!
LIVE THIS WEEKEND THE FLIPS !
MATAGNE SHOP
HEY! WATCH WHERE YOU'RE GOIN'!

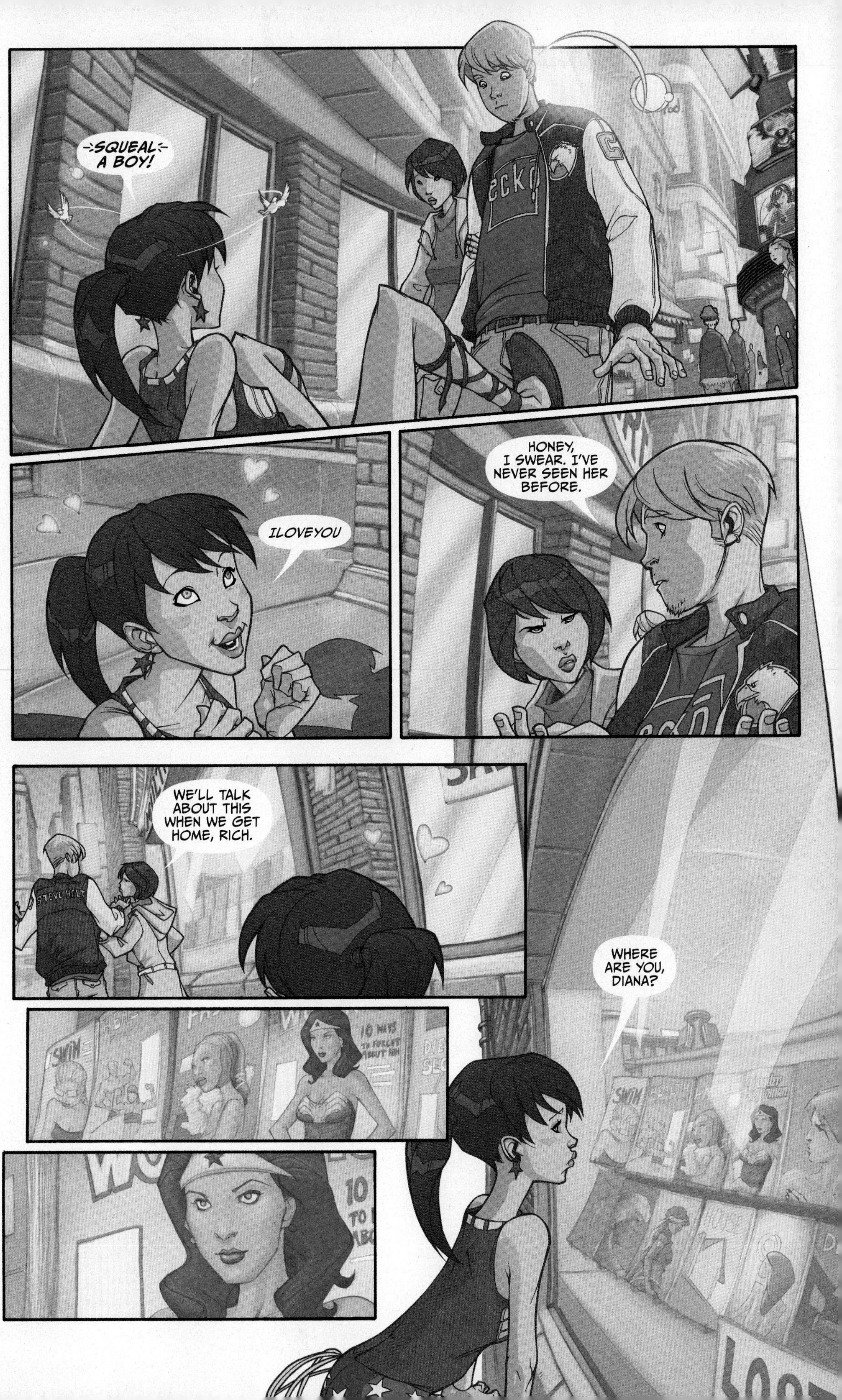
-SQUEAL- A BOY!
ILOVEYOU
HONEY, I SWEAR. I'VE NEVER SEEN HER BEFORE.
WE'LL TALK ABOUT THIS WHEN WE GET HOME, RICH.
WHERE ARE YOU, DIANA?

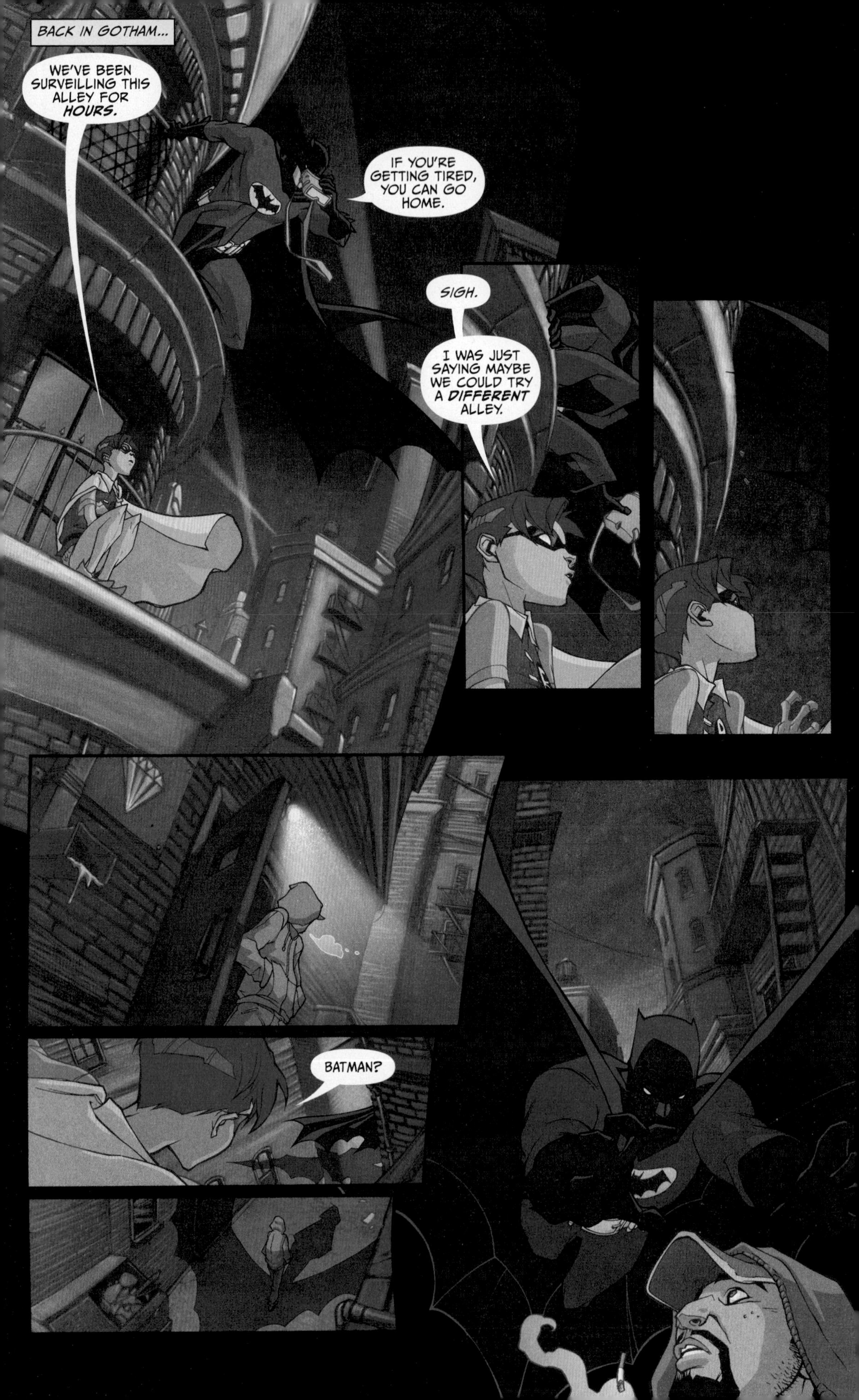
BACK IN GOTHAM...
WE'VE BEEN SURVEILLING THIS ALLEY FOR HOURS.
IF YOU'RE GETTING TIRED, YOU CAN GO HOME.
SIGH.
I WAS JUST SAYING MAYBE WE COULD TRY A DIFFERENT ALLEY.
BATMAN?

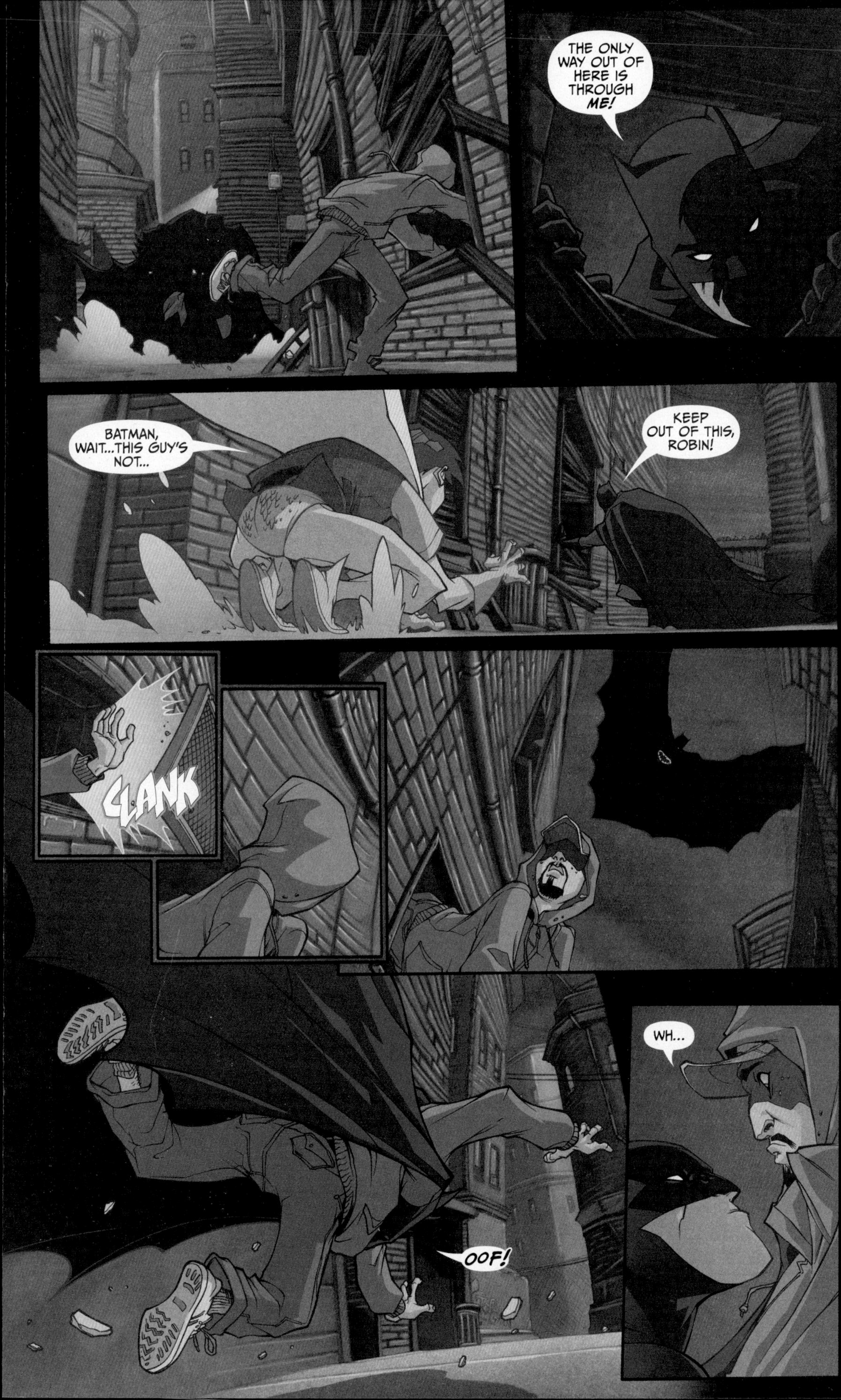
THE ONLY WAY OUT OF HERE IS THROUGH *ME!*
BATMAN, WAIT...THIS GUY'S NOT...
KEEP OUT OF THIS, ROBIN!
CLANK
OOF!
WH...

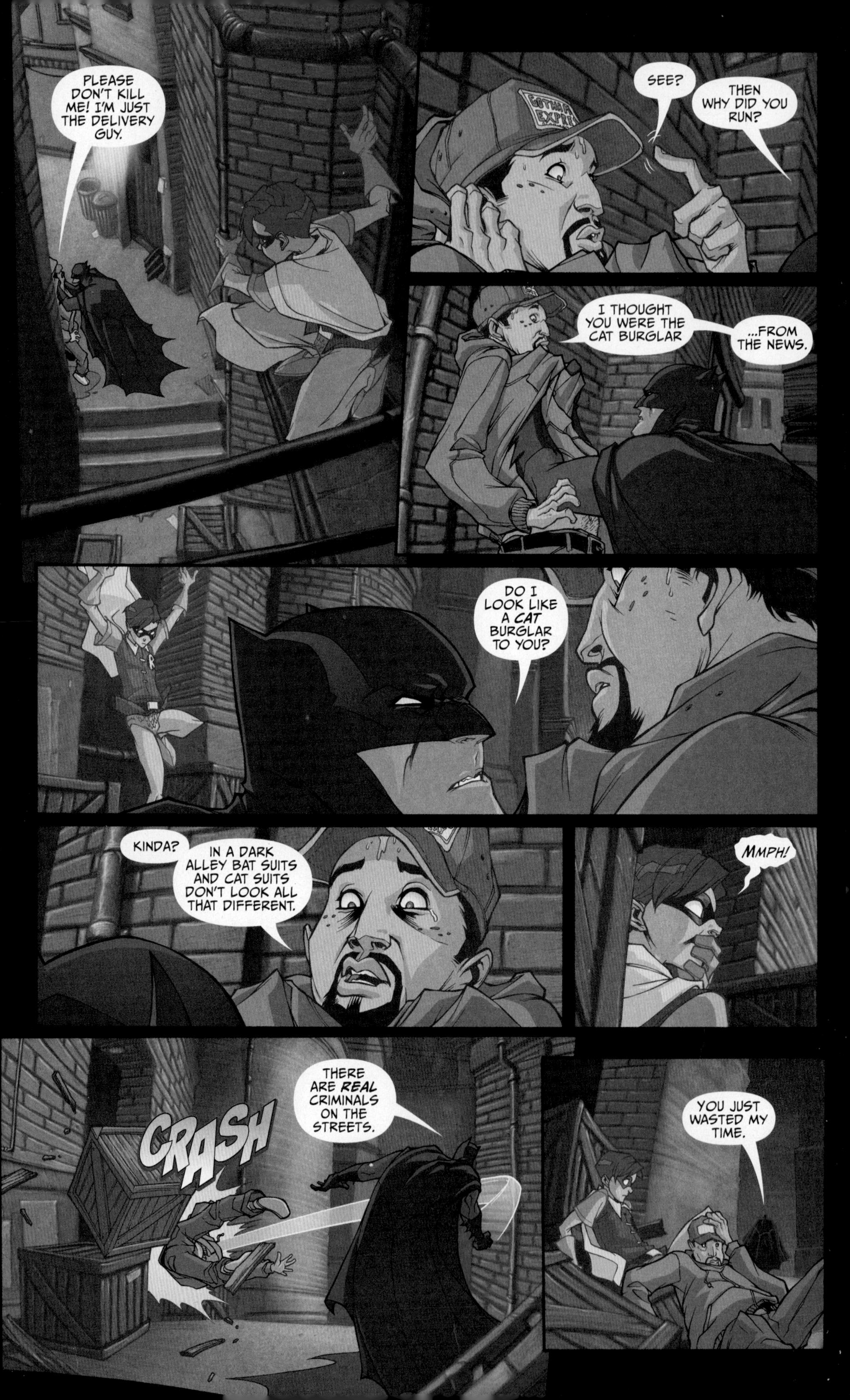
PLEASE DON'T KILL ME! I'M JUST THE DELIVERY GUY.
SEE?
THEN WHY DID YOU RUN?
I THOUGHT YOU WERE THE CAT BURGLAR
...FROM THE NEWS.
DO I LOOK LIKE A CAT BURGLAR TO YOU?
KINDA?
IN A DARK ALLEY BAT SUITS AND CAT SUITS DON'T LOOK ALL THAT DIFFERENT.
MMPH!
CRASH
THERE ARE REAL CRIMINALS ON THE STREETS.
YOU JUST WASTED MY TIME.

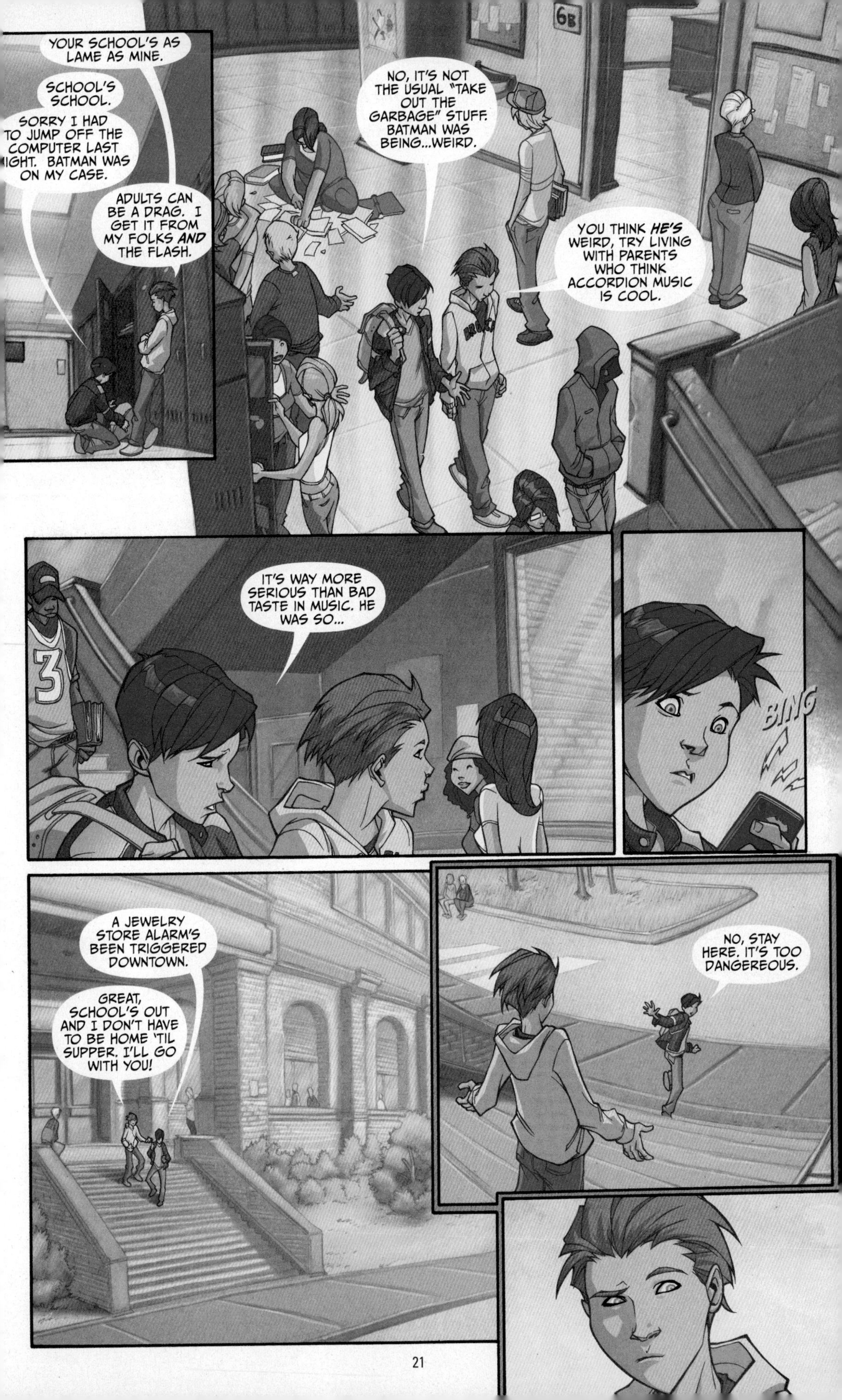

YOUR SCHOOL'S AS LAME AS MINE.
SCHOOL'S SCHOOL.
SORRY I HAD TO JUMP OFF THE COMPUTER LAST NIGHT. BATMAN WAS ON MY CASE.
ADULTS CAN BE A DRAG. I GET IT FROM MY FOLKS AND THE FLASH.
NO, IT'S NOT THE USUAL "TAKE OUT THE GARBAGE" STUFF. BATMAN WAS BEING...WEIRD.
YOU THINK HE'S WEIRD, TRY LIVING WITH PARENTS WHO THINK ACCORDION MUSIC IS COOL.
IT'S WAY MORE SERIOUS THAN BAD TASTE IN MUSIC. HE WAS SO...
BING
A JEWELRY STORE ALARM'S BEEN TRIGGERED DOWNTOWN.
GREAT, SCHOOL'S OUT AND I DON'T HAVE TO BE HOME 'TIL SUPPER. I'LL GO WITH YOU!
NO, STAY HERE. IT'S TOO DANGEROUS.

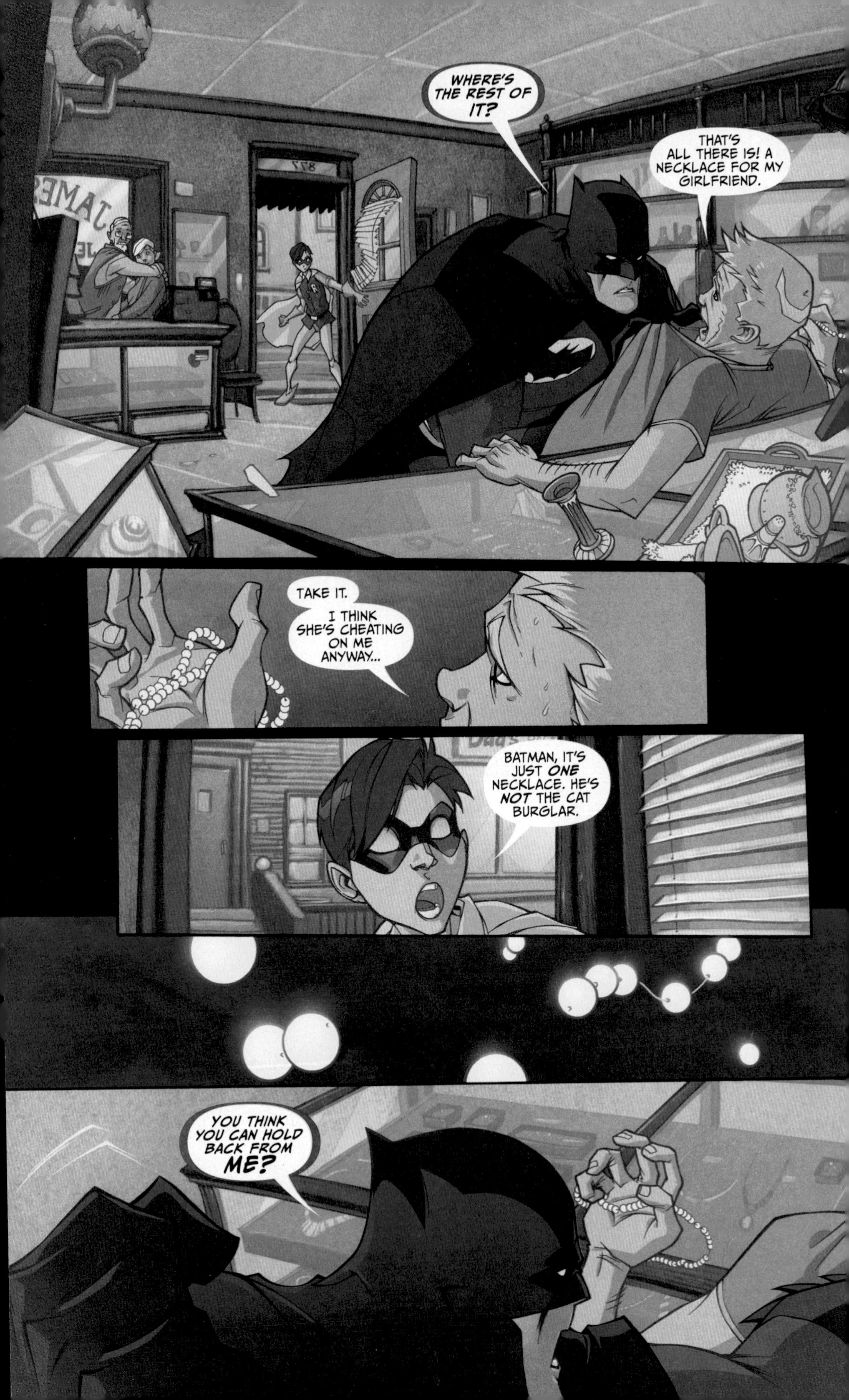
WHERE'S THE REST OF IT?
THAT'S ALL THERE IS! A NECKLACE FOR MY GIRLFRIEND.
TAKE IT.
I THINK SHE'S CHEATING ON ME ANYWAY...
BATMAN, IT'S JUST ONE NECKLACE. HE'S NOT THE CAT BURGLAR.
YOU THINK YOU CAN HOLD BACK FROM ME?

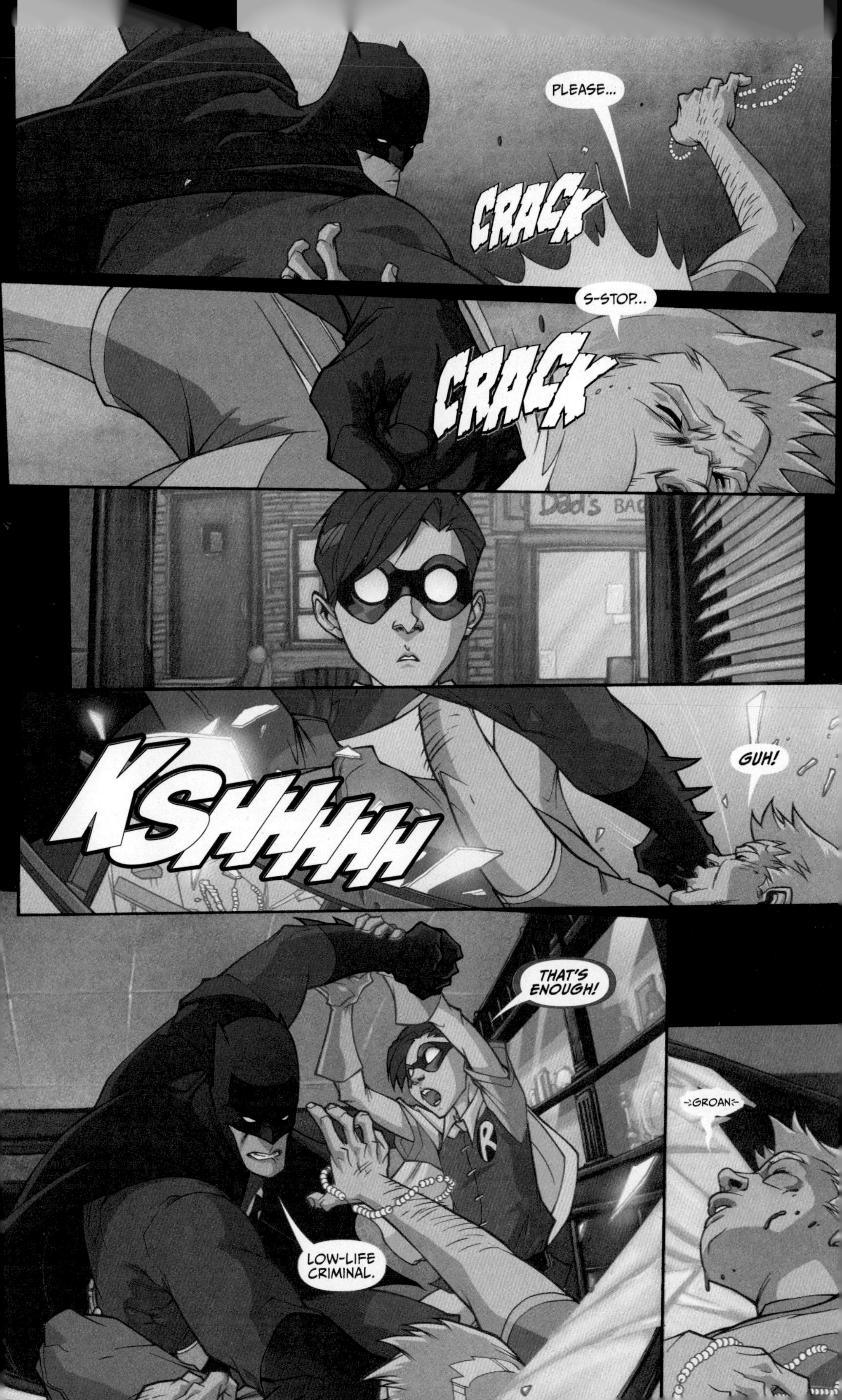
PLEASE...
CRACK
S-STOP...
CRACK
Dad's BA
KSHHHHH
GUH!
THAT'S ENOUGH!
LOW-LIFE CRIMINAL.
GROAN

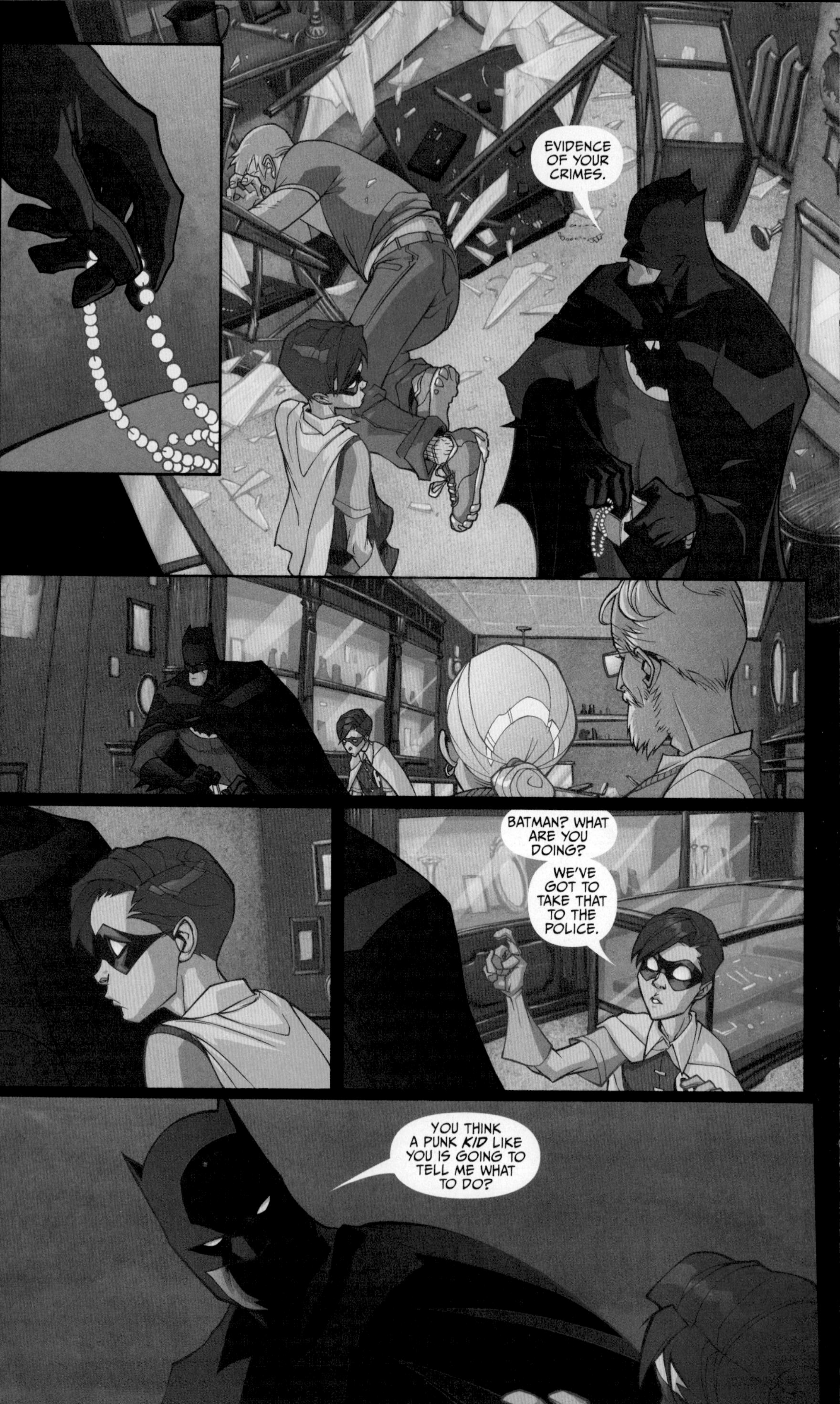
EVIDENCE OF YOUR CRIMES.
BATMAN? WHAT ARE YOU DOING?
WE'VE GOT TO TAKE THAT TO THE POLICE.
YOU THINK A PUNK *KID* LIKE YOU IS GOING TO TELL ME WHAT TO DO?

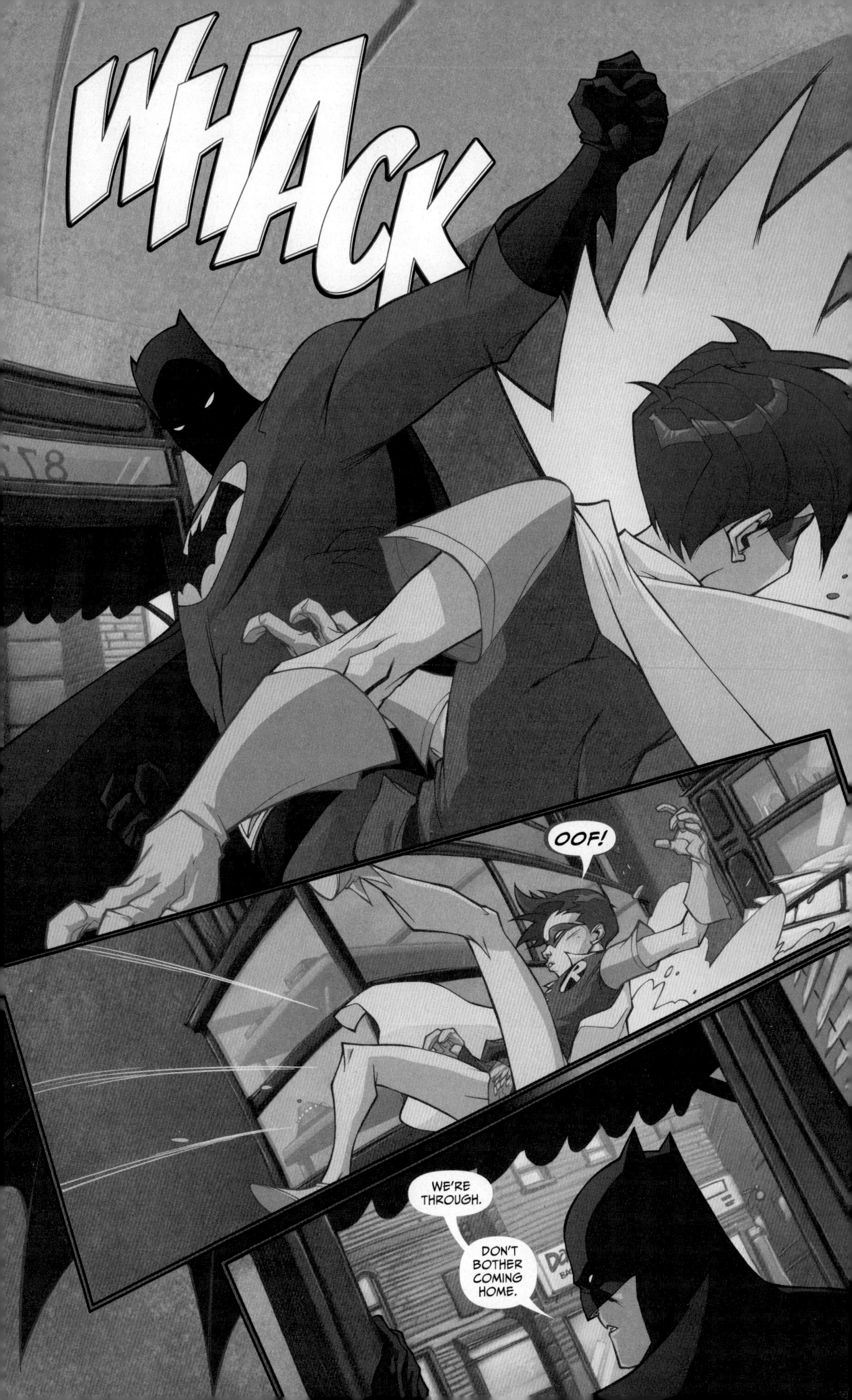
WHACK
OOF!
WE'RE THROUGH.
DON'T BOTHER COMING HOME.

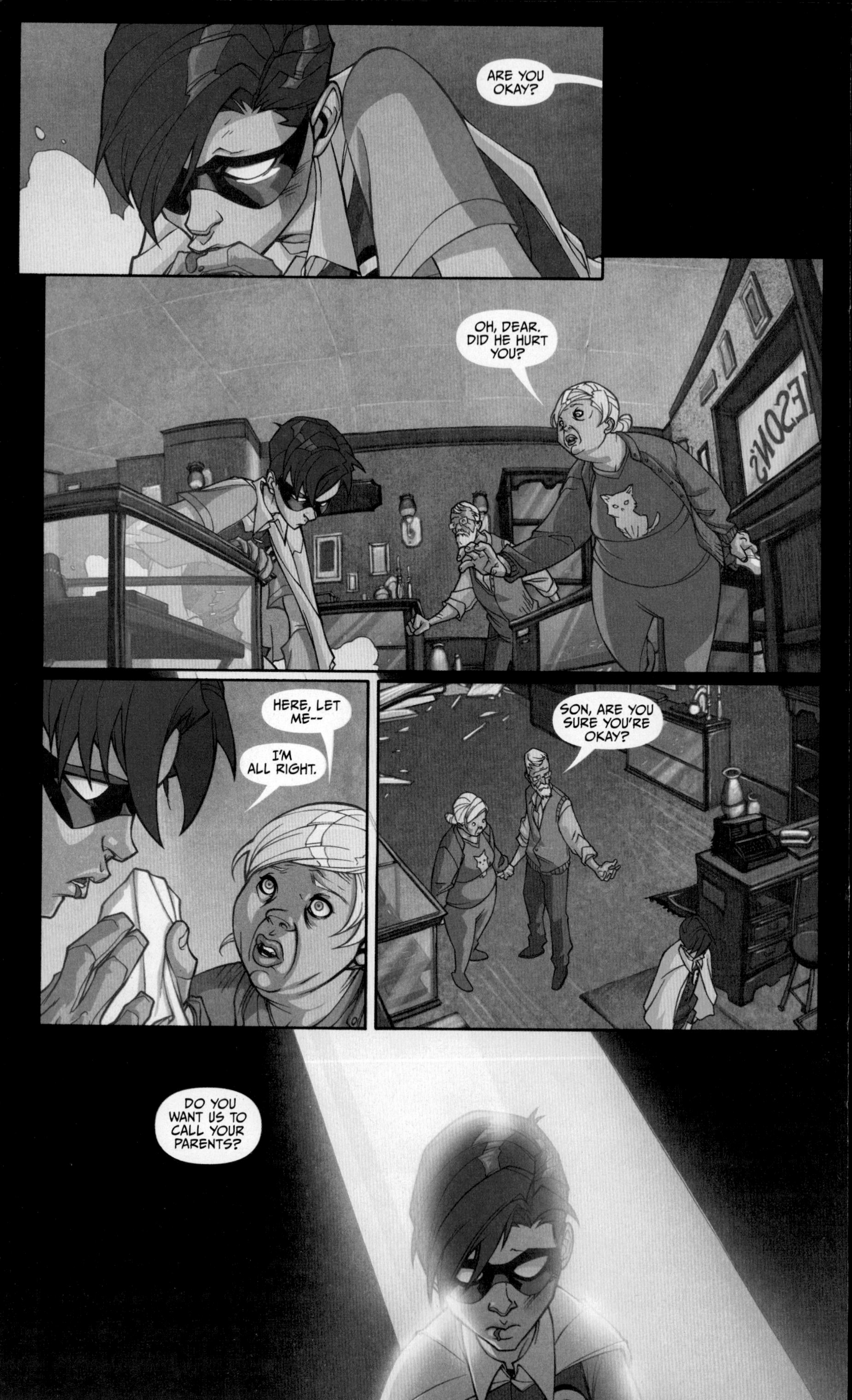
ARE YOU OKAY?
OH, DEAR. DID HE HURT YOU?
ESON'S
HERE, LET ME--
I'M ALL RIGHT.
SON, ARE YOU SURE YOU'RE OKAY?
DO YOU WANT US TO CALL YOUR PARENTS?

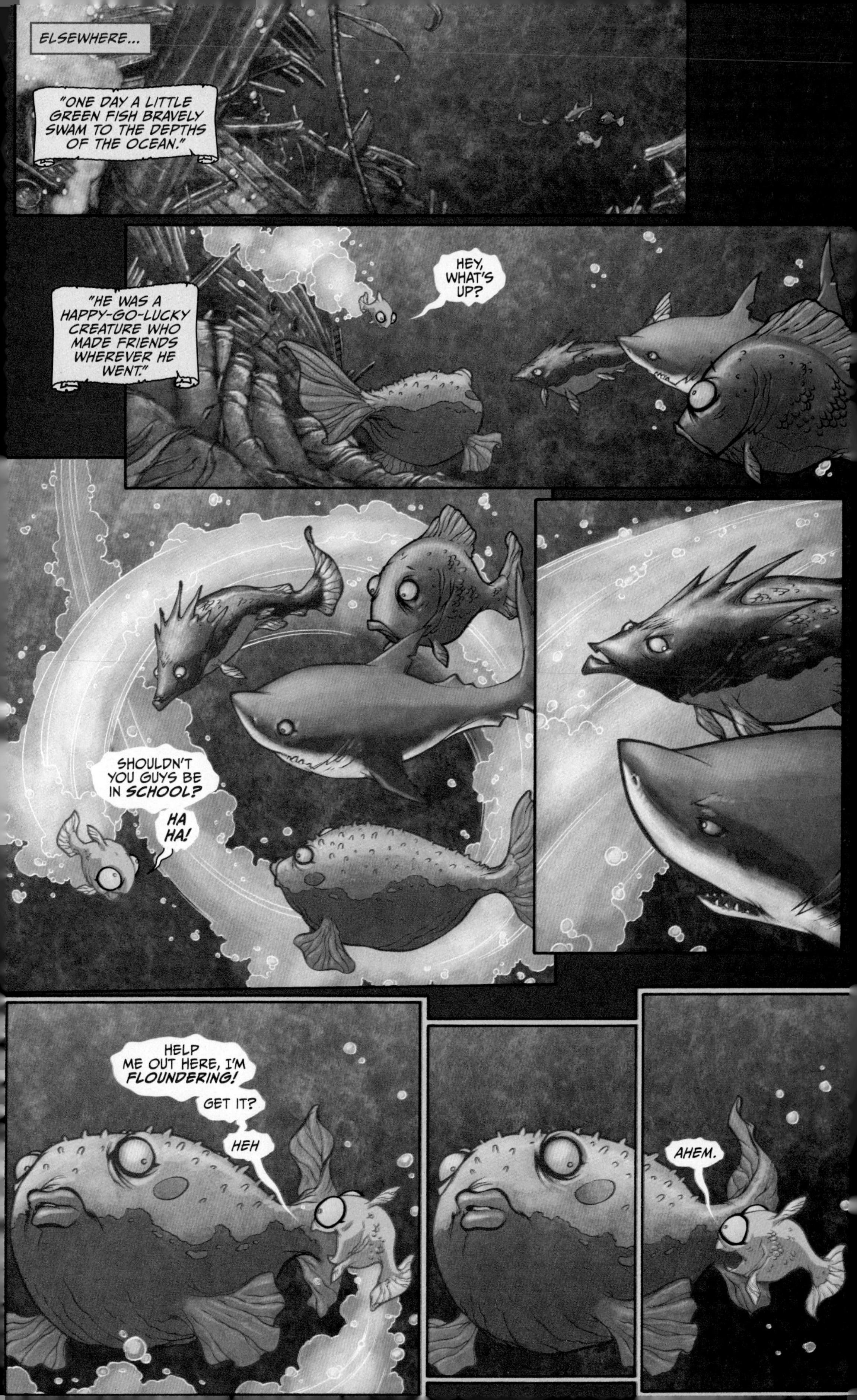
ELSEWHERE...
"ONE DAY A LITTLE GREEN FISH BRAVELY SWAM TO THE DEPTHS OF THE OCEAN."
"HE WAS A HAPPY-GO-LUCKY CREATURE WHO MADE FRIENDS WHEREVER HE WENT."
HEY, WHAT'S UP?
SHOULDN'T YOU GUYS BE IN SCHOOL?
HA HA!
HELP ME OUT HERE, I'M FLOUNDERING!
GET IT?
HEH
AHEM.

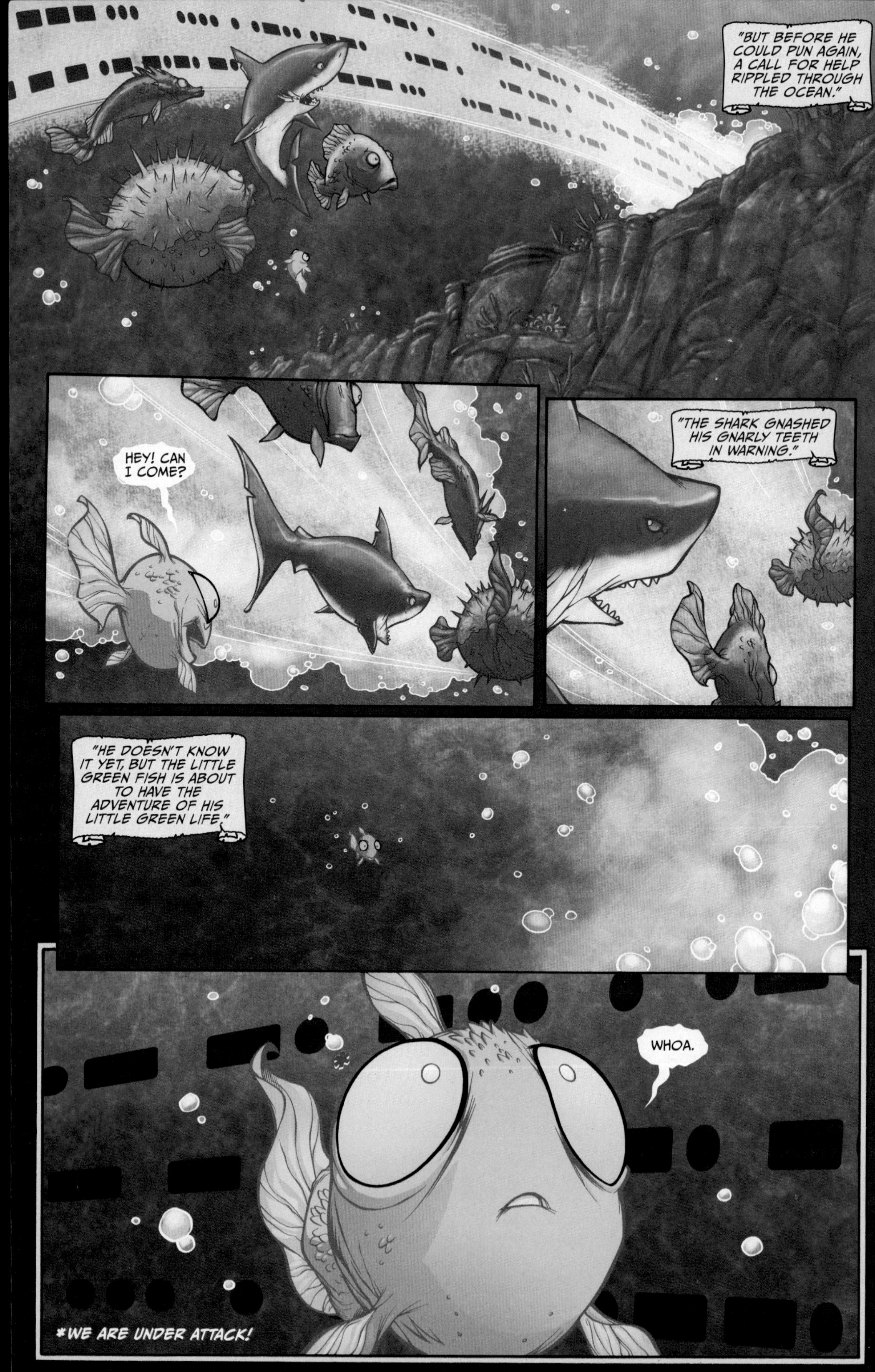
"BUT BEFORE HE COULD PUN AGAIN, A CALL FOR HELP RIPPLED THROUGH THE OCEAN."
HEY! CAN I COME?
"THE SHARK GNASHED HIS GNARLY TEETH IN WARNING."
"HE DOESN'T KNOW IT YET, BUT THE LITTLE GREEN FISH IS ABOUT TO HAVE THE ADVENTURE OF HIS LITTLE GREEN LIFE."
WHOA.
*WE ARE UNDER ATTACK!

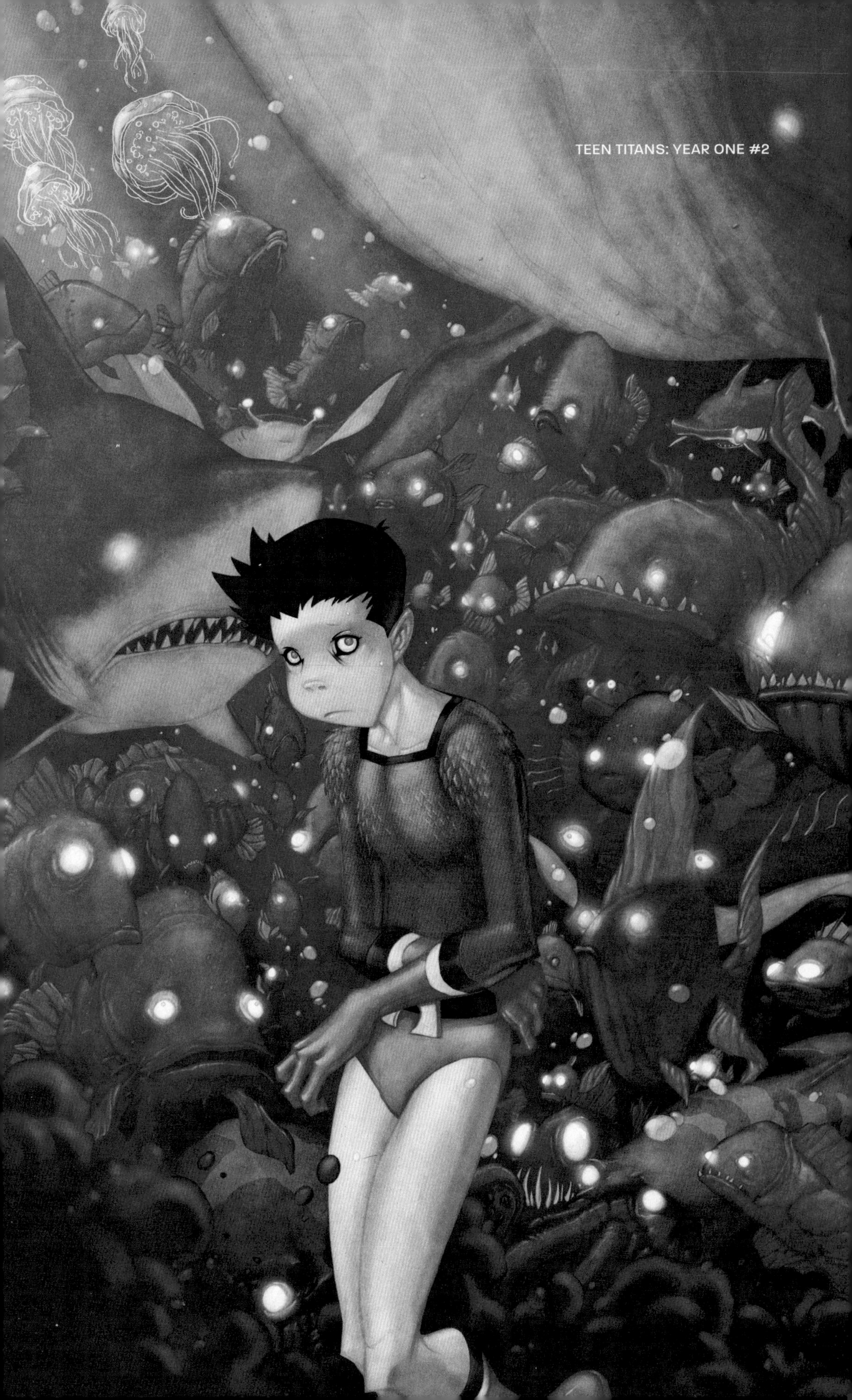
TEEN TITANS: YEAR ONE #2

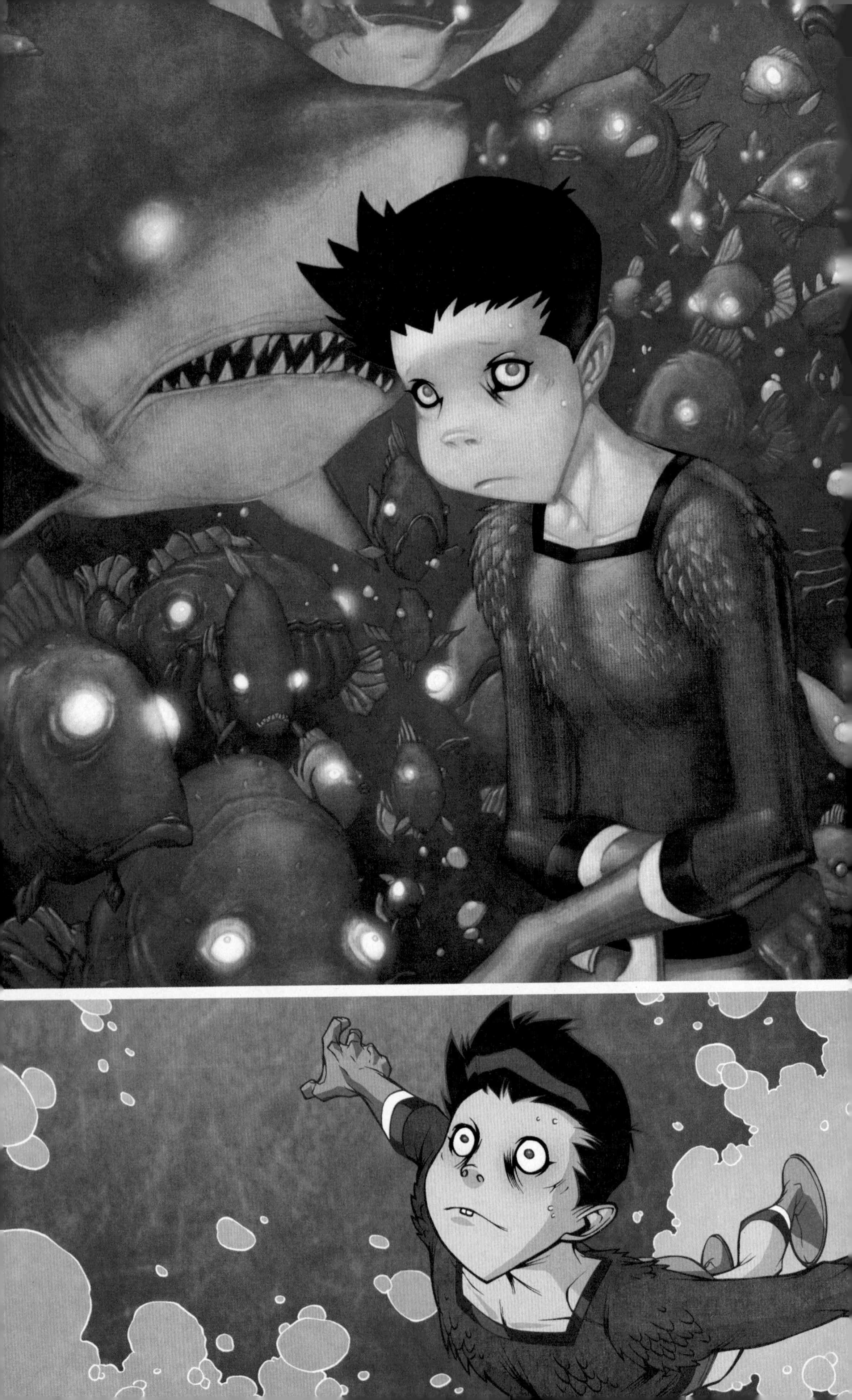

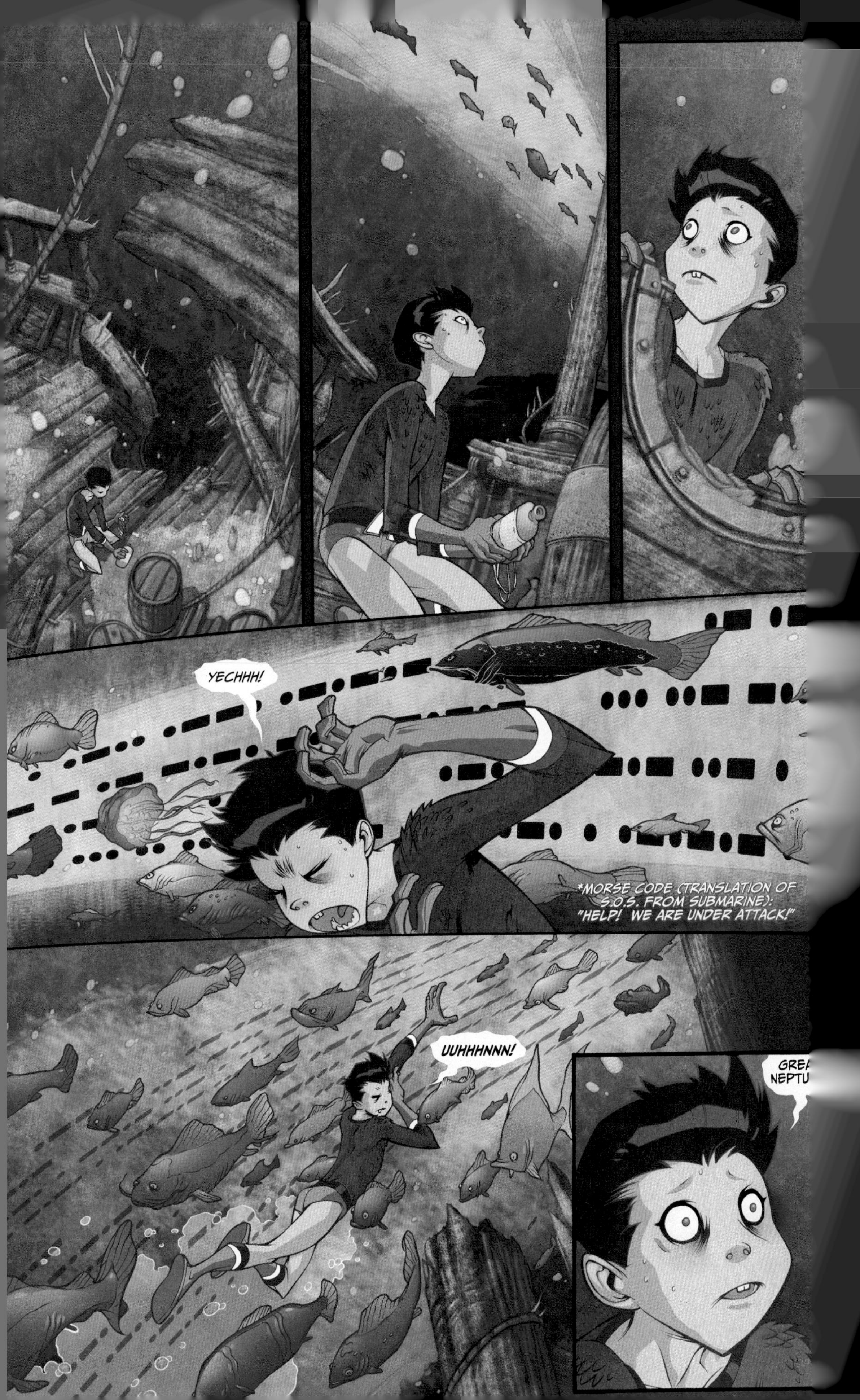
YECHHH!
*MORSE CODE (TRANSLATION OF S.O.S. FROM SUBMARINE): "HELP! WE ARE UNDER ATTACK!"
UUHHHNNN!
GREA
NEPTU

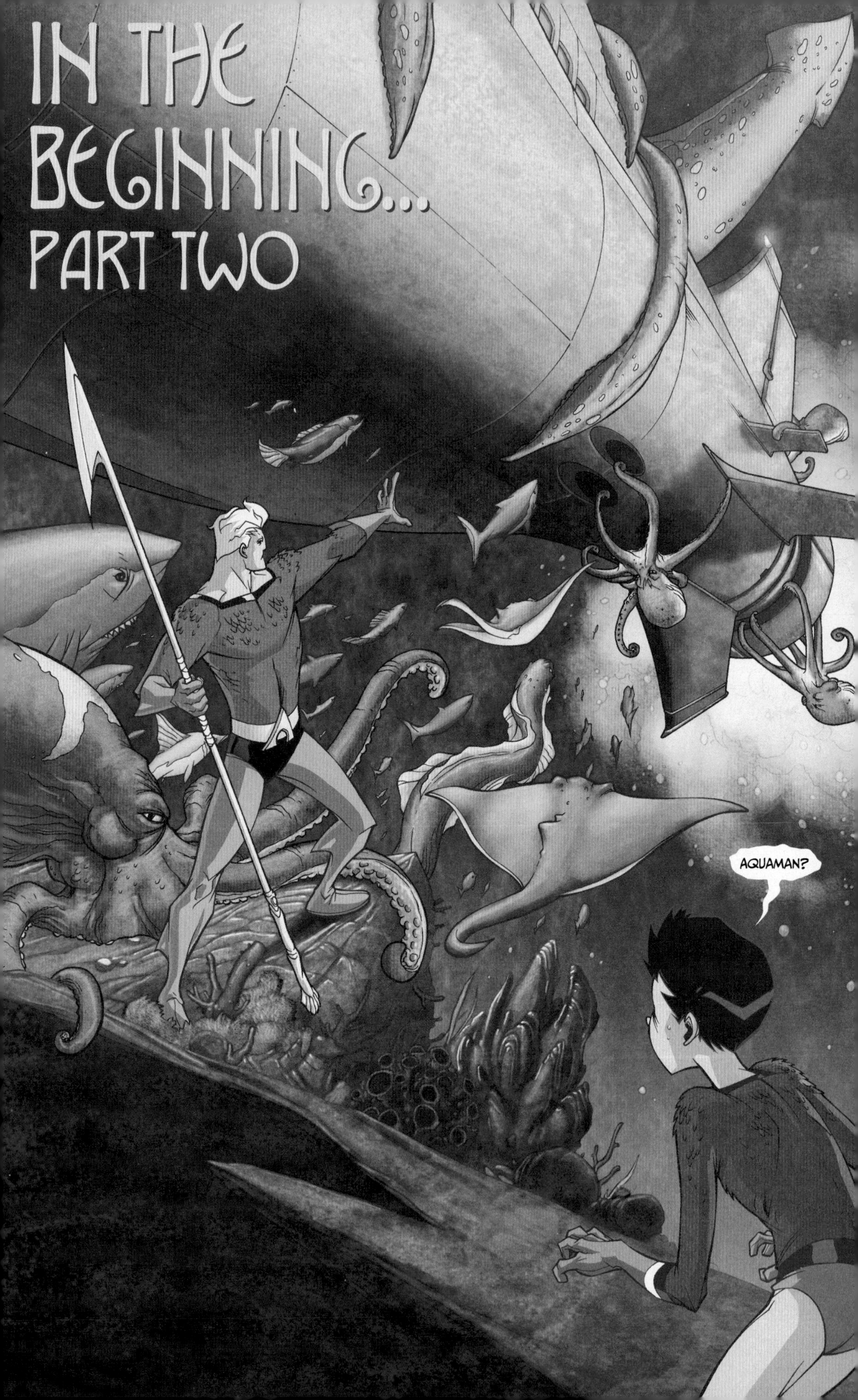
IN THE BEGINNING... PART TWO
AQUAMAN?

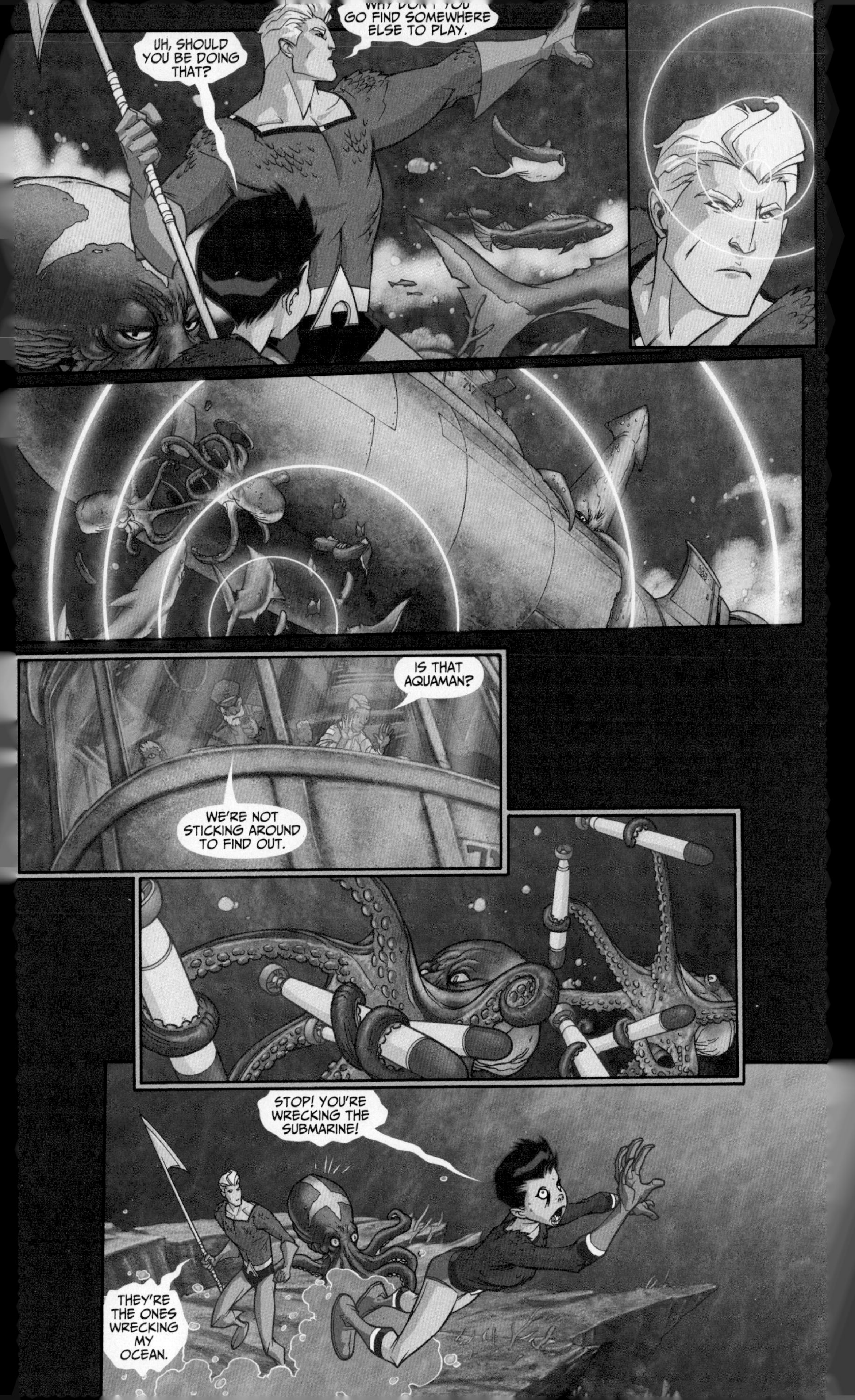
WHY DON'T YOU GO FIND SOMEWHERE ELSE TO PLAY.
UH, SHOULD YOU BE DOING THAT?
IS THAT AQUAMAN?
WE'RE NOT STICKING AROUND TO FIND OUT.
STOP! YOU'RE WRECKING THE SUBMARINE!
THEY'RE THE ONES WRECKING MY OCEAN.

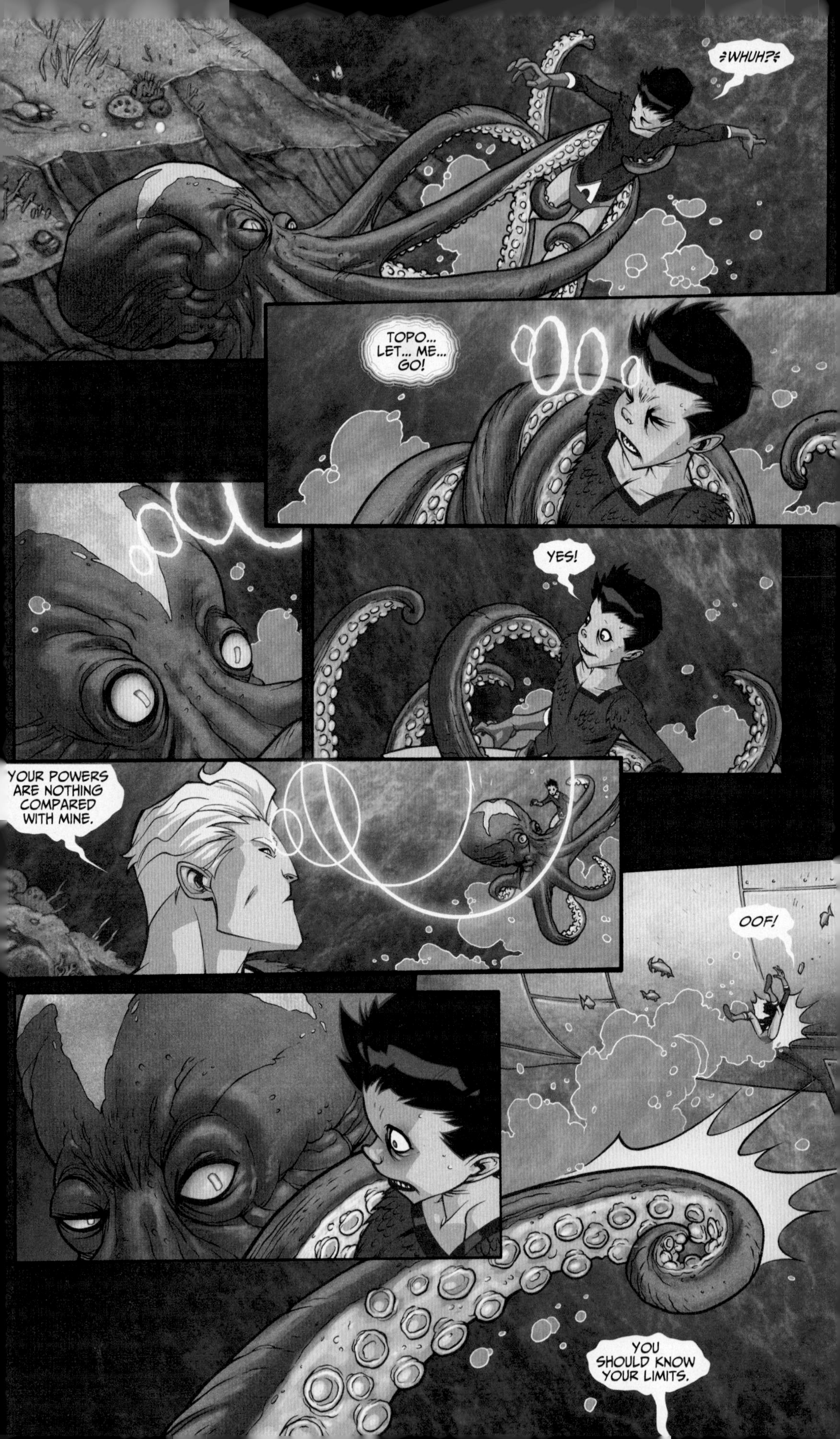
WHUH?
TOPO... LET... ME... GO!
YES!
YOUR POWERS ARE NOTHING COMPARED WITH MINE.
OOF!
YOU SHOULD KNOW YOUR LIMITS.

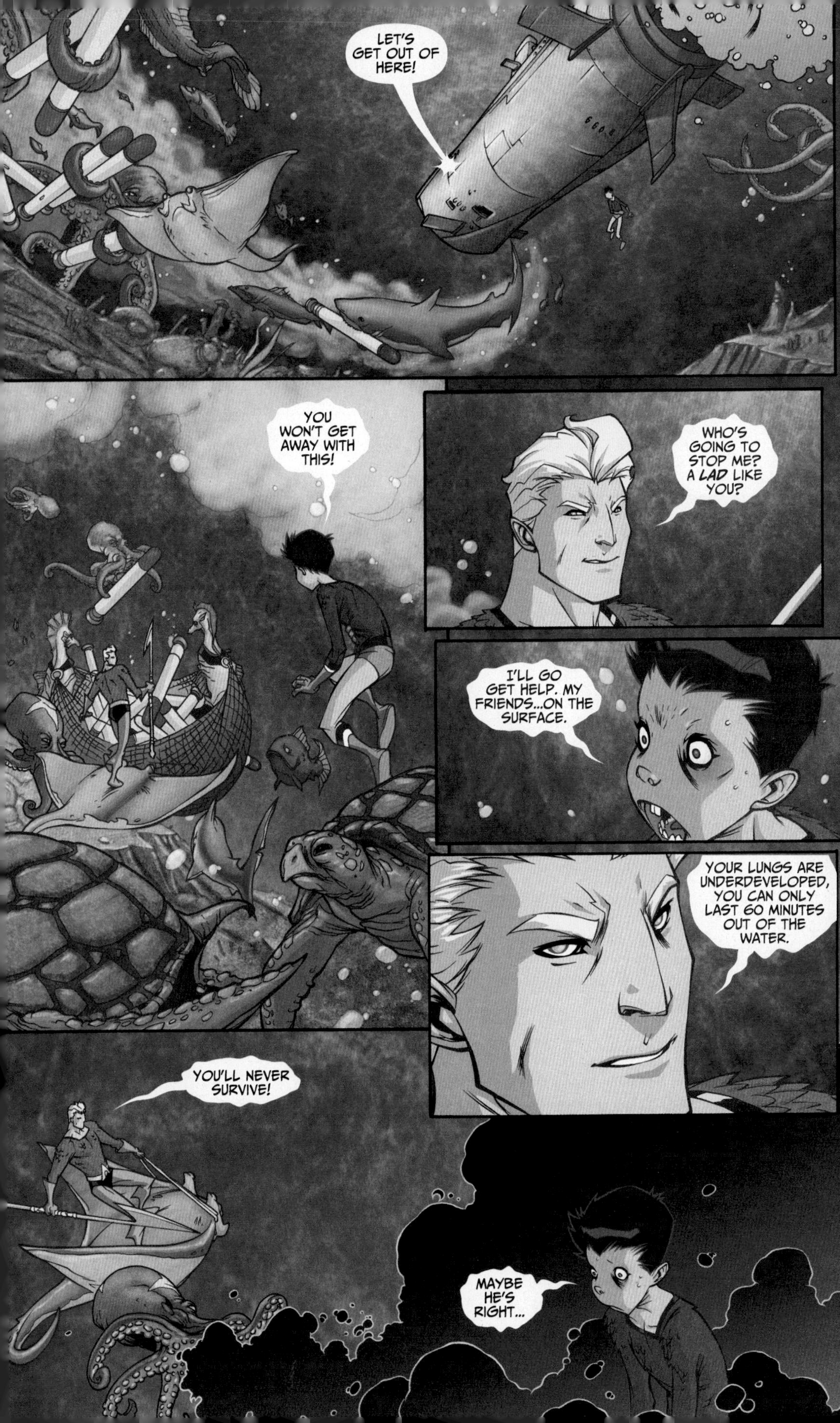
LET'S GET OUT OF HERE!
YOU WON'T GET AWAY WITH THIS!
WHO'S GOING TO STOP ME? A LAD LIKE YOU?
I'LL GO GET HELP. MY FRIENDS...ON THE SURFACE.
YOUR LUNGS ARE UNDERDEVELOPED, YOU CAN ONLY LAST 60 MINUTES OUT OF THE WATER.
YOU'LL NEVER SURVIVE!
MAYBE HE'S RIGHT...

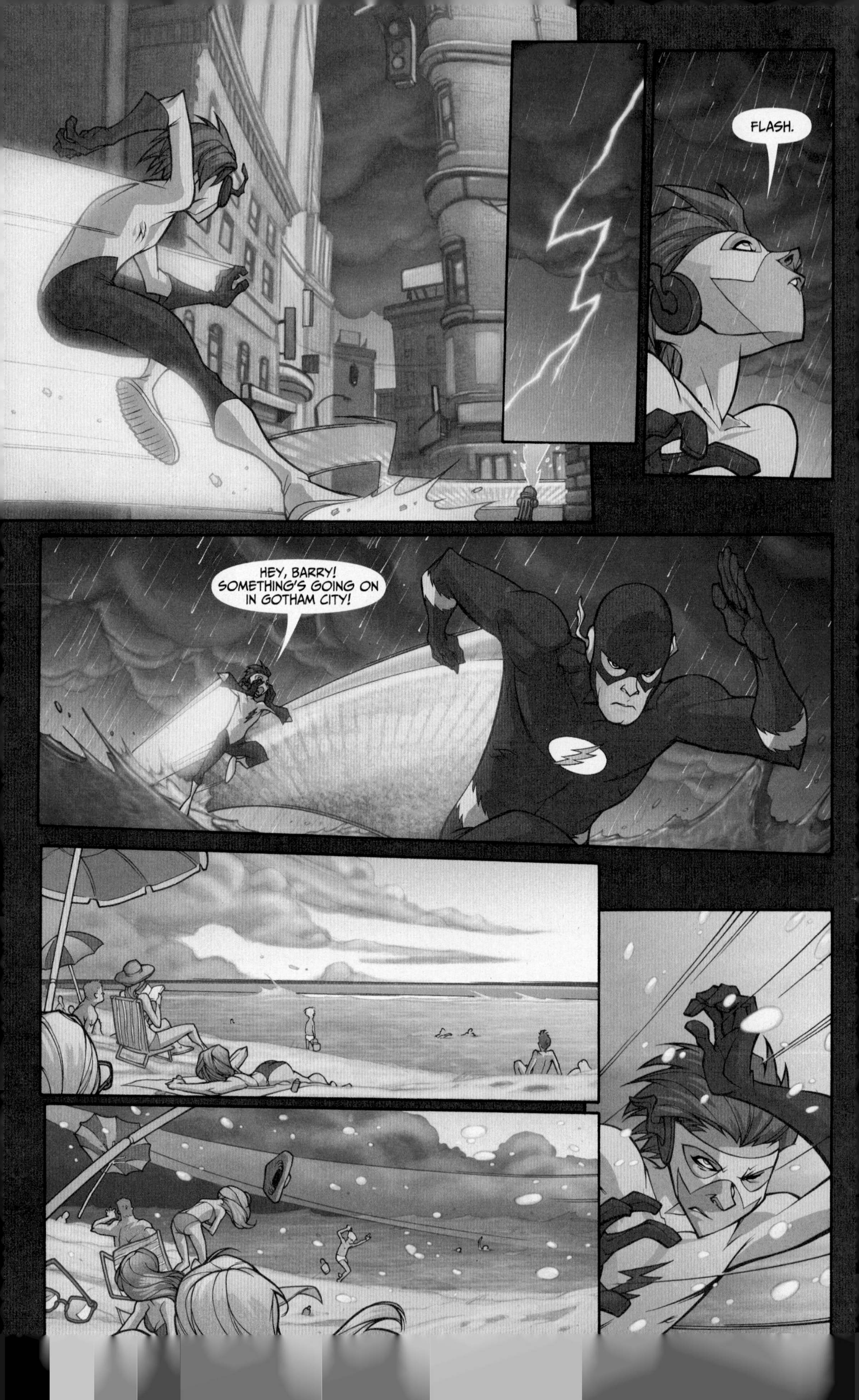
FLASH.
HEY, BARRY! SOMETHING'S GOING ON IN GOTHAM CITY!

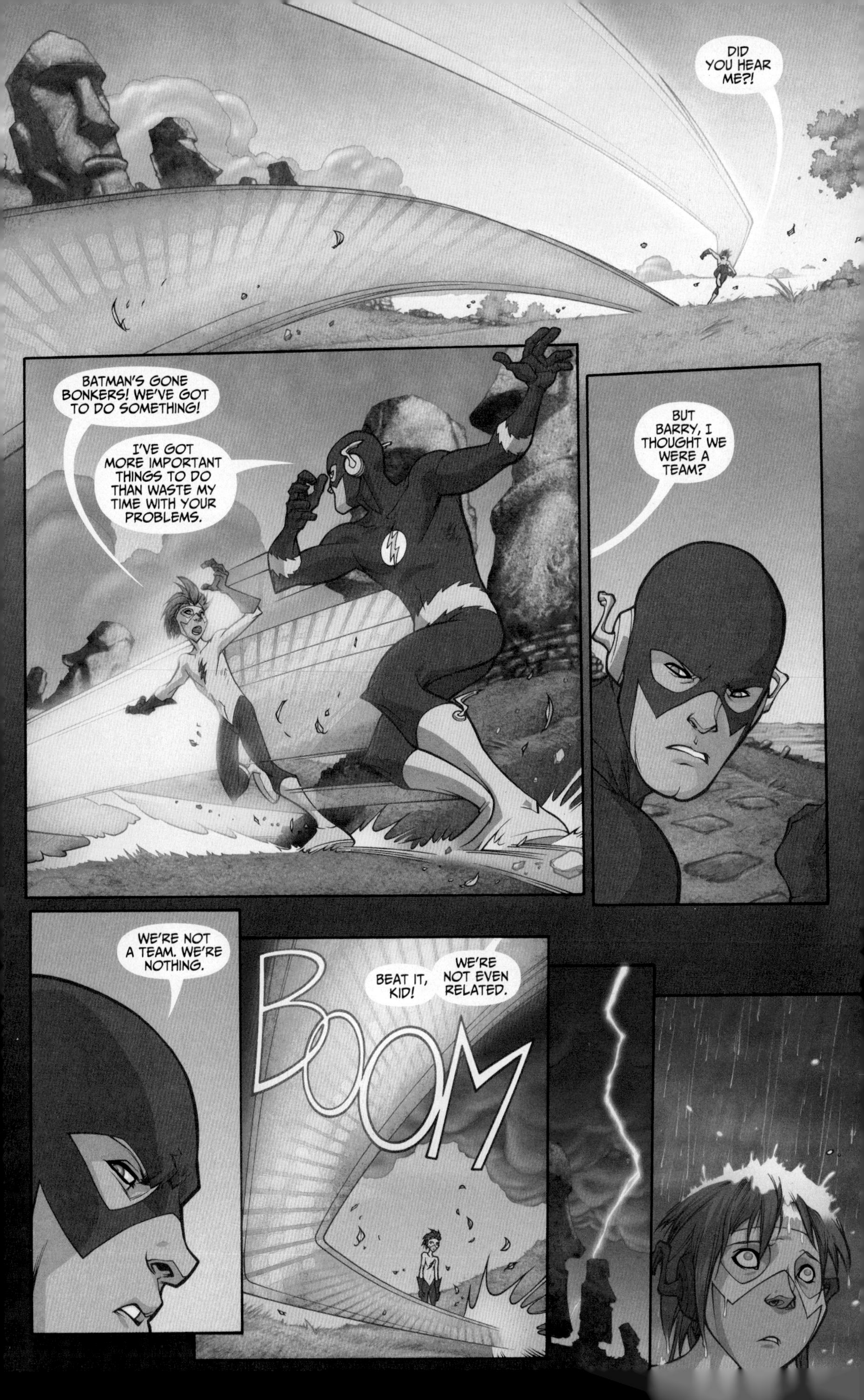
DID YOU HEAR ME?!
BATMAN'S GONE BONKERS! WE'VE GOT TO DO SOMETHING!
I'VE GOT MORE IMPORTANT THINGS TO DO THAN WASTE MY TIME WITH YOUR PROBLEMS.
BUT BARRY, I THOUGHT WE WERE A TEAM?
WE'RE NOT A TEAM. WE'RE NOTHING.
WE'RE NOT EVEN RELATED.
BEAT IT, KID!
BOOM

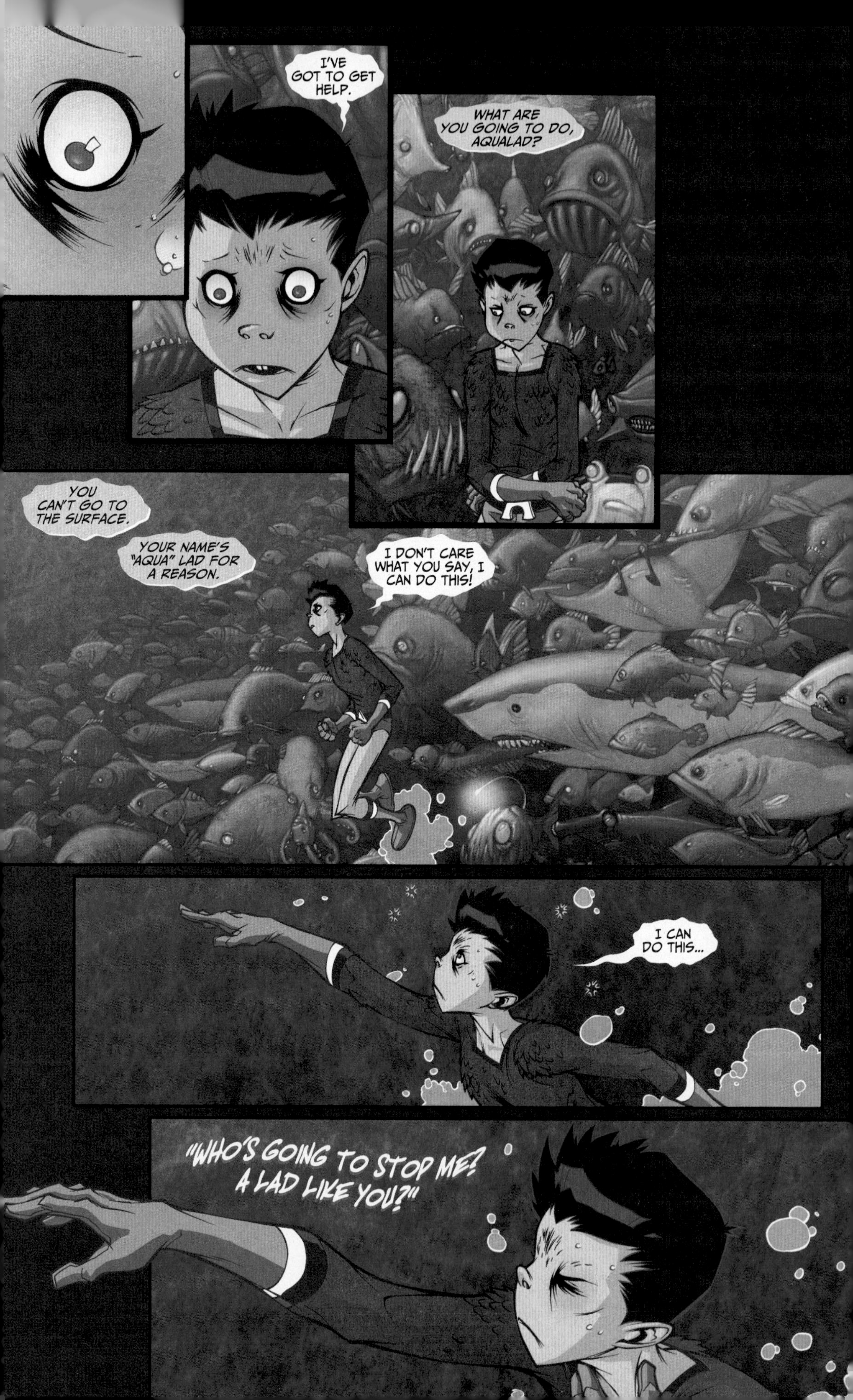
I'VE GOT TO GET HELP.
WHAT ARE YOU GOING TO DO, AQUALAD?
YOU CAN'T GO TO THE SURFACE.
YOUR NAME'S "AQUA" LAD FOR A REASON.
I DON'T CARE WHAT YOU SAY, I CAN DO THIS!
I CAN DO THIS...
"WHO'S GOING TO STOP ME? A LAD LIKE YOU?"

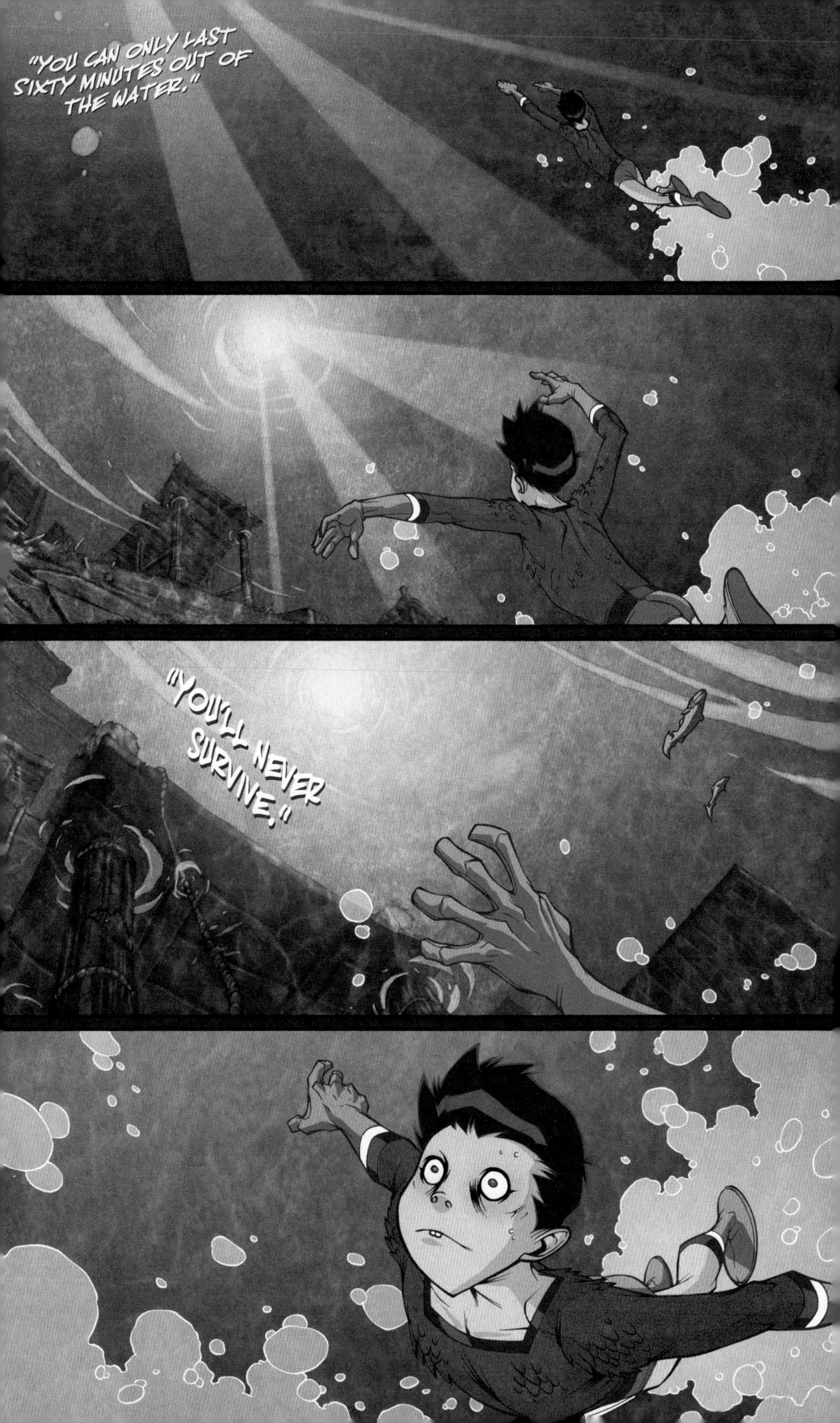
"YOU CAN ONLY LAST SIXTY MINUTES OUT OF THE WATER."
"YOU'LL NEVER SURVIVE."

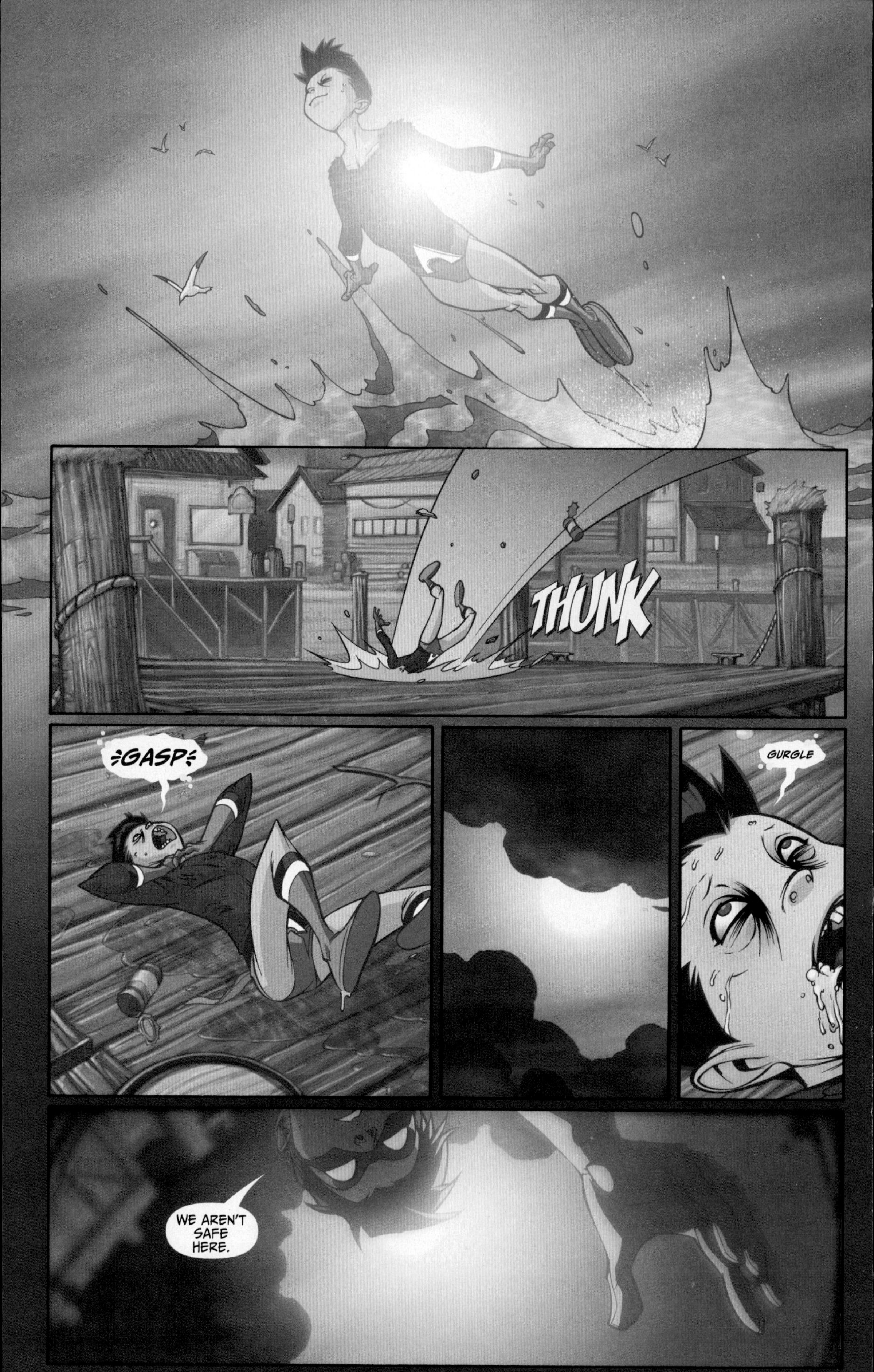
THUNK
GASP
GURGLE
WE AREN'T SAFE HERE.

GARTH, ARE YOU ALL RIGHT?

I'M ≑GASP≑ OKA--

≑GASP≑

EEEEEEEEEEEEEEEEEEEEEEEEEEEEEE

IT'S JUST A SQUIRREL, GILLS FOR BRAINS. SHEESH.

BE NICE.

WHY ARE YOU HERE?

AQUAMAN ≑INHALE≑... HAS BECOME ≑GASP≑ A...

PI- ≑GASP≑

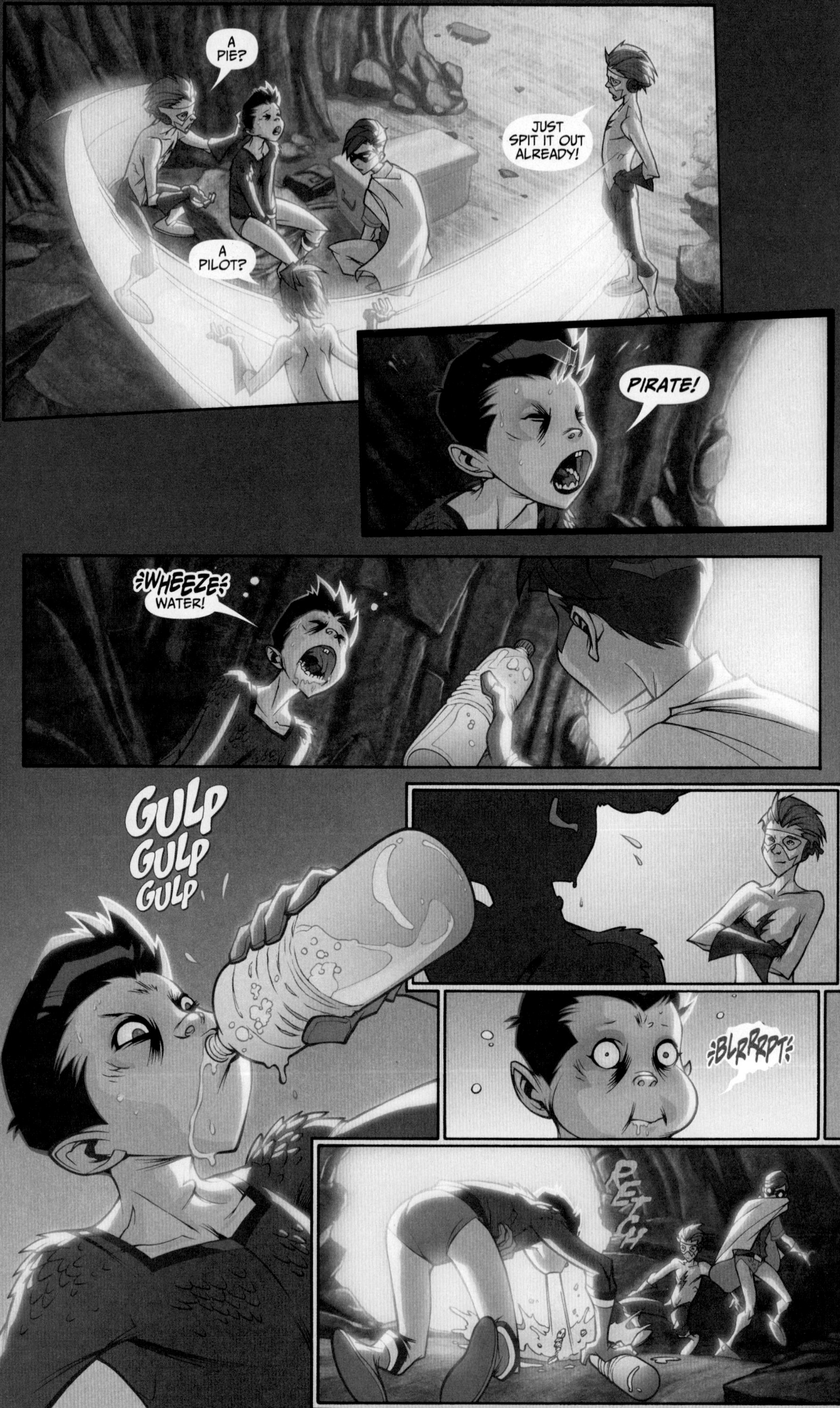
A PIE?
JUST SPIT IT OUT ALREADY!
A PILOT?
PIRATE!
WHEEZE
WATER!
GULP
GULP
GULP
BLRRRPT
PLEGH

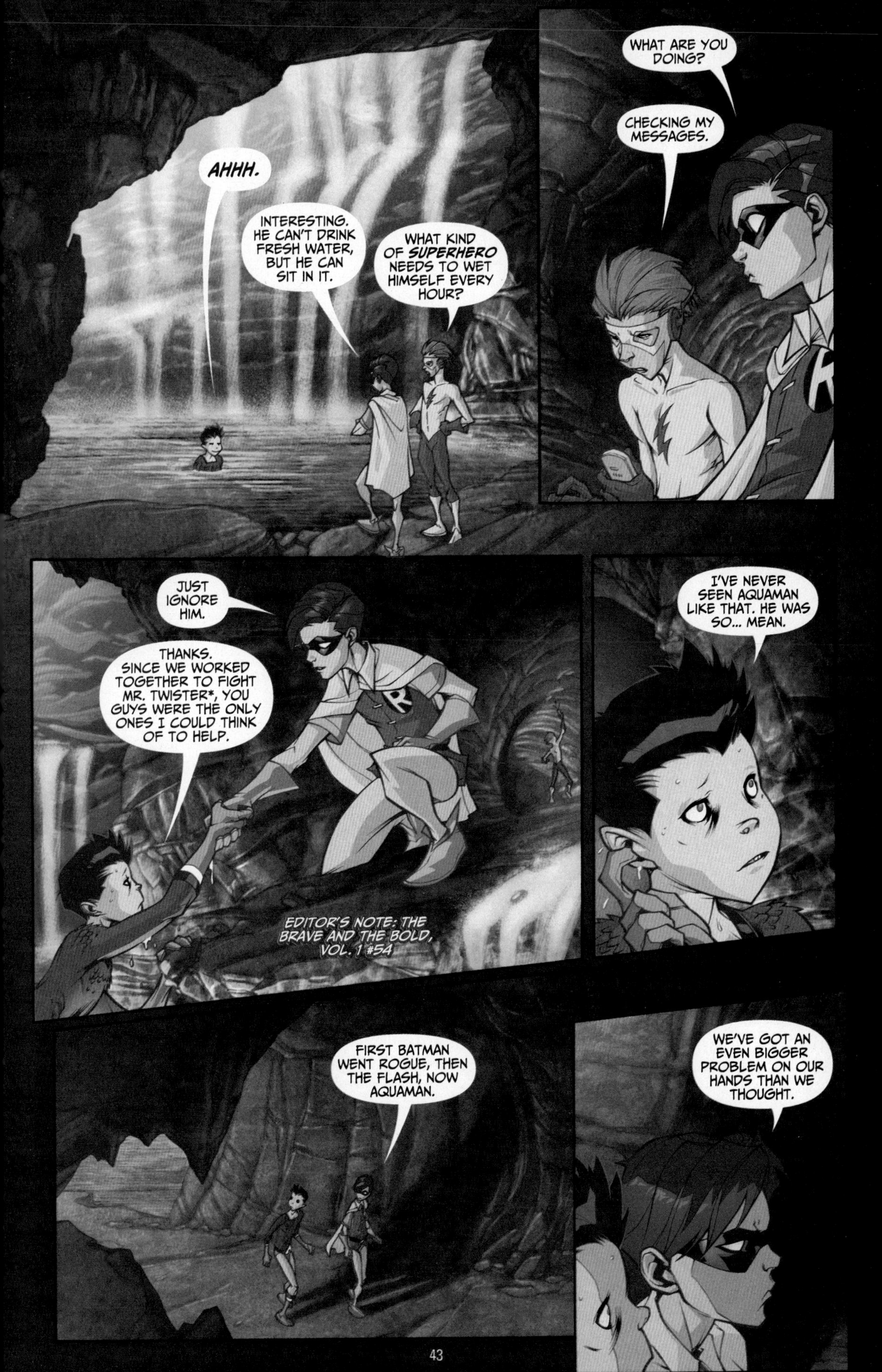
AHHH.
INTERESTING. HE CAN'T DRINK FRESH WATER, BUT HE CAN SIT IN IT.
WHAT KIND OF SUPERHERO NEEDS TO WET HIMSELF EVERY HOUR?
WHAT ARE YOU DOING?
CHECKING MY MESSAGES.
JUST IGNORE HIM.
THANKS. SINCE WE WORKED TOGETHER TO FIGHT MR. TWISTER*, YOU GUYS WERE THE ONLY ONES I COULD THINK OF TO HELP.
EDITOR'S NOTE: THE BRAVE AND THE BOLD, VOL. 1 #54
I'VE NEVER SEEN AQUAMAN LIKE THAT. HE WAS SO... MEAN.
FIRST BATMAN WENT ROGUE, THEN THE FLASH, NOW AQUAMAN.
WE'VE GOT AN EVEN BIGGER PROBLEM ON OUR HANDS THAN WE THOUGHT.

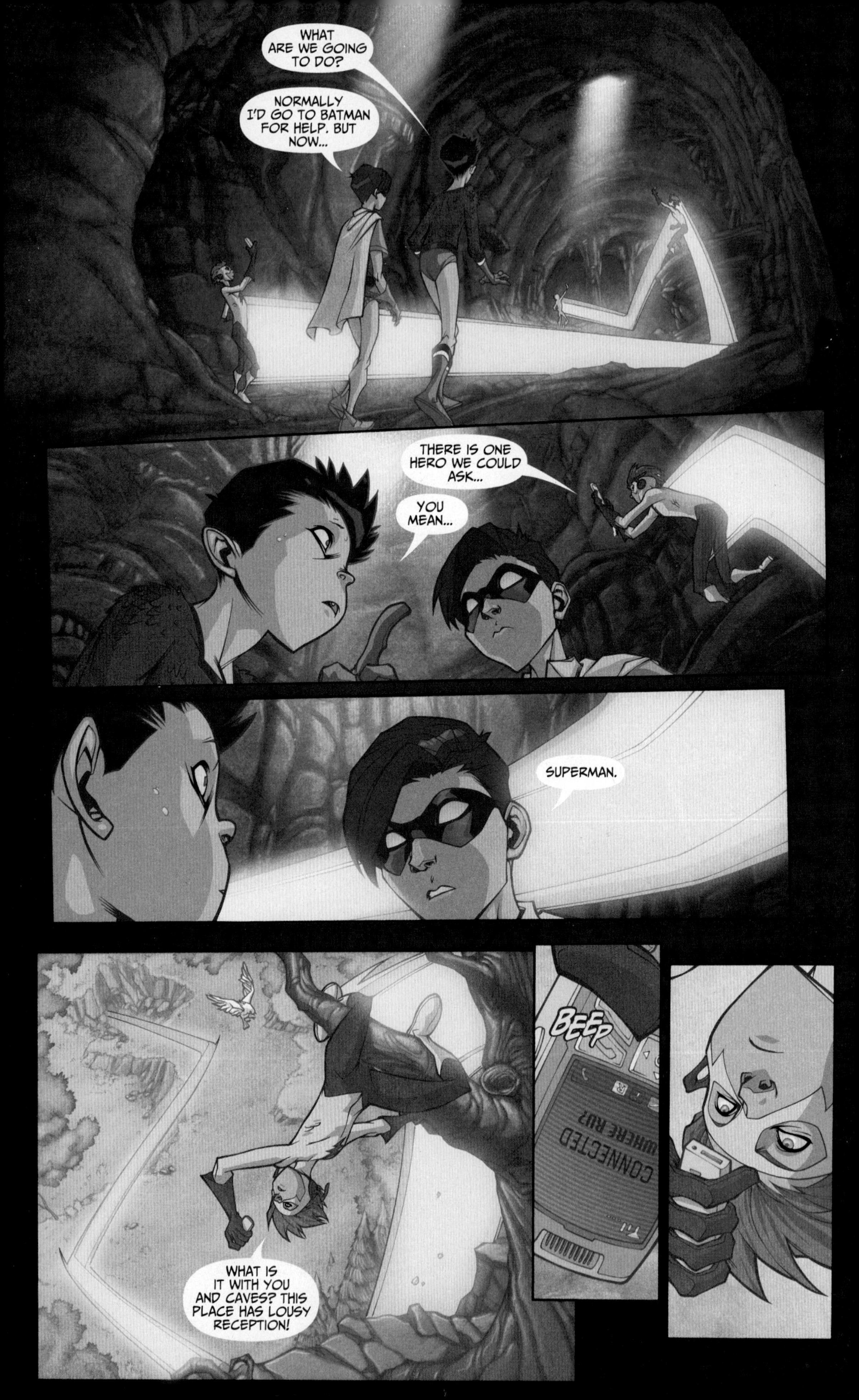
WHAT ARE WE GOING TO DO?
NORMALLY I'D GO TO BATMAN FOR HELP. BUT NOW...
THERE IS ONE HERO WE COULD ASK...
YOU MEAN...
SUPERMAN.
WHAT IS IT WITH YOU AND CAVES? THIS PLACE HAS LOUSY RECEPTION!
BEEP
CONNECTED
WHERE RU?

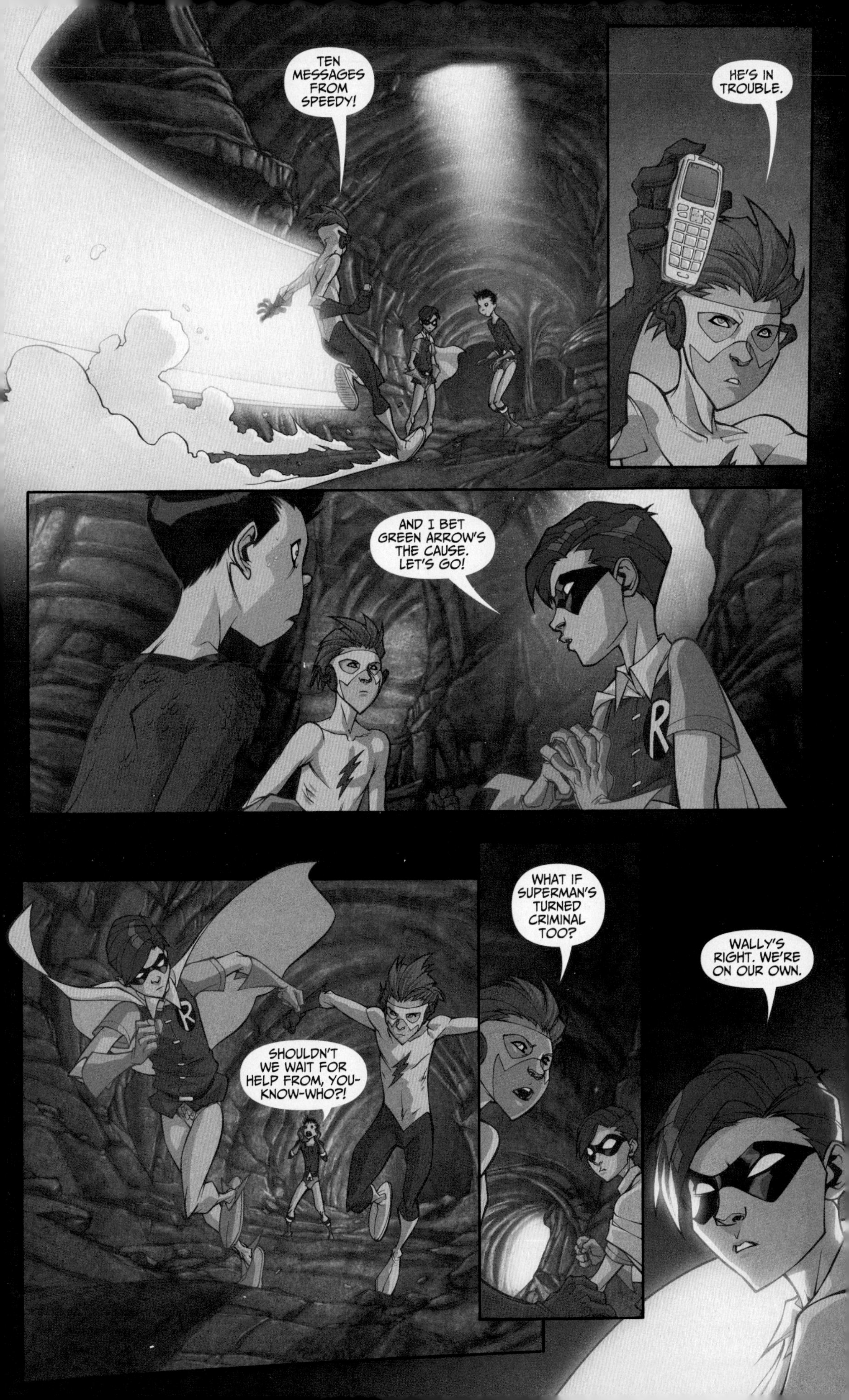
TEN MESSAGES FROM SPEEDY!
HE'S IN TROUBLE.
AND I BET GREEN ARROW'S THE CAUSE. LET'S GO!
SHOULDN'T WE WAIT FOR HELP FROM, YOU-KNOW-WHO?!
WHAT IF SUPERMAN'S TURNED CRIMINAL TOO?
WALLY'S RIGHT. WE'RE ON OUR OWN.

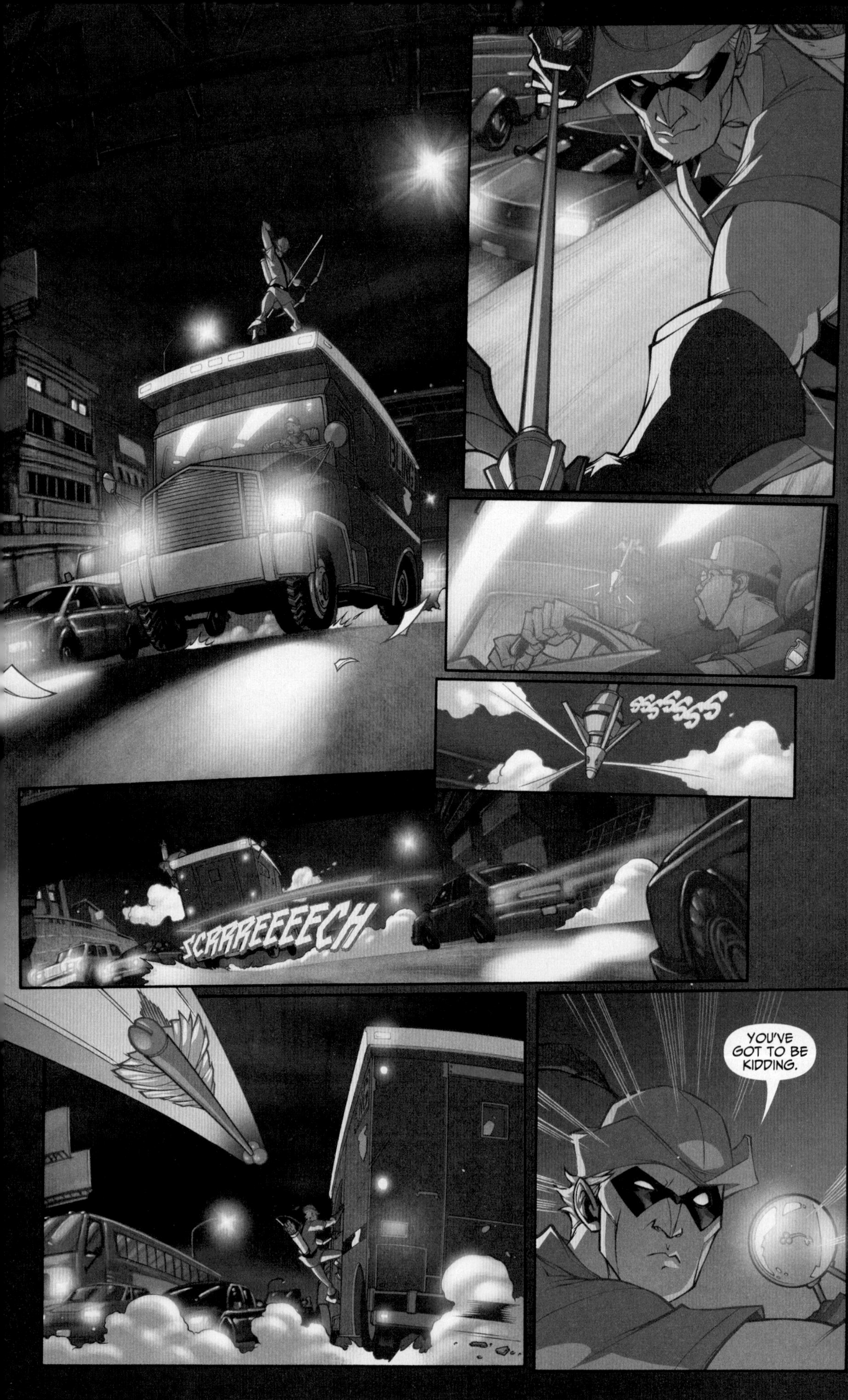
SSSSSSS
SCRRREEEEECH
YOU'VE GOT TO BE KIDDING.

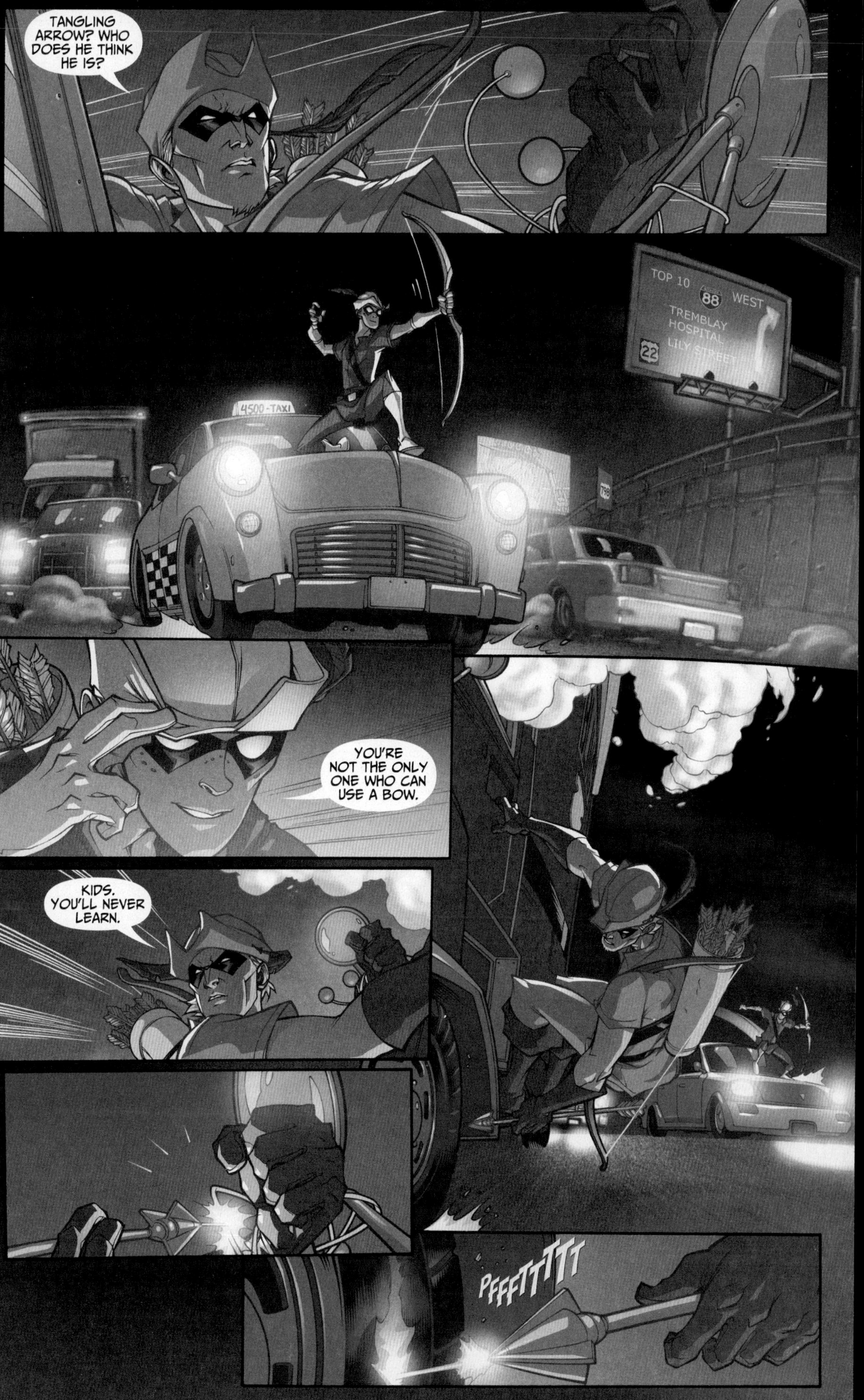
TANGLING ARROW? WHO DOES HE THINK HE IS?
TOP 10 88 WEST
TREMBLAY HOSPITAL
22 LILY STREET
4500-TAXI
YOU'RE NOT THE ONLY ONE WHO CAN USE A BOW.
KIDS. YOU'LL NEVER LEARN.
PFFFTTTTT

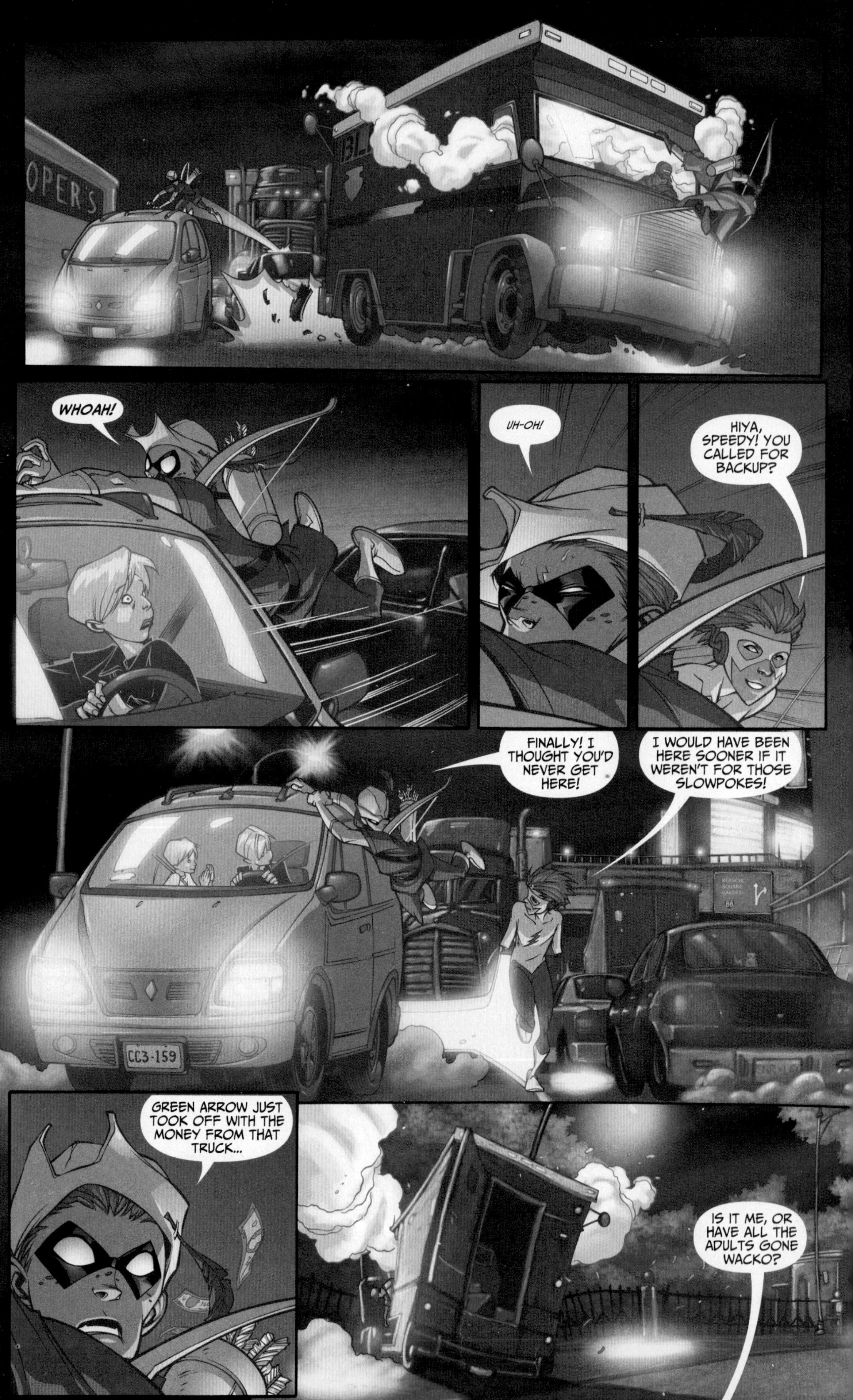
OPER'S
WHOAH!
UH-OH!
HIYA, SPEEDY! YOU CALLED FOR BACKUP?
FINALLY! I THOUGHT YOU'D NEVER GET HERE!
I WOULD HAVE BEEN HERE SOONER IF IT WEREN'T FOR THOSE SLOWPOKES!
CC3-159
GREEN ARROW JUST TOOK OFF WITH THE MONEY FROM THAT TRUCK...
IS IT ME, OR HAVE ALL THE ADULTS GONE WACKO?

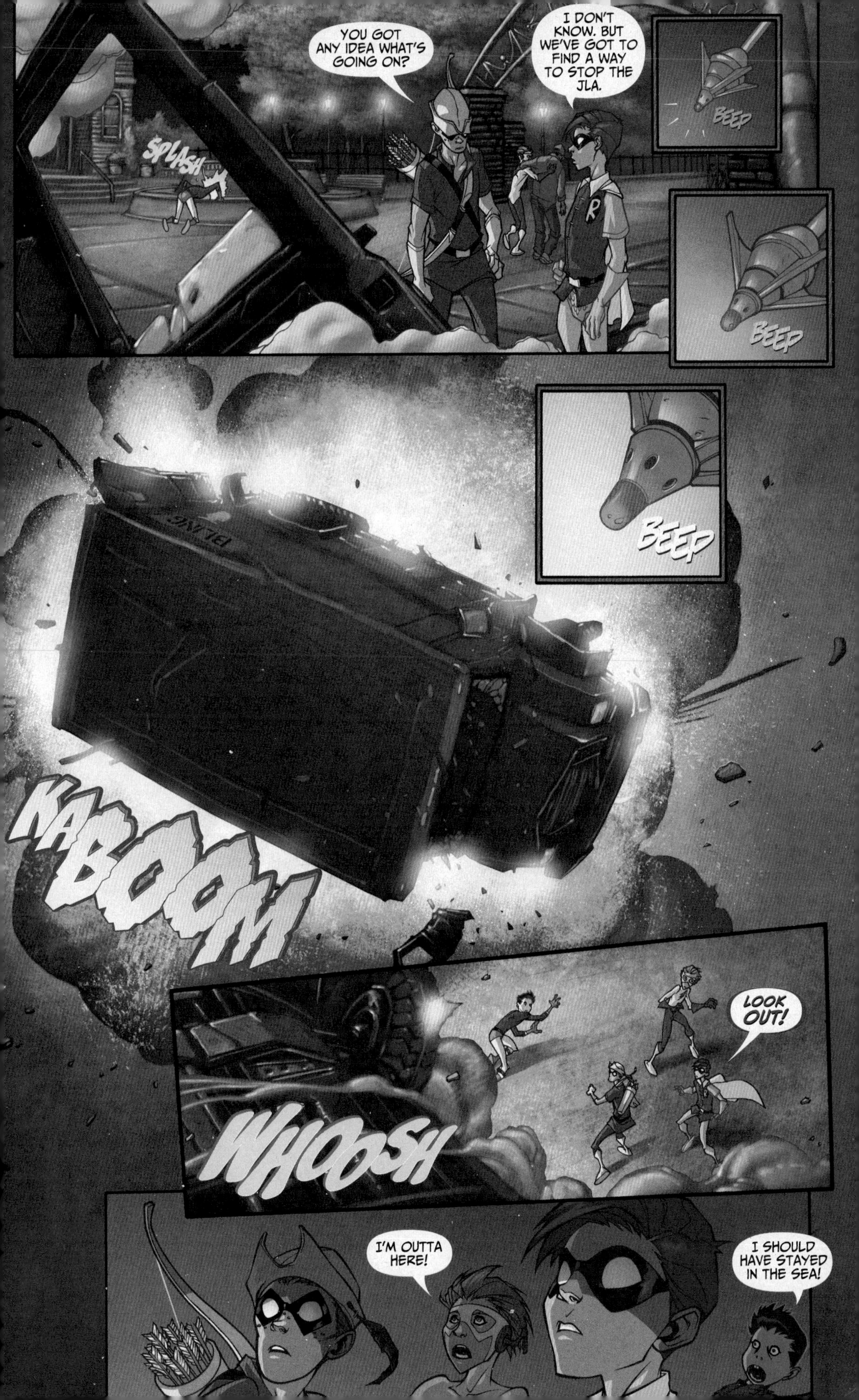
SPLASH
YOU GOT ANY IDEA WHAT'S GOING ON?
I DON'T KNOW. BUT WE'VE GOT TO FIND A WAY TO STOP THE JLA.
BEEP
BEEP
BEEP
KABOOM
WHOOSH
LOOK OUT!
I'M OUTTA HERE!
I SHOULD HAVE STAYED IN THE SEA!

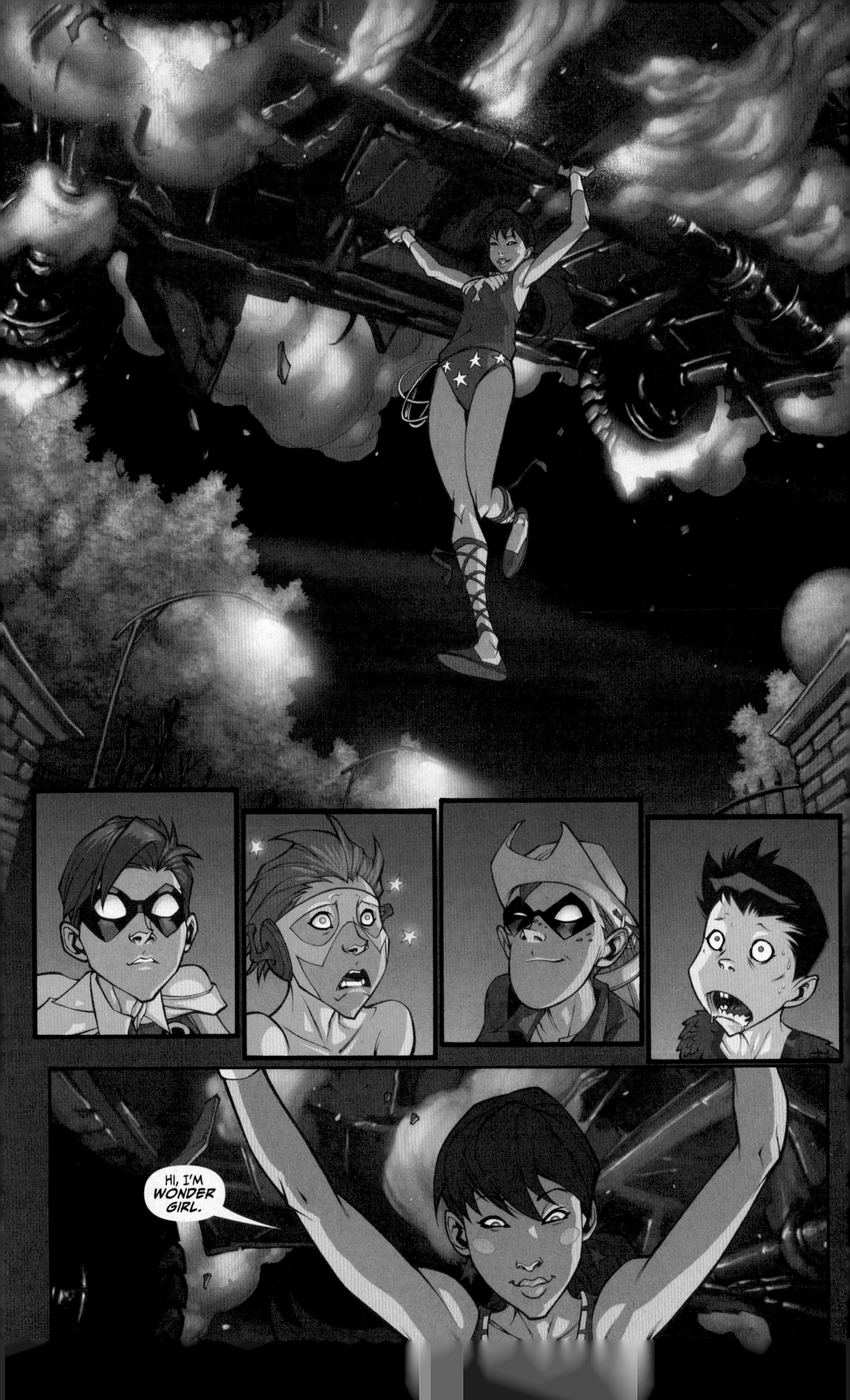
HI, I'M WONDER GIRL.

TEEN TITANS: YEAR ONE #3

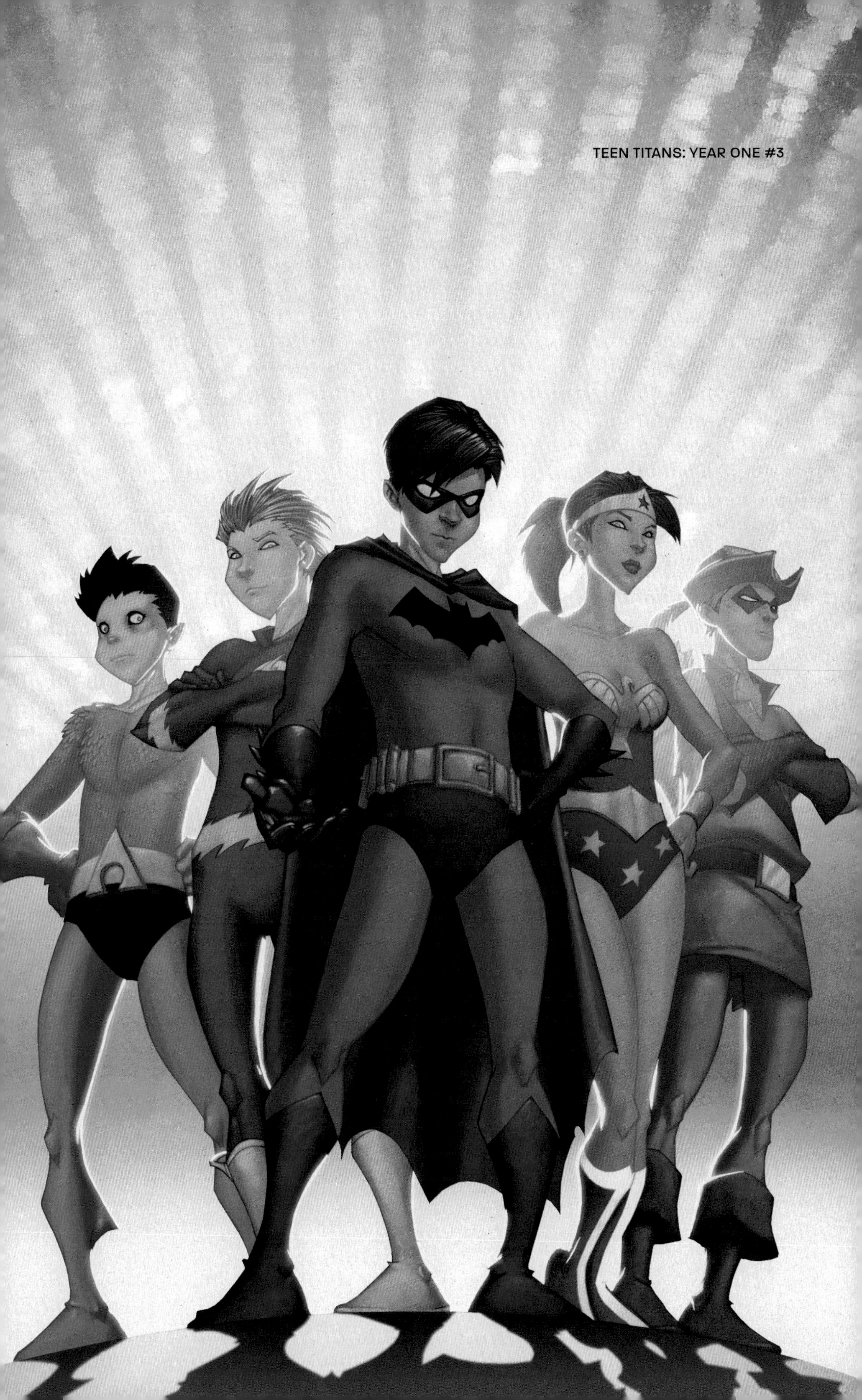

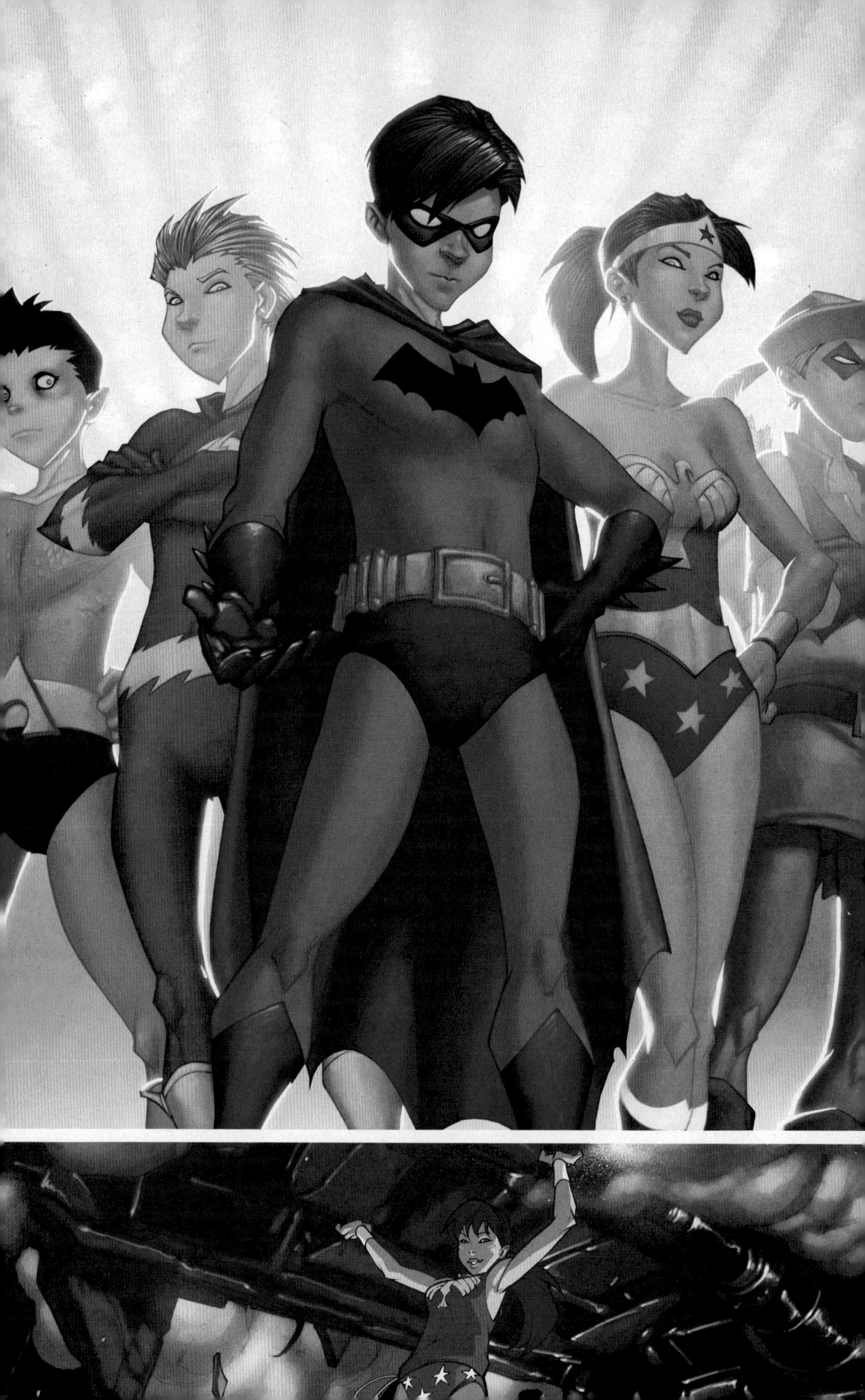

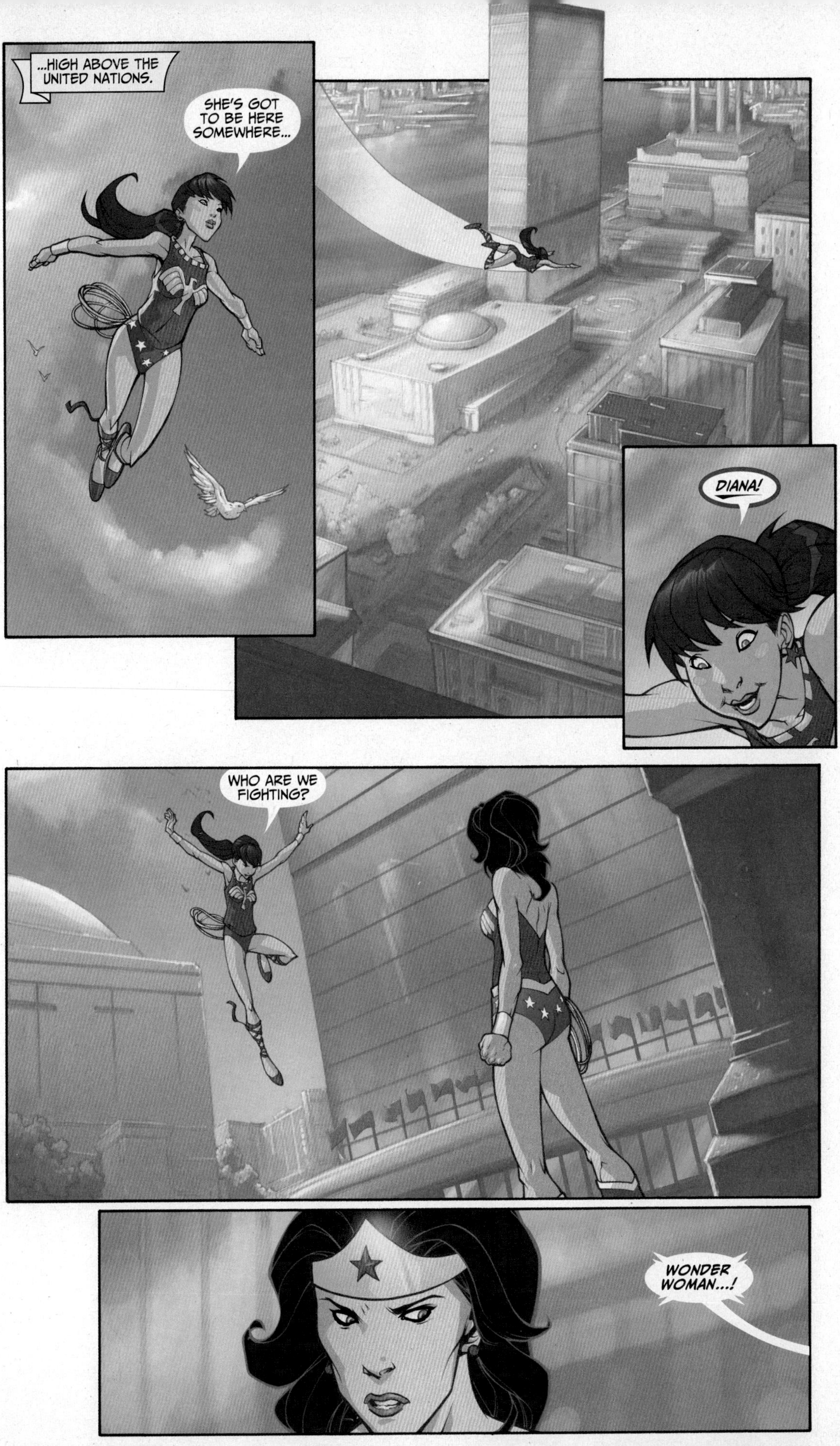
...HIGH ABOVE THE UNITED NATIONS.
SHE'S GOT TO BE HERE SOMEWHERE...
DIANA!
WHO ARE WE FIGHTING?
WONDER WOMAN...!

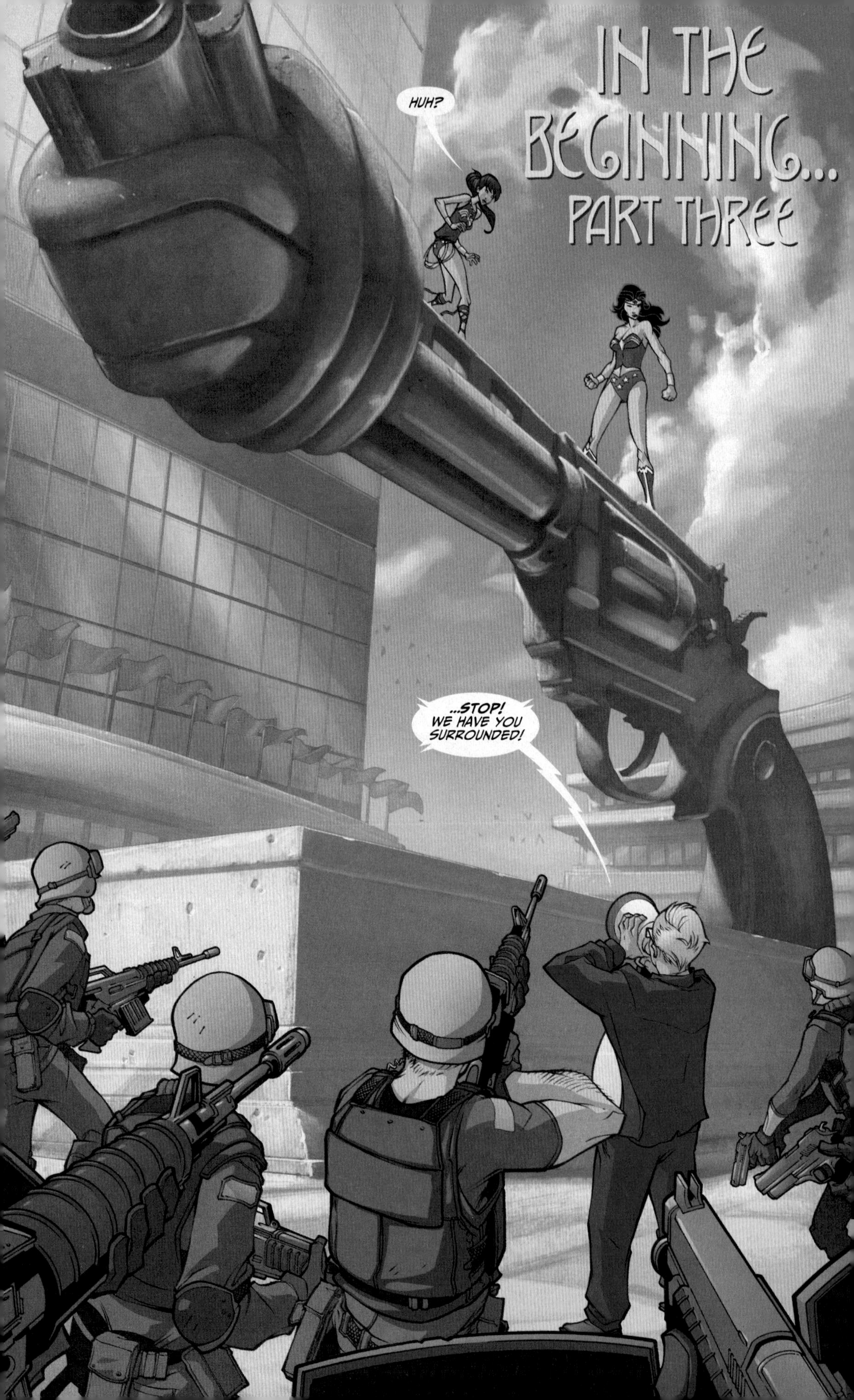
IN THE BEGINNING... PART THREE
HUH?
...STOP! WE HAVE YOU SURROUNDED!

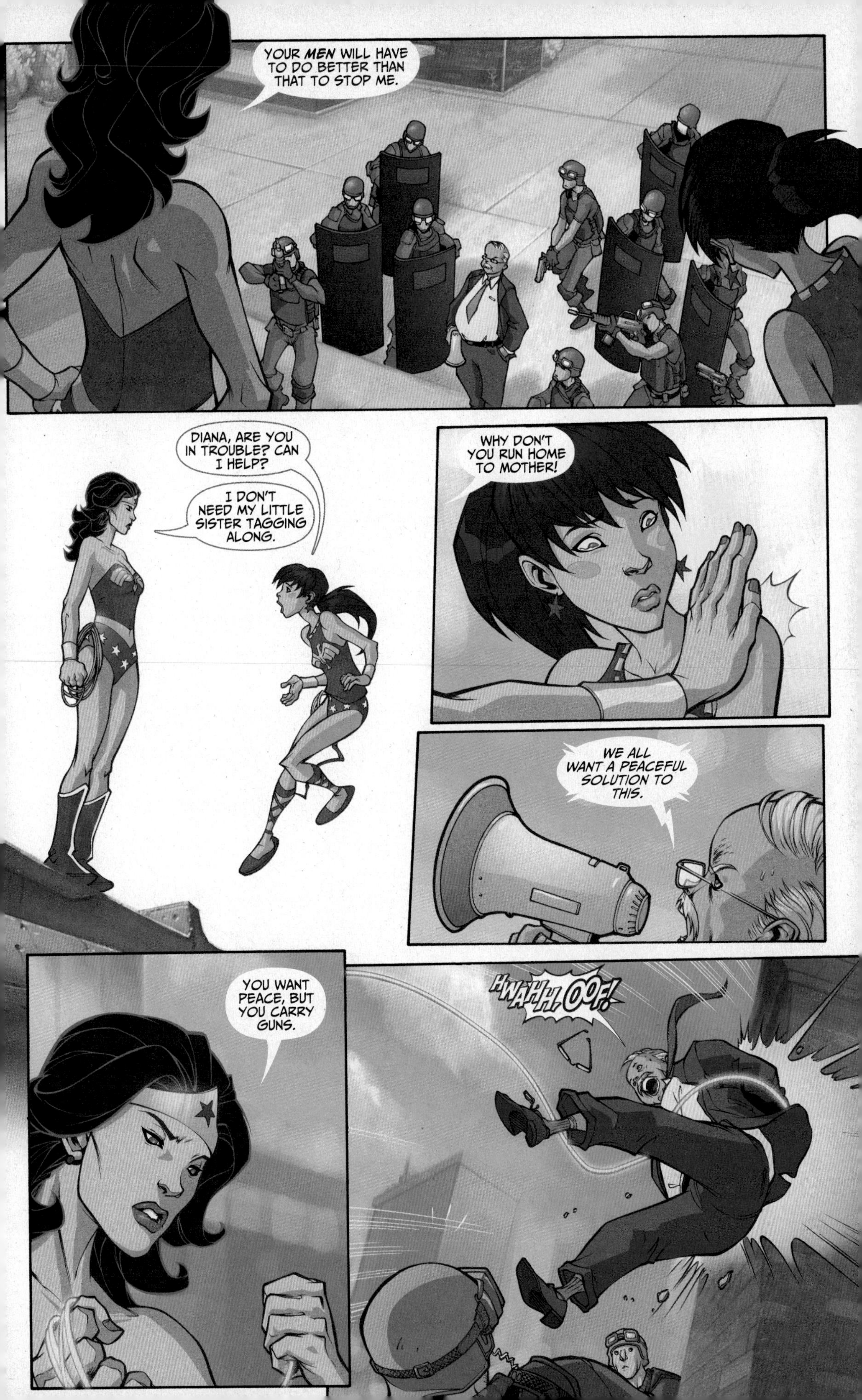
YOUR MEN WILL HAVE TO DO BETTER THAN THAT TO STOP ME.
DIANA, ARE YOU IN TROUBLE? CAN I HELP?
I DON'T NEED MY LITTLE SISTER TAGGING ALONG.
WHY DON'T YOU RUN HOME TO MOTHER!
WE ALL WANT A PEACEFUL SOLUTION TO THIS.
YOU WANT PEACE, BUT YOU CARRY GUNS.
HWAHH, OOF!

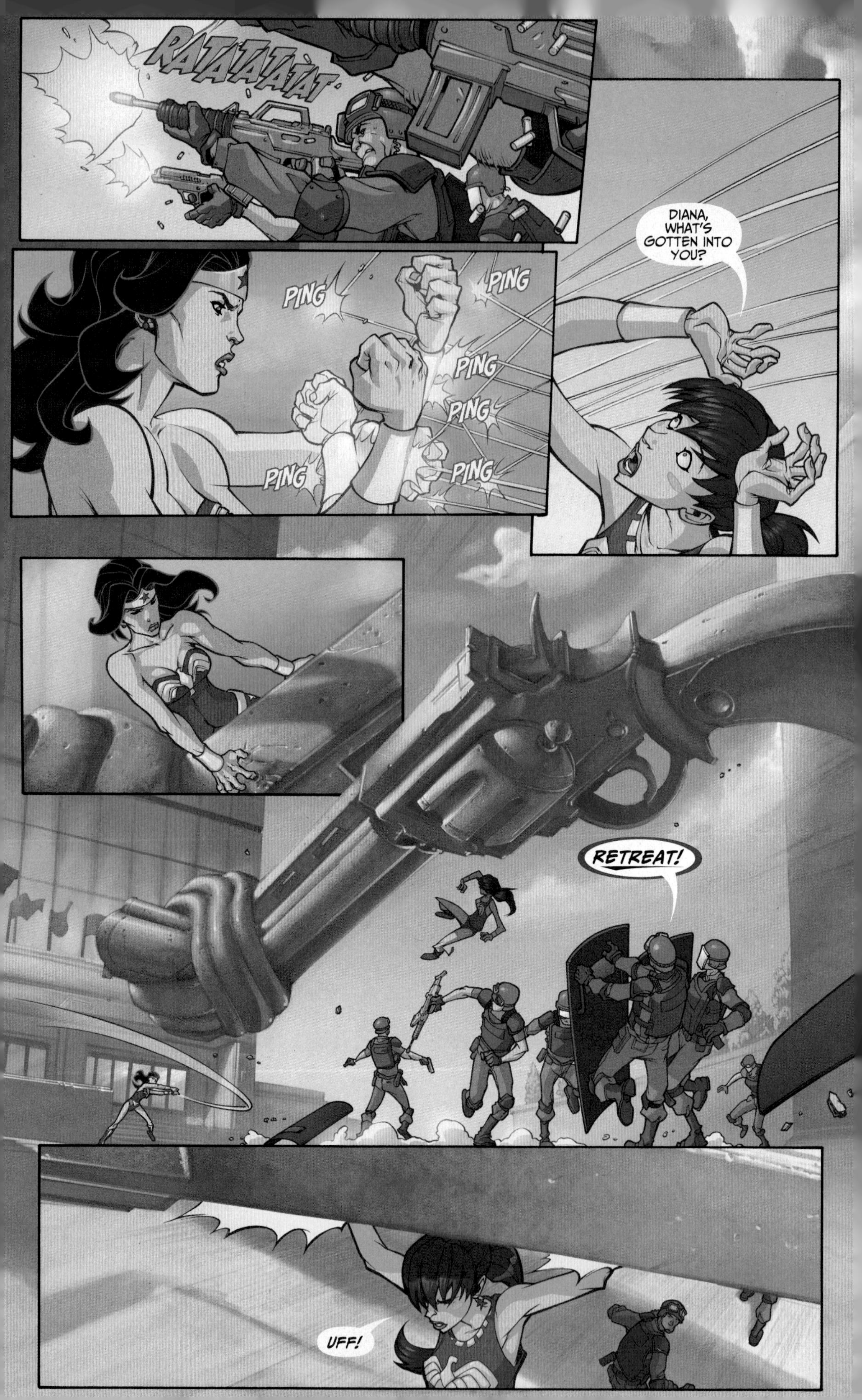
RATATATATAT
PING
PING
PING
PING
PING
PING
DIANA, WHAT'S GOTTEN INTO YOU?
RETREAT!
UFF!

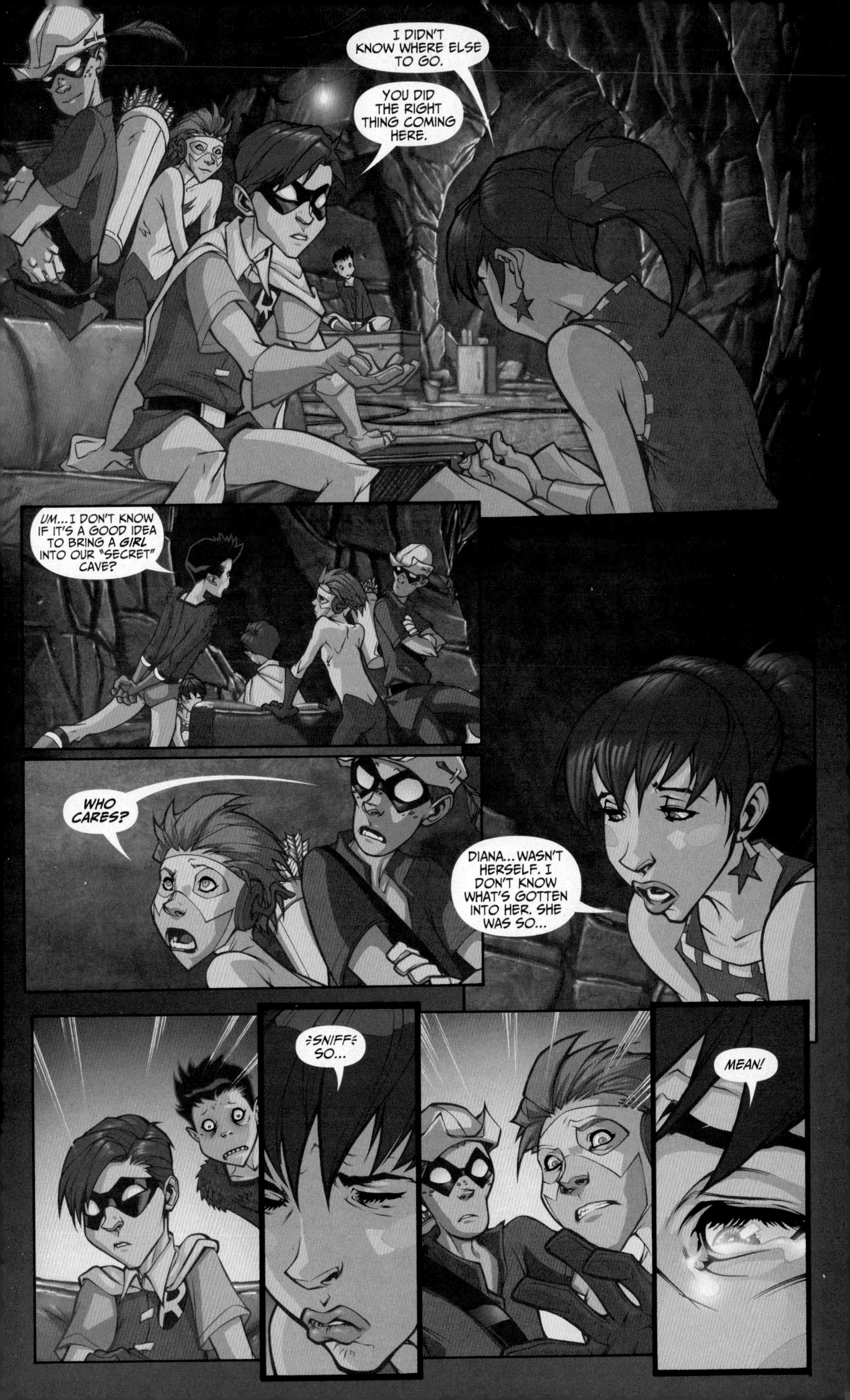
I DIDN'T KNOW WHERE ELSE TO GO.
YOU DID THE RIGHT THING COMING HERE.
UM...I DON'T KNOW IF IT'S A GOOD IDEA TO BRING A GIRL INTO OUR "SECRET" CAVE?
WHO CARES?
DIANA...WASN'T HERSELF. I DON'T KNOW WHAT'S GOTTEN INTO HER. SHE WAS SO...
SNIFF SO...
MEAN!

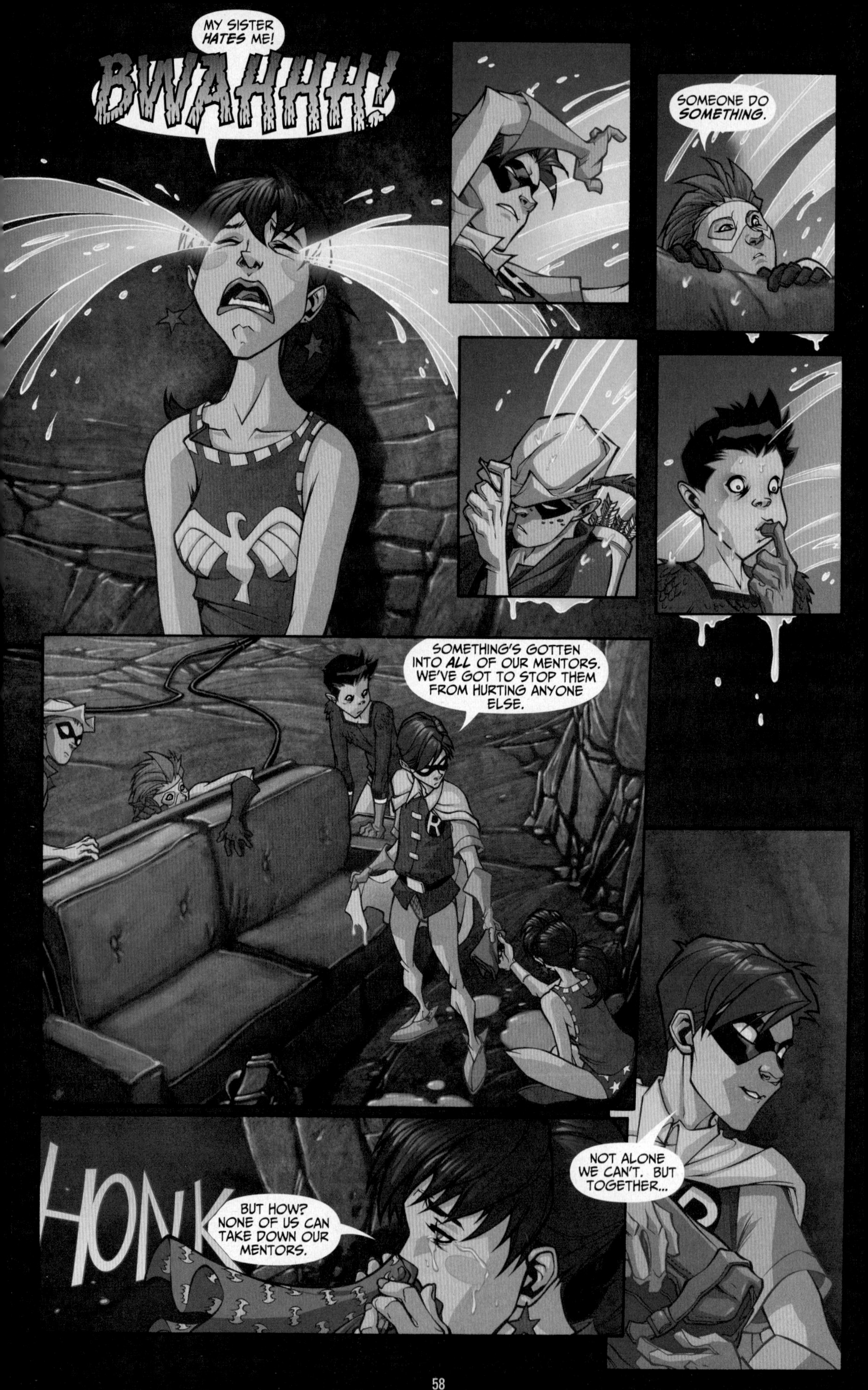
MY SISTER HATES ME!
BWAHHH!
SOMEONE DO SOMETHING.
SOMETHING'S GOTTEN INTO ALL OF OUR MENTORS. WE'VE GOT TO STOP THEM FROM HURTING ANYONE ELSE.
HONK
BUT HOW? NONE OF US CAN TAKE DOWN OUR MENTORS.
NOT ALONE WE CAN'T. BUT TOGETHER...

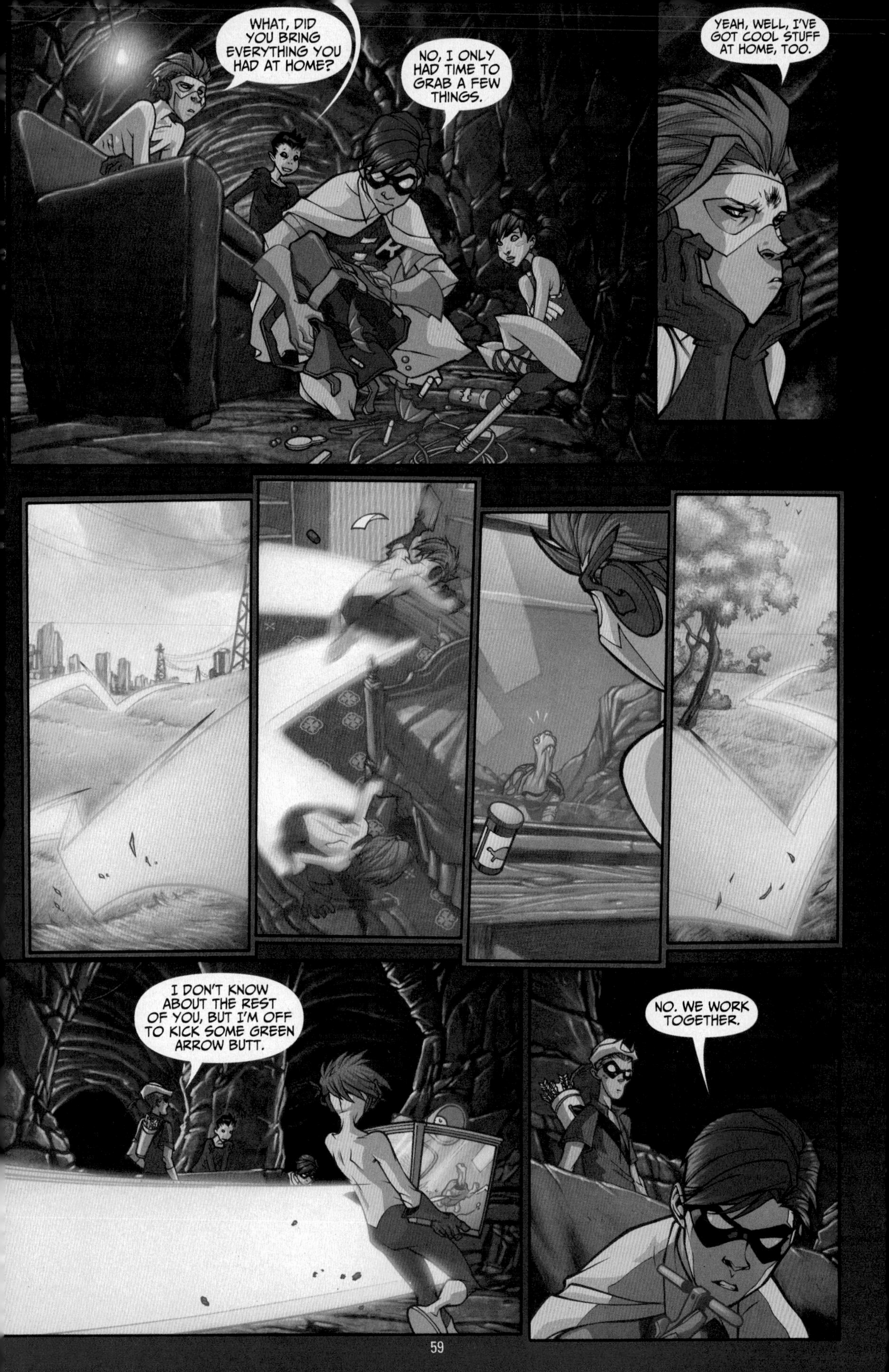

WHAT, DID YOU BRING EVERYTHING YOU HAD AT HOME?
NO, I ONLY HAD TIME TO GRAB A FEW THINGS.
YEAH, WELL, I'VE GOT COOL STUFF AT HOME, TOO.
I DON'T KNOW ABOUT THE REST OF YOU, BUT I'M OFF TO KICK SOME GREEN ARROW BUTT.
NO. WE WORK TOGETHER.

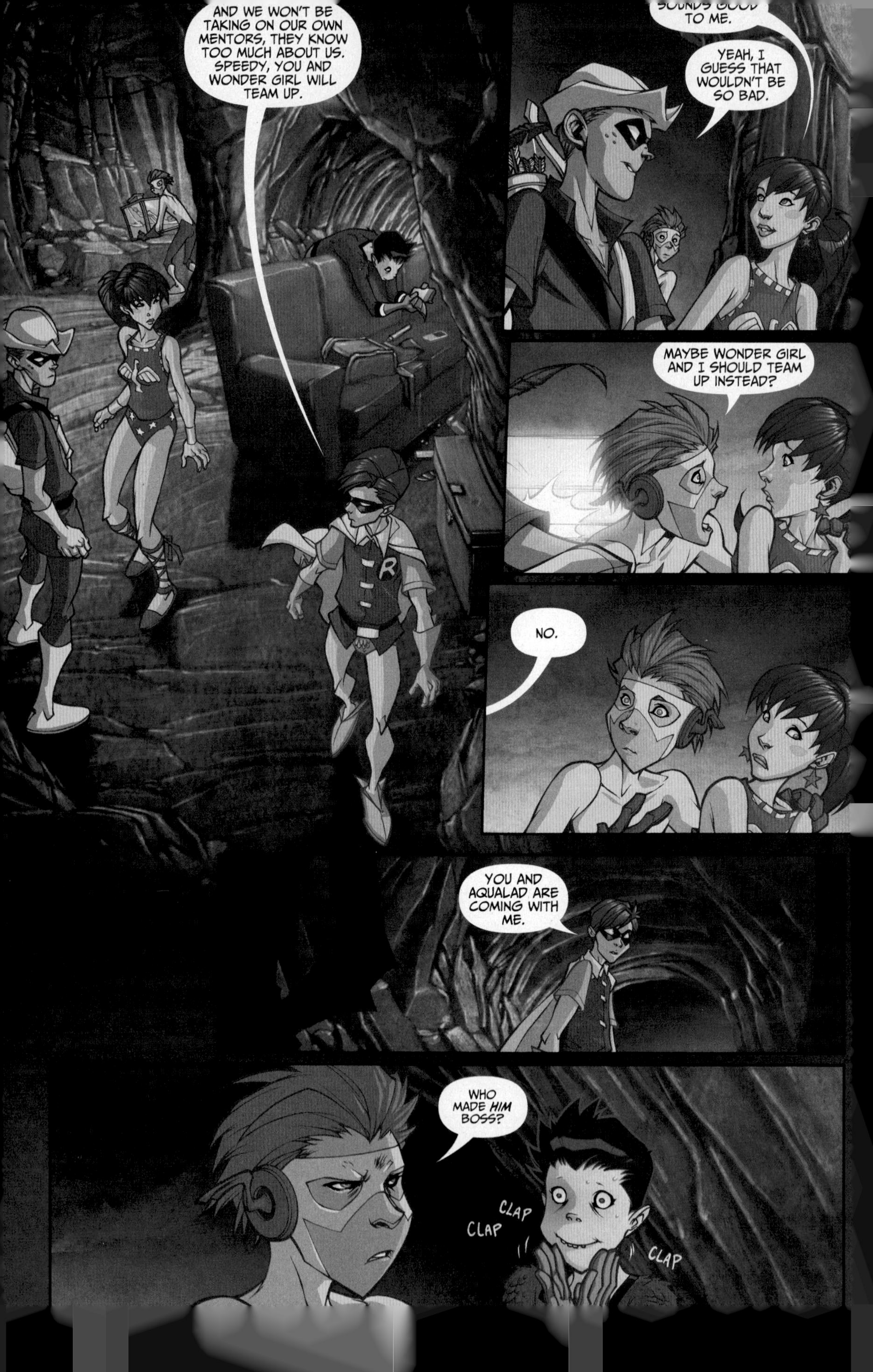
AND WE WON'T BE TAKING ON OUR OWN MENTORS, THEY KNOW TOO MUCH ABOUT US. SPEEDY, YOU AND WONDER GIRL WILL TEAM UP.
TO ME.
YEAH, I GUESS THAT WOULDN'T BE SO BAD.
MAYBE WONDER GIRL AND I SHOULD TEAM UP INSTEAD?
NO.
YOU AND AQUALAD ARE COMING WITH ME.
WHO MADE *HIM* BOSS?
CLAP
CLAP
CLAP

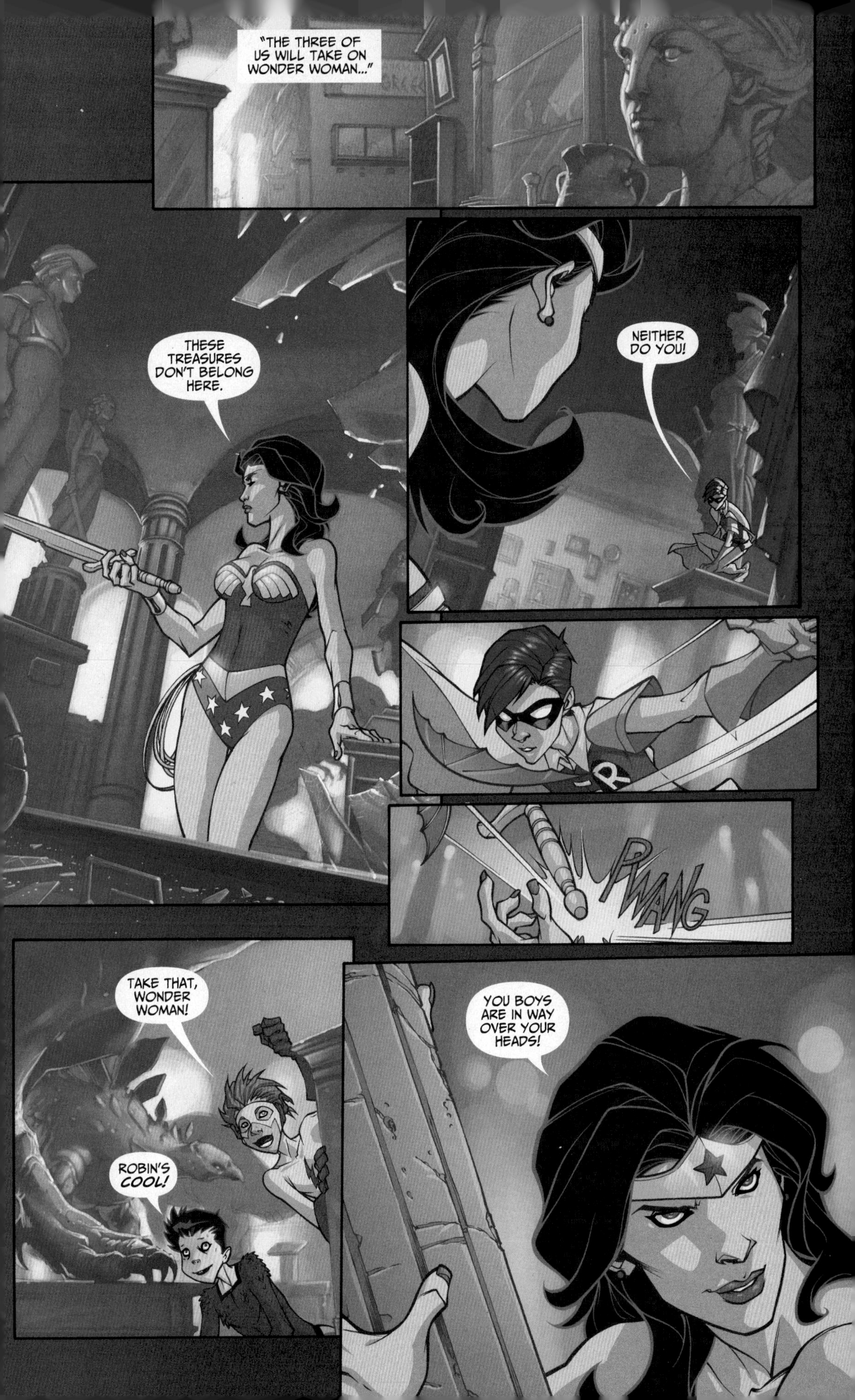
"THE THREE OF US WILL TAKE ON WONDER WOMAN..."
THESE TREASURES DON'T BELONG HERE.
NEITHER DO YOU!
PWANG
TAKE THAT, WONDER WOMAN!
ROBIN'S COOL!
YOU BOYS ARE IN WAY OVER YOUR HEADS!

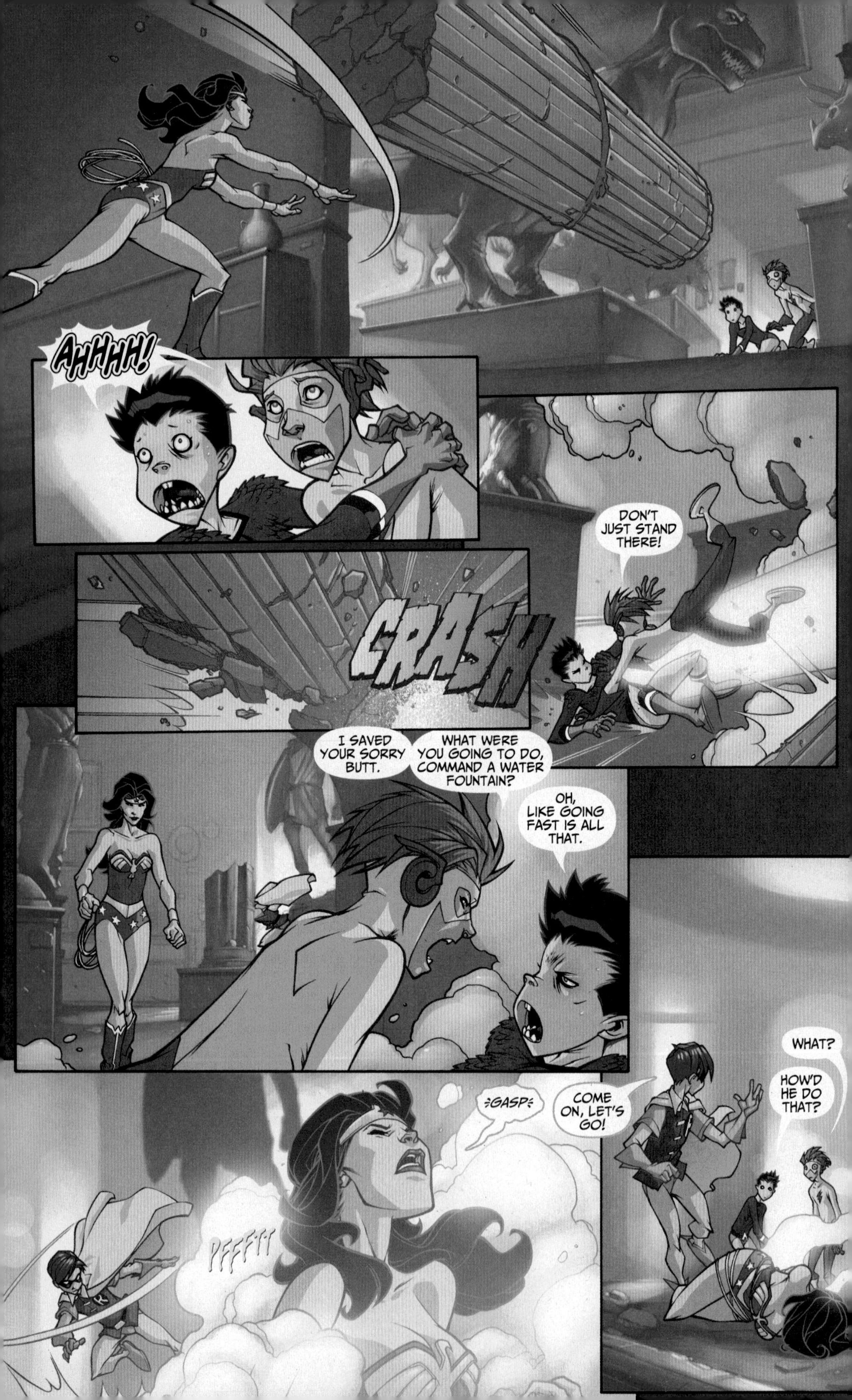
AHHHH!
DON'T JUST STAND THERE!
CRASH
I SAVED YOUR SORRY BUTT.
WHAT WERE YOU GOING TO DO, COMMAND A WATER FOUNTAIN?
OH, LIKE GOING FAST IS ALL THAT.
PFFFTT
GASP
COME ON, LET'S GO!
WHAT?
HOW'D HE DO THAT?

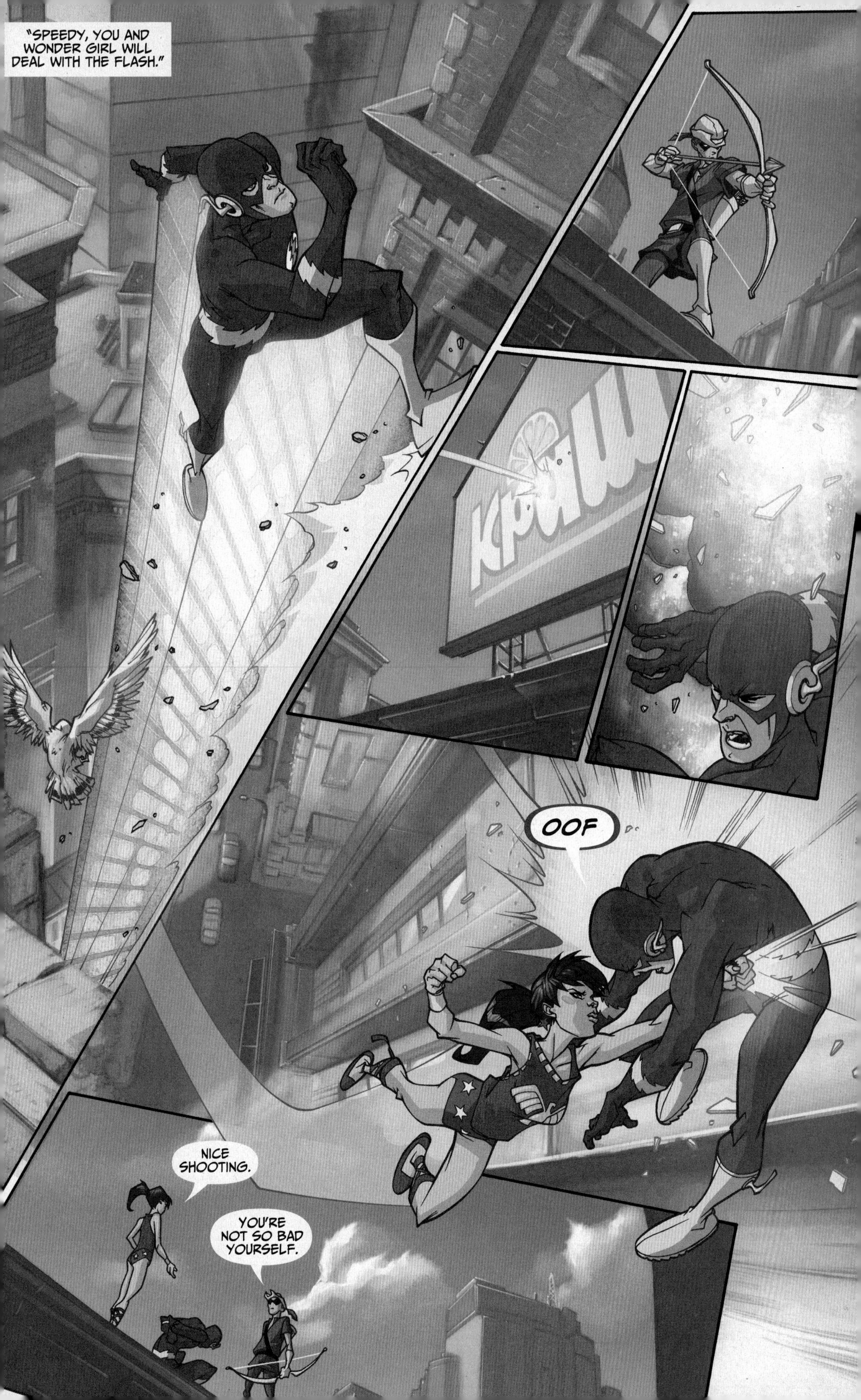
"SPEEDY, YOU AND WONDER GIRL WILL DEAL WITH THE FLASH."
КРИШ
OOF
NICE SHOOTING.
YOU'RE NOT SO BAD YOURSELF.

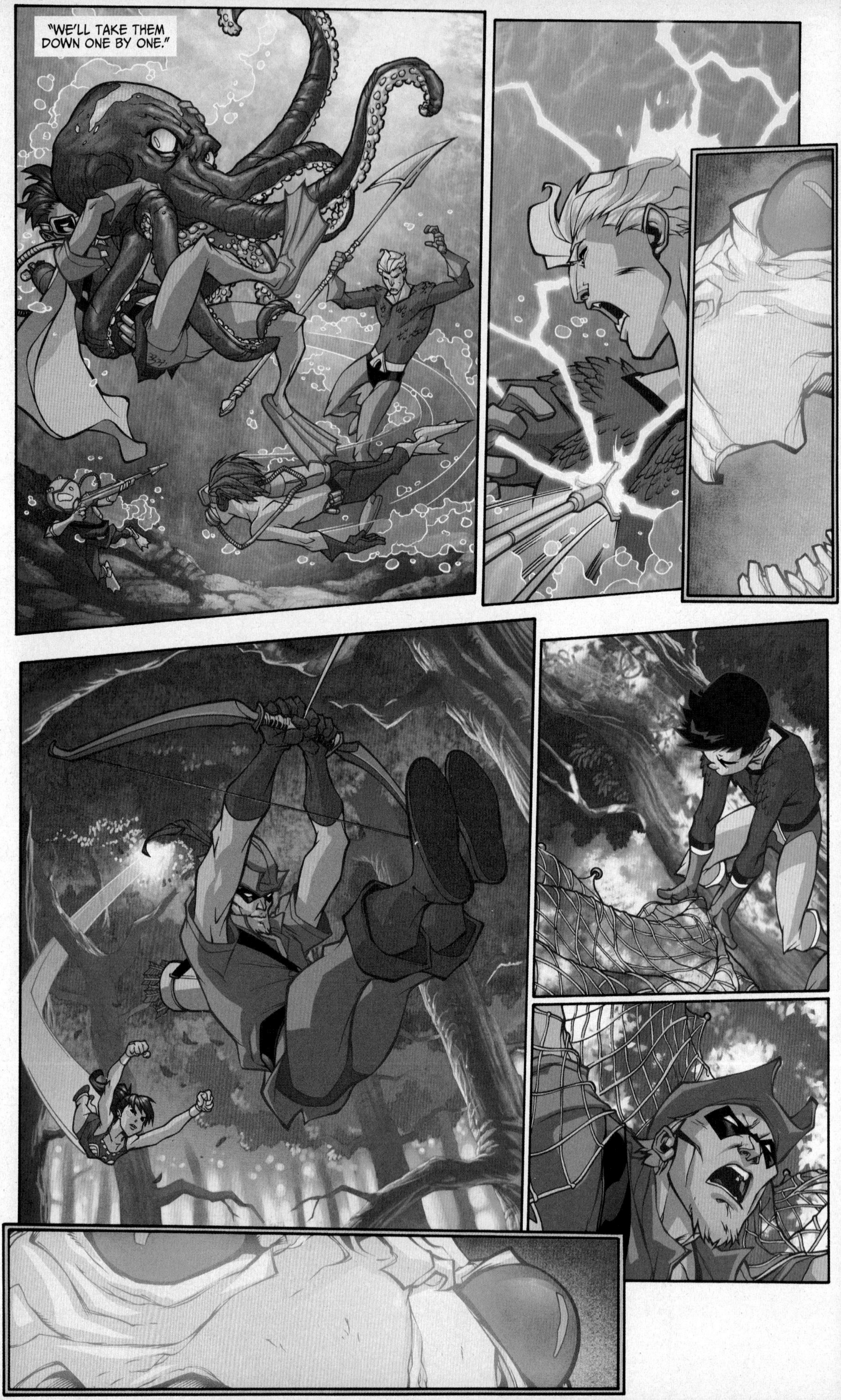
"WE'LL TAKE THEM DOWN ONE BY ONE."

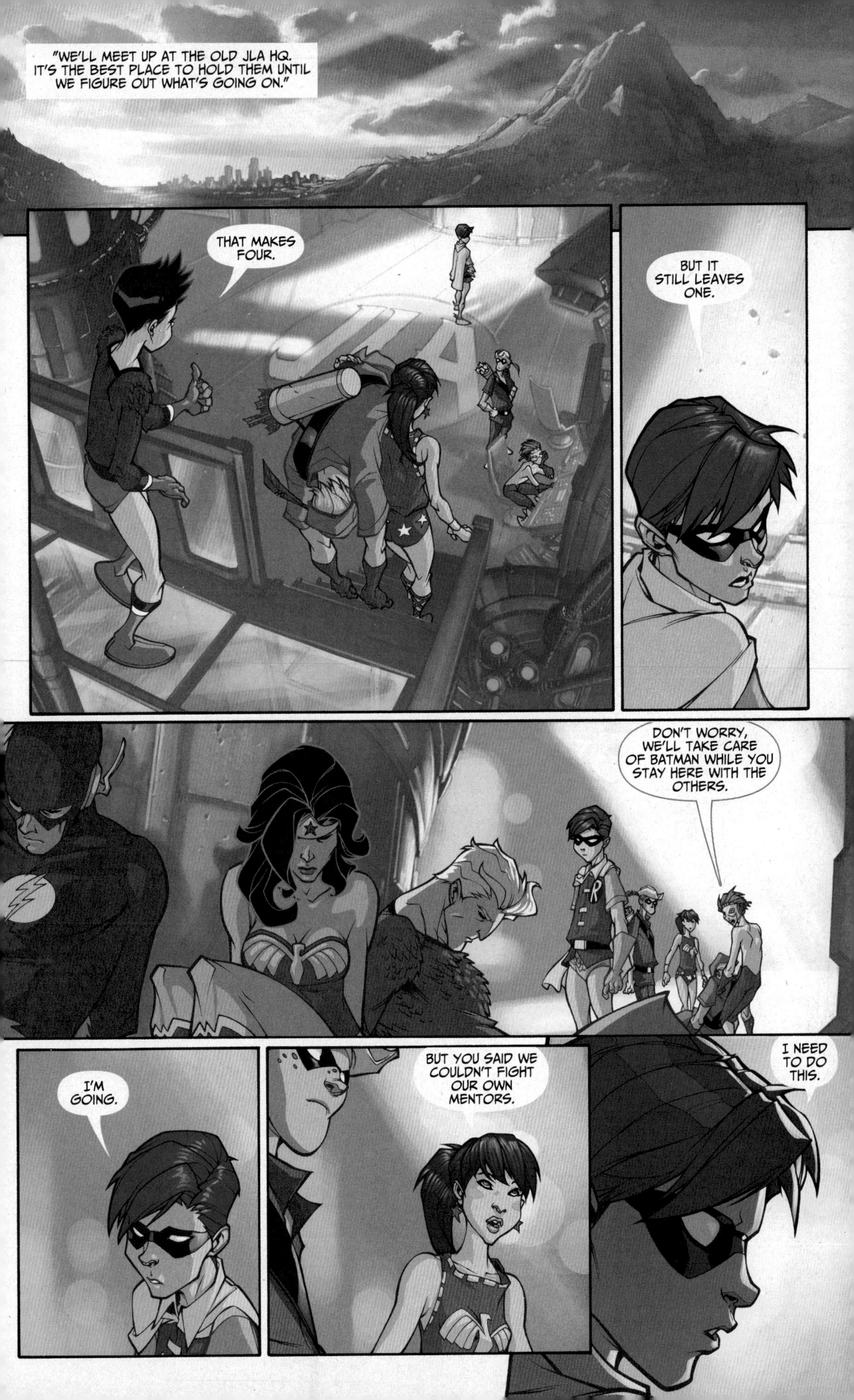
"WE'LL MEET UP AT THE OLD JLA HQ. IT'S THE BEST PLACE TO HOLD THEM UNTIL WE FIGURE OUT WHAT'S GOING ON."
THAT MAKES FOUR.
BUT IT STILL LEAVES ONE.
DON'T WORRY, WE'LL TAKE CARE OF BATMAN WHILE YOU STAY HERE WITH THE OTHERS.
I'M GOING.
BUT YOU SAID WE COULDN'T FIGHT OUR OWN MENTORS.
I NEED TO DO THIS.

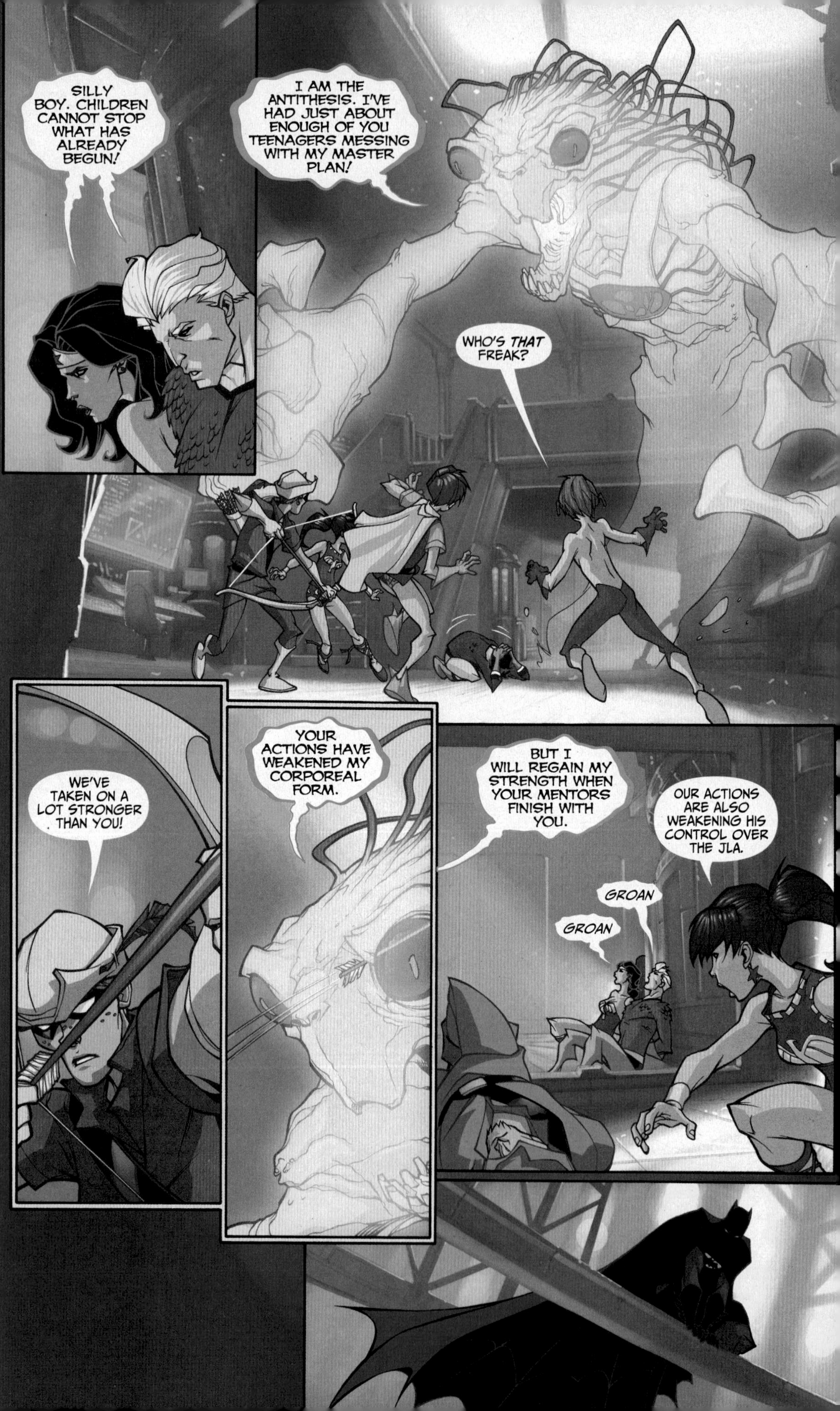
SILLY BOY. CHILDREN CANNOT STOP WHAT HAS ALREADY BEGUN!
I AM THE ANTITHESIS. I'VE HAD JUST ABOUT ENOUGH OF YOU TEENAGERS MESSING WITH MY MASTER PLAN!
WHO'S *THAT* FREAK?
WE'VE TAKEN ON A LOT STRONGER THAN YOU!
YOUR ACTIONS HAVE WEAKENED MY CORPOREAL FORM.
BUT I WILL REGAIN MY STRENGTH WHEN YOUR MENTORS FINISH WITH YOU.
OUR ACTIONS ARE ALSO WEAKENING HIS CONTROL OVER THE JLA.
GROAN
GROAN

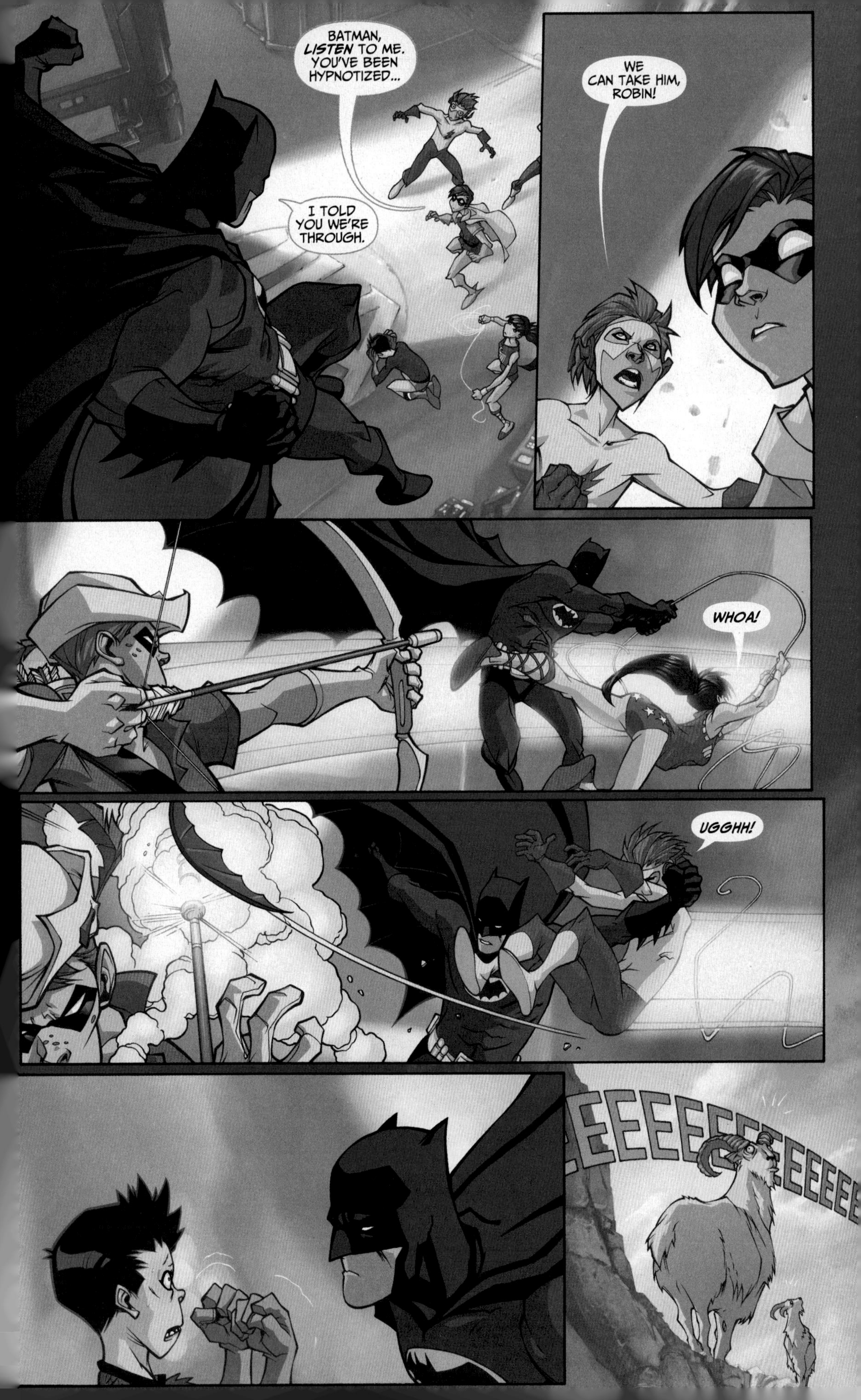
BATMAN, LISTEN TO ME. YOU'VE BEEN HYPNOTIZED...
I TOLD YOU WE'RE THROUGH.
WE CAN TAKE HIM, ROBIN!
WHOA!
UGGHH!
EEEEEEEEEEEEEEEEE

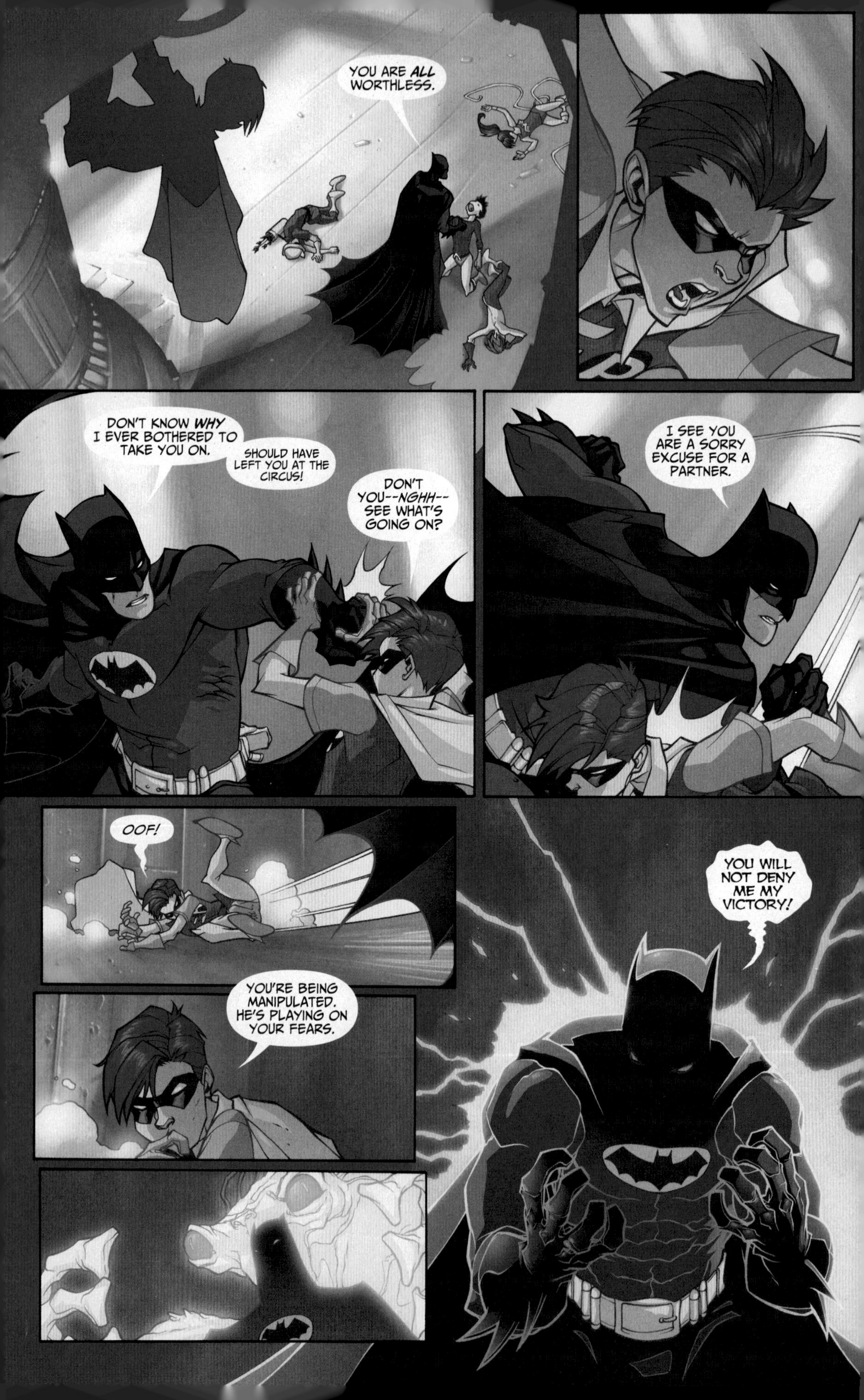
YOU ARE *ALL* WORTHLESS.
DON'T KNOW *WHY* I EVER BOTHERED TO TAKE YOU ON.
SHOULD HAVE LEFT YOU AT THE CIRCUS!
DON'T YOU--*NGHH*--SEE WHAT'S GOING ON?
I SEE YOU ARE A SORRY EXCUSE FOR A PARTNER.
OOF!
YOU'RE BEING MANIPULATED. HE'S PLAYING ON YOUR FEARS.
YOU WILL NOT DENY ME MY VICTORY!

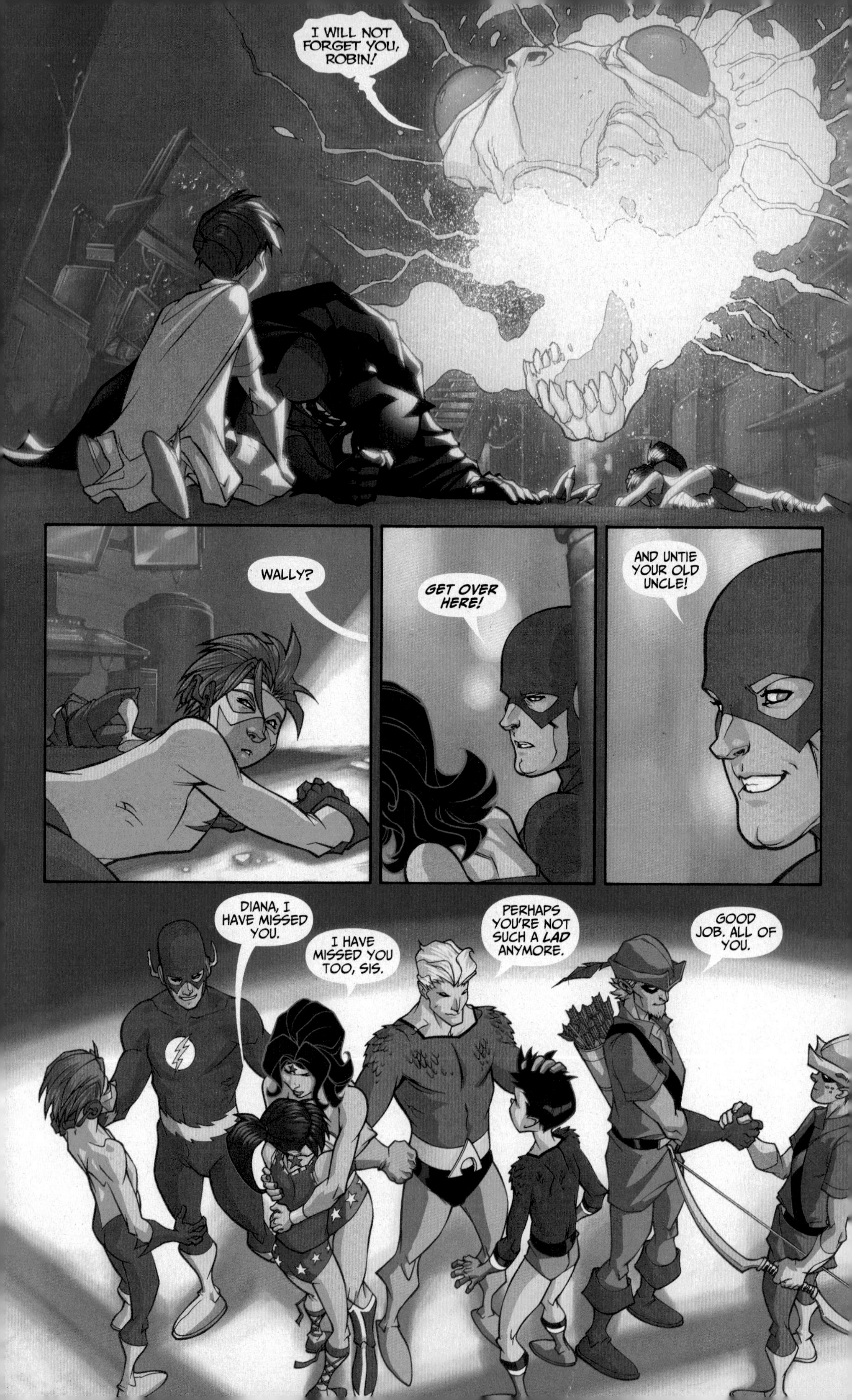
I WILL NOT FORGET YOU, ROBIN!
WALLY?
GET OVER HERE!
AND UNTIE YOUR OLD UNCLE!
DIANA, I HAVE MISSED YOU.
I HAVE MISSED YOU TOO, SIS.
PERHAPS YOU'RE NOT SUCH A LAD ANYMORE.
GOOD JOB. ALL OF YOU.

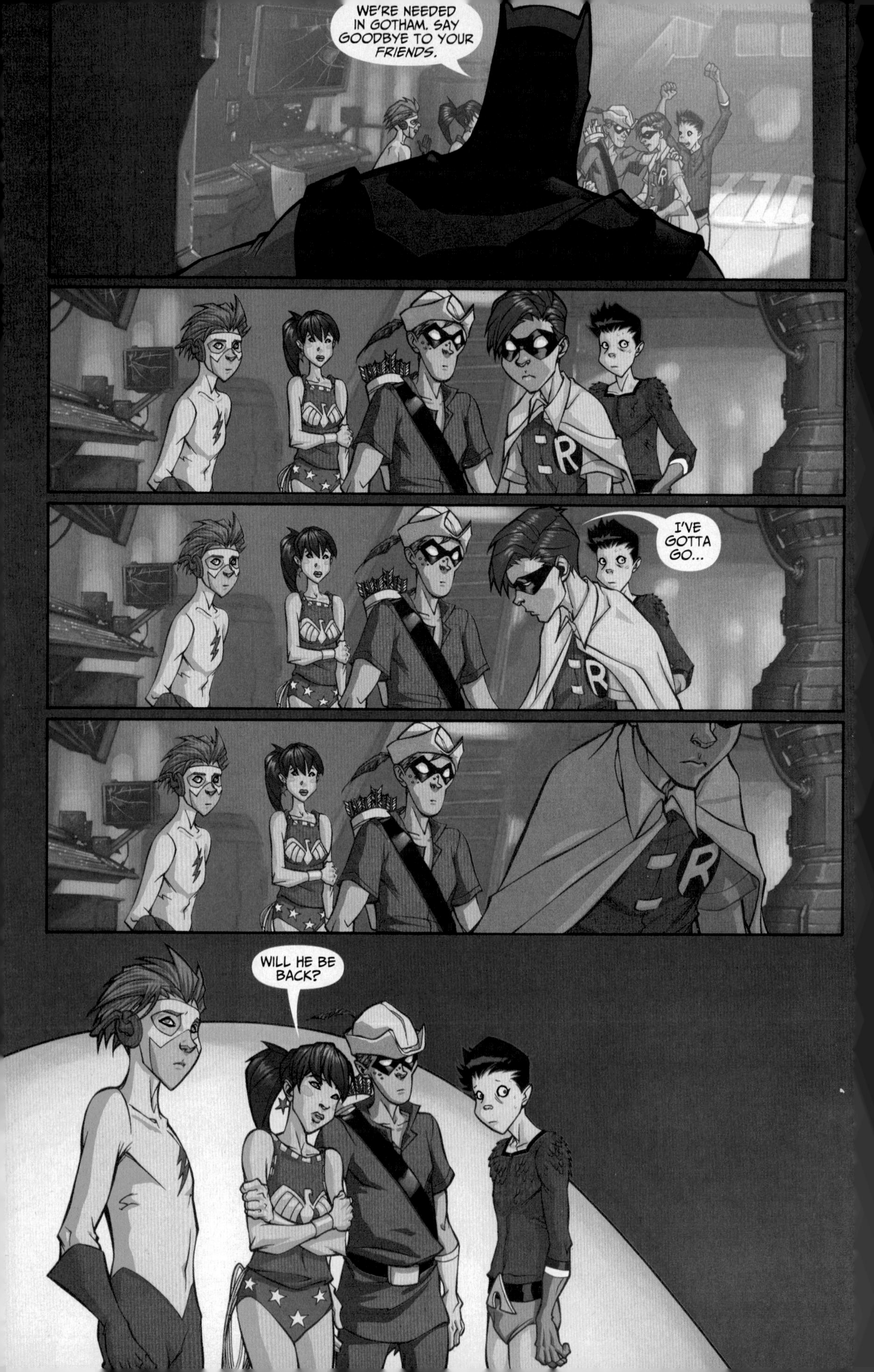
WE'RE NEEDED IN GOTHAM. SAY GOODBYE TO YOUR FRIENDS.
I'VE GOTTA GO...
WILL HE BE BACK?

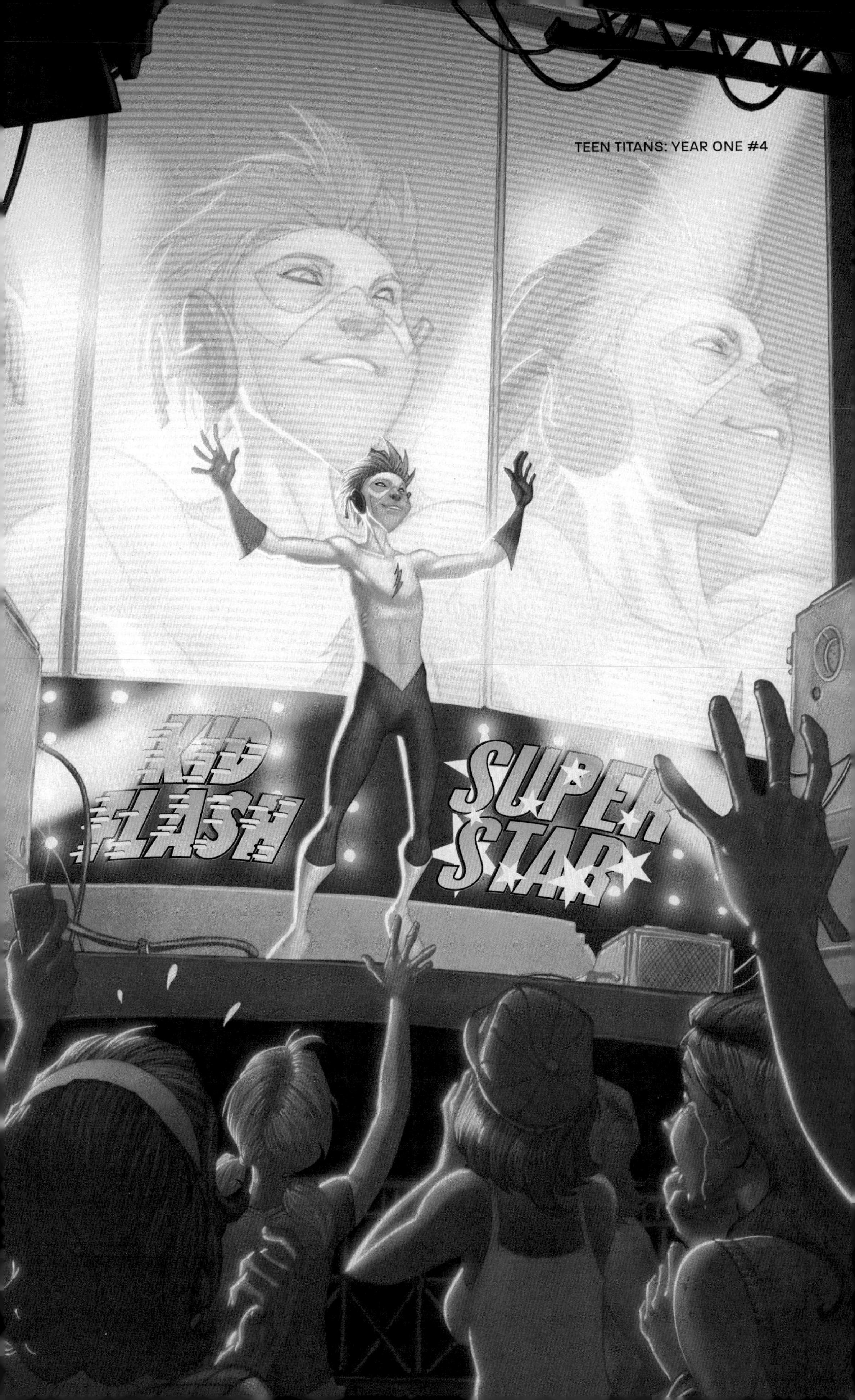
TEEN TITANS: YEAR ONE #4
KID FLASH
SUPER STAR

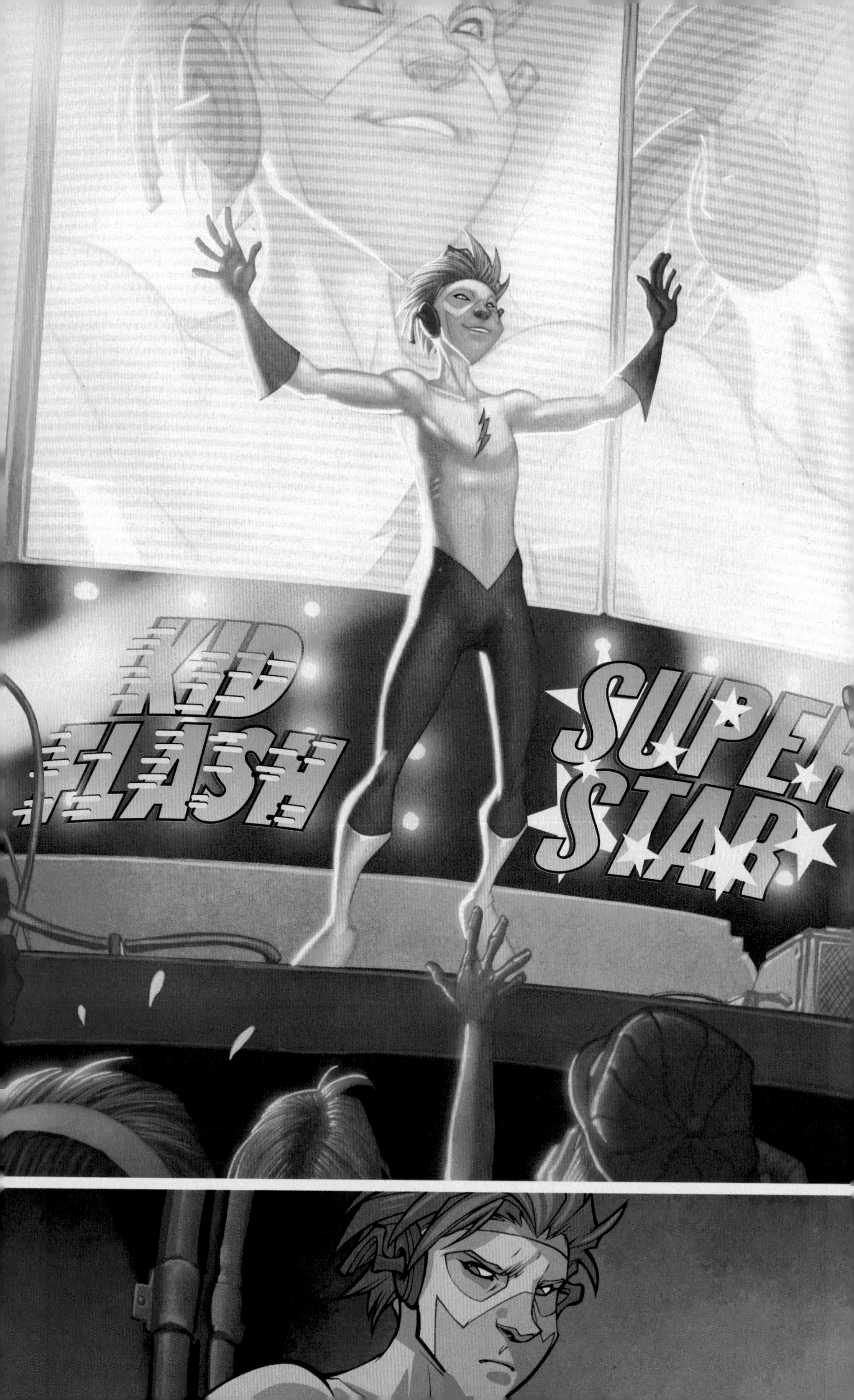
KID FLASH
SUPER STAR

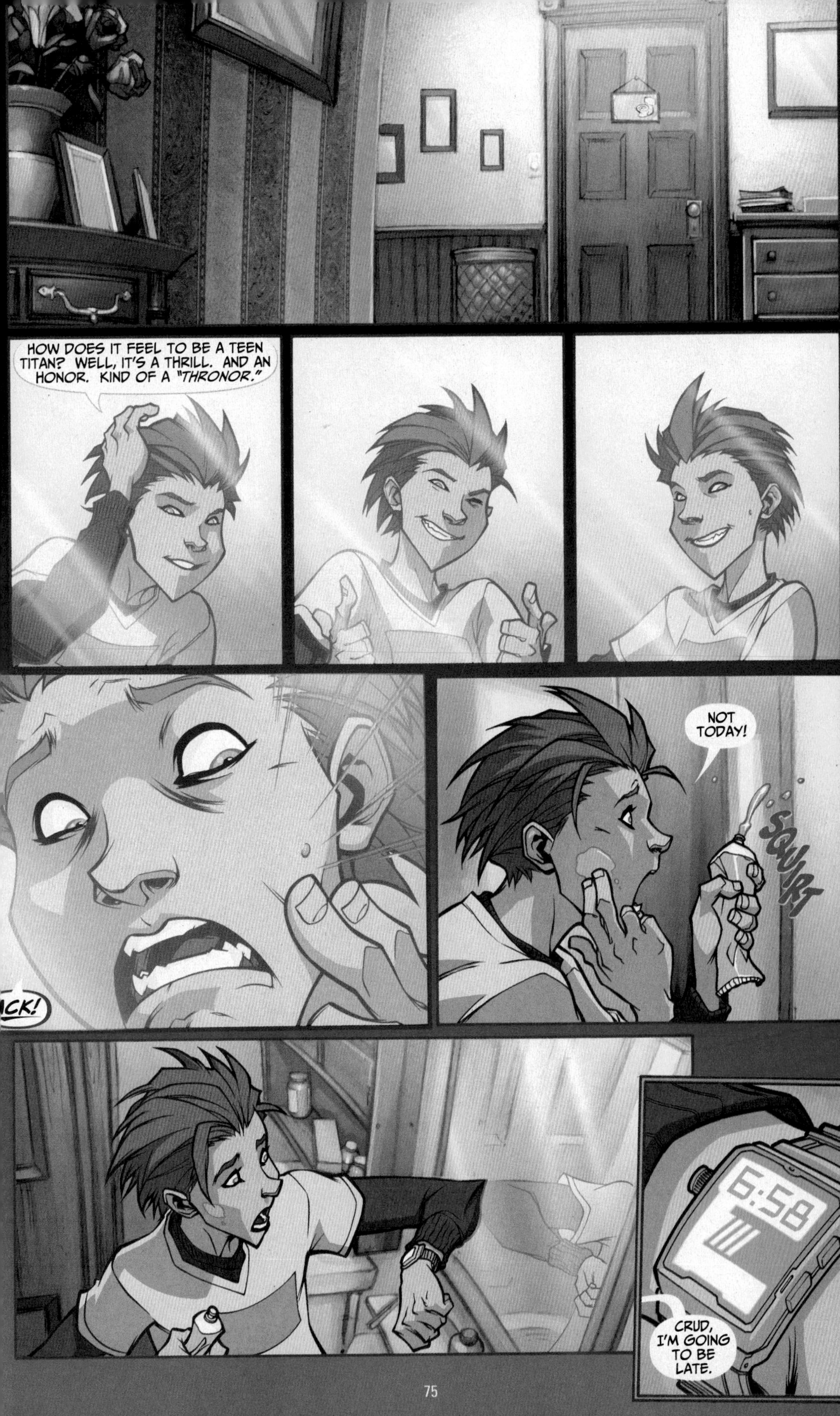

HOW DOES IT FEEL TO BE A TEEN TITAN? WELL, IT'S A THRILL. AND AN HONOR. KIND OF A "THRONOR."
CK!
NOT TODAY!
SQUIRT
6:58
CRUD, I'M GOING TO BE LATE.

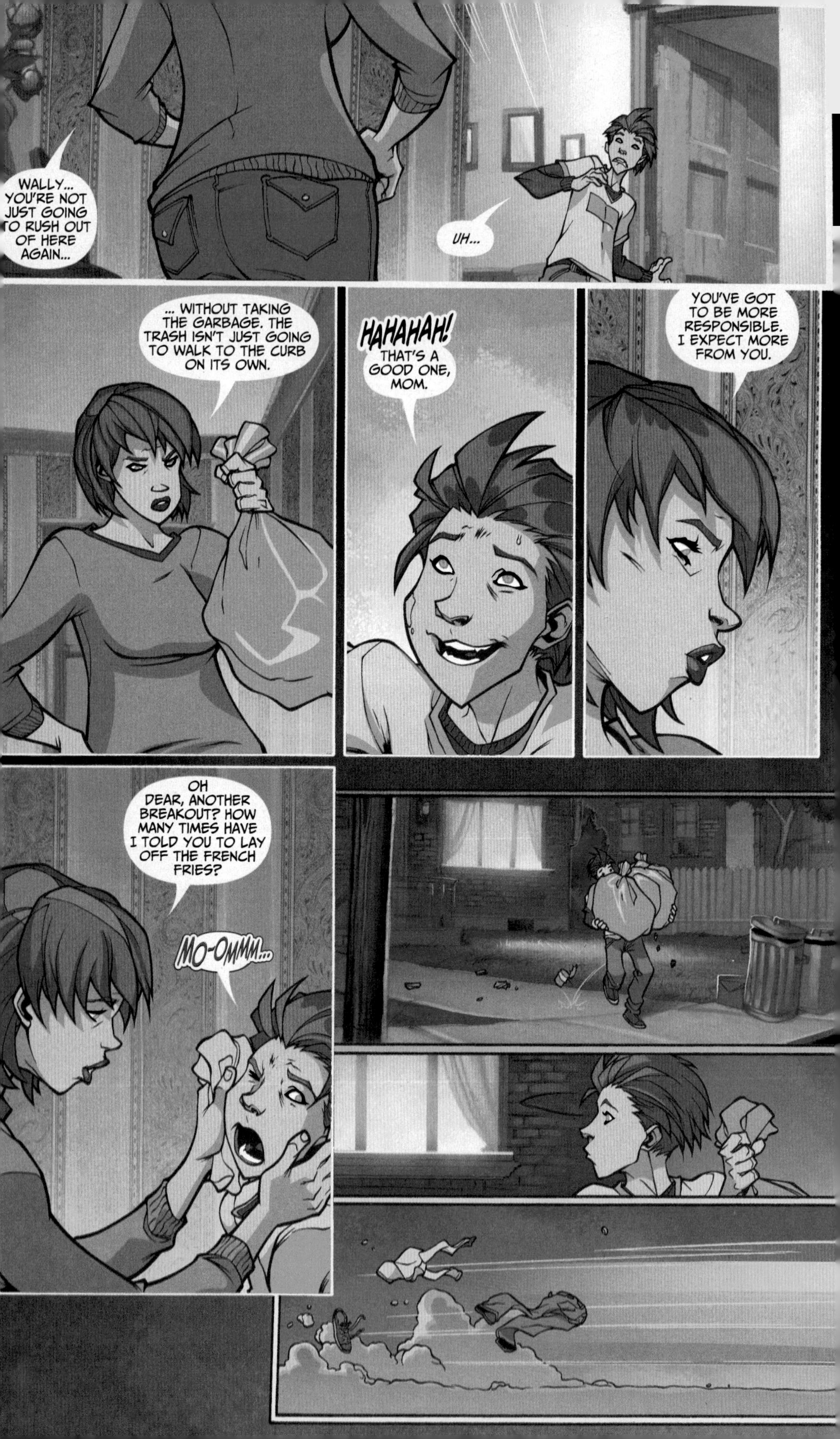
WALLY... YOU'RE NOT JUST GOING TO RUSH OUT OF HERE AGAIN...
UH...
... WITHOUT TAKING THE GARBAGE. THE TRASH ISN'T JUST GOING TO WALK TO THE CURB ON ITS OWN.
HAHAHAH!
THAT'S A GOOD ONE, MOM.
YOU'VE GOT TO BE MORE RESPONSIBLE. I EXPECT MORE FROM YOU.
OH DEAR, ANOTHER BREAKOUT? HOW MANY TIMES HAVE I TOLD YOU TO LAY OFF THE FRENCH FRIES?
MO-OMMM...

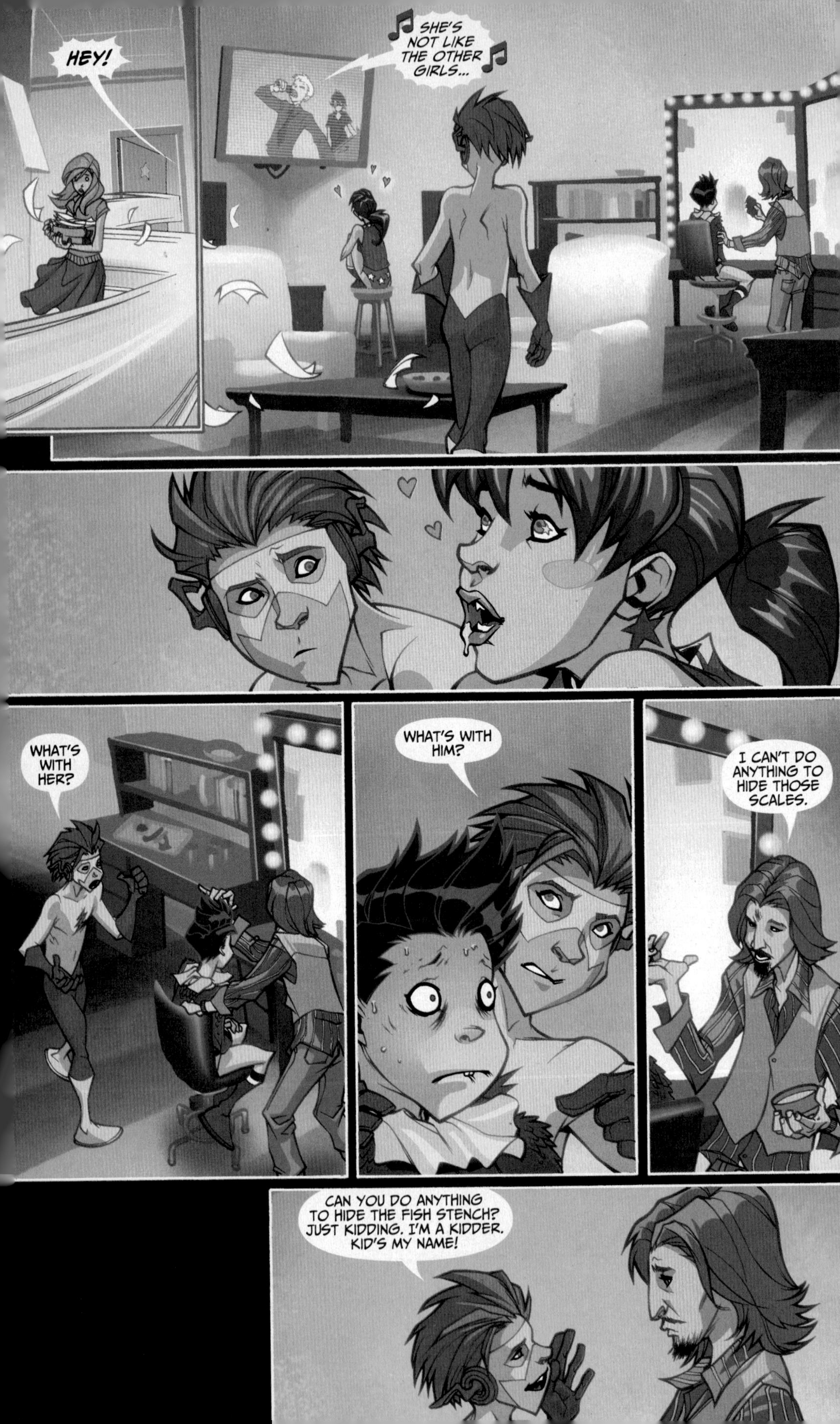
HEY!
SHE'S NOT LIKE THE OTHER GIRLS...
WHAT'S WITH HER?
WHAT'S WITH HIM?
I CAN'T DO ANYTHING TO HIDE THOSE SCALES.
CAN YOU DO ANYTHING TO HIDE THE FISH STENCH? JUST KIDDING. I'M A KIDDER. KID'S MY NAME!

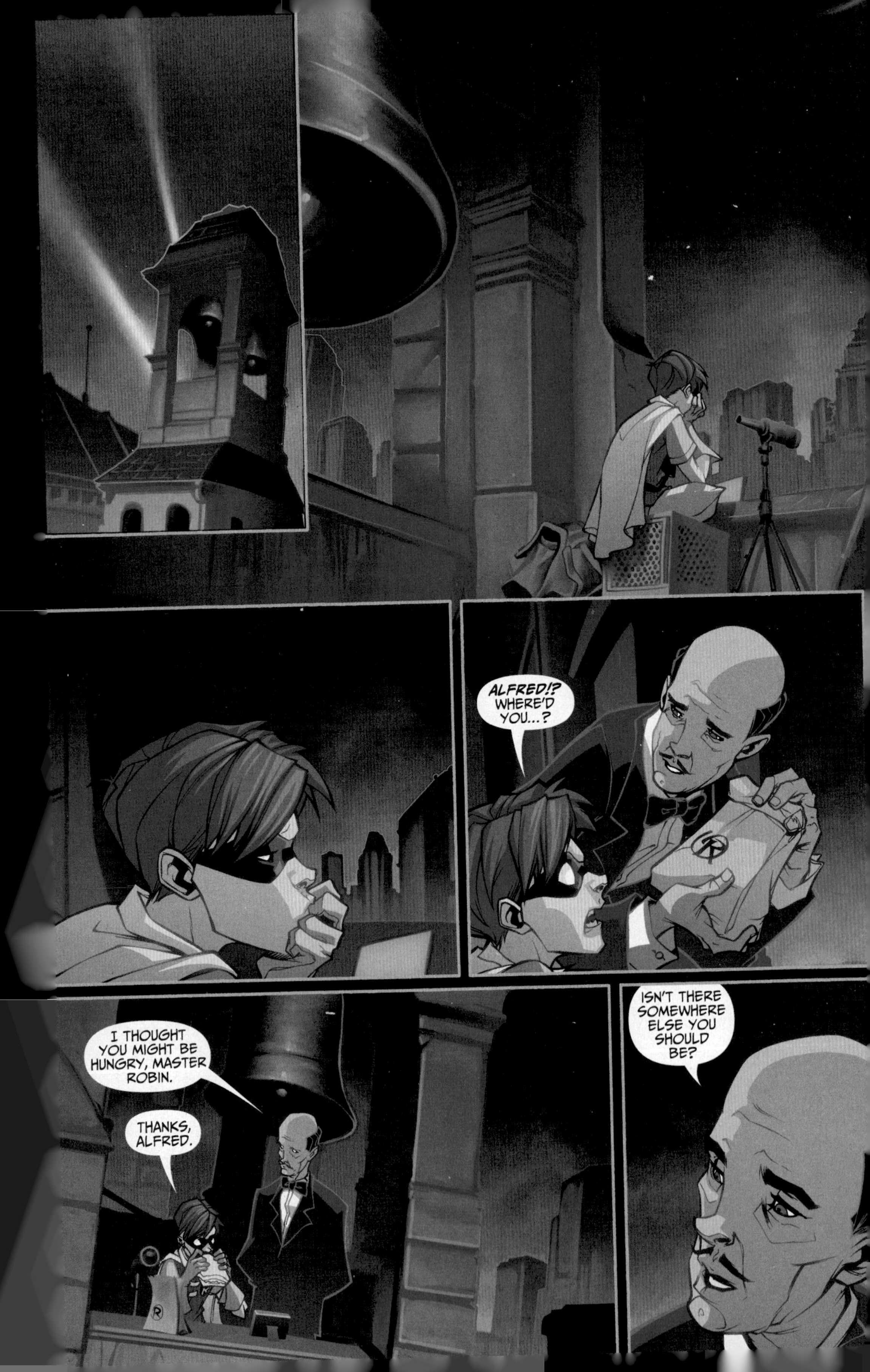
ALFRED!? WHERE'D YOU...?
I THOUGHT YOU MIGHT BE HUNGRY, MASTER ROBIN.
THANKS, ALFRED.
ISN'T THERE SOMEWHERE ELSE YOU SHOULD BE?

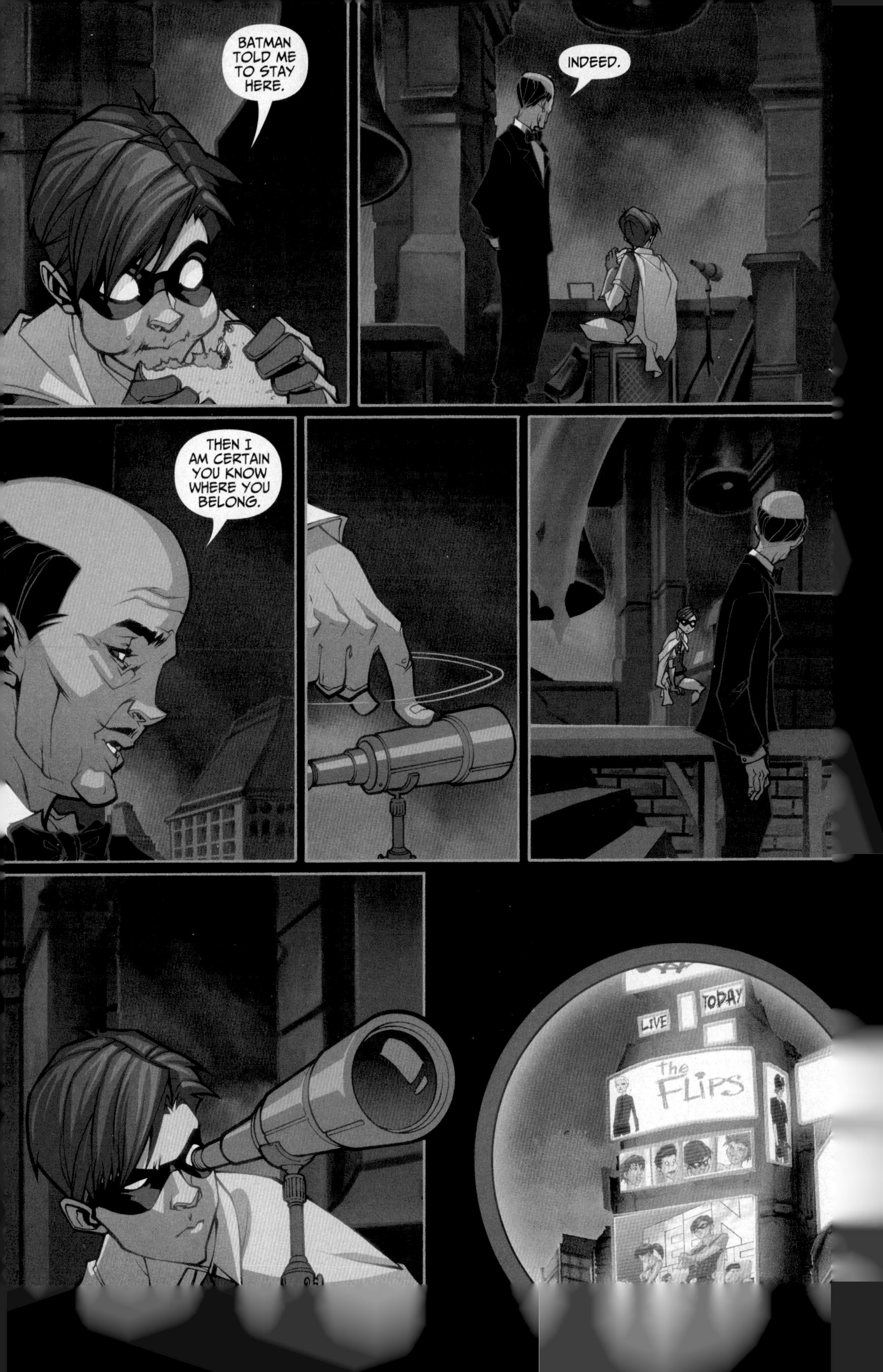
BATMAN TOLD ME TO STAY HERE.
INDEED.
THEN I AM CERTAIN YOU KNOW WHERE YOU BELONG.
LIVE
TODAY
the FLIPS

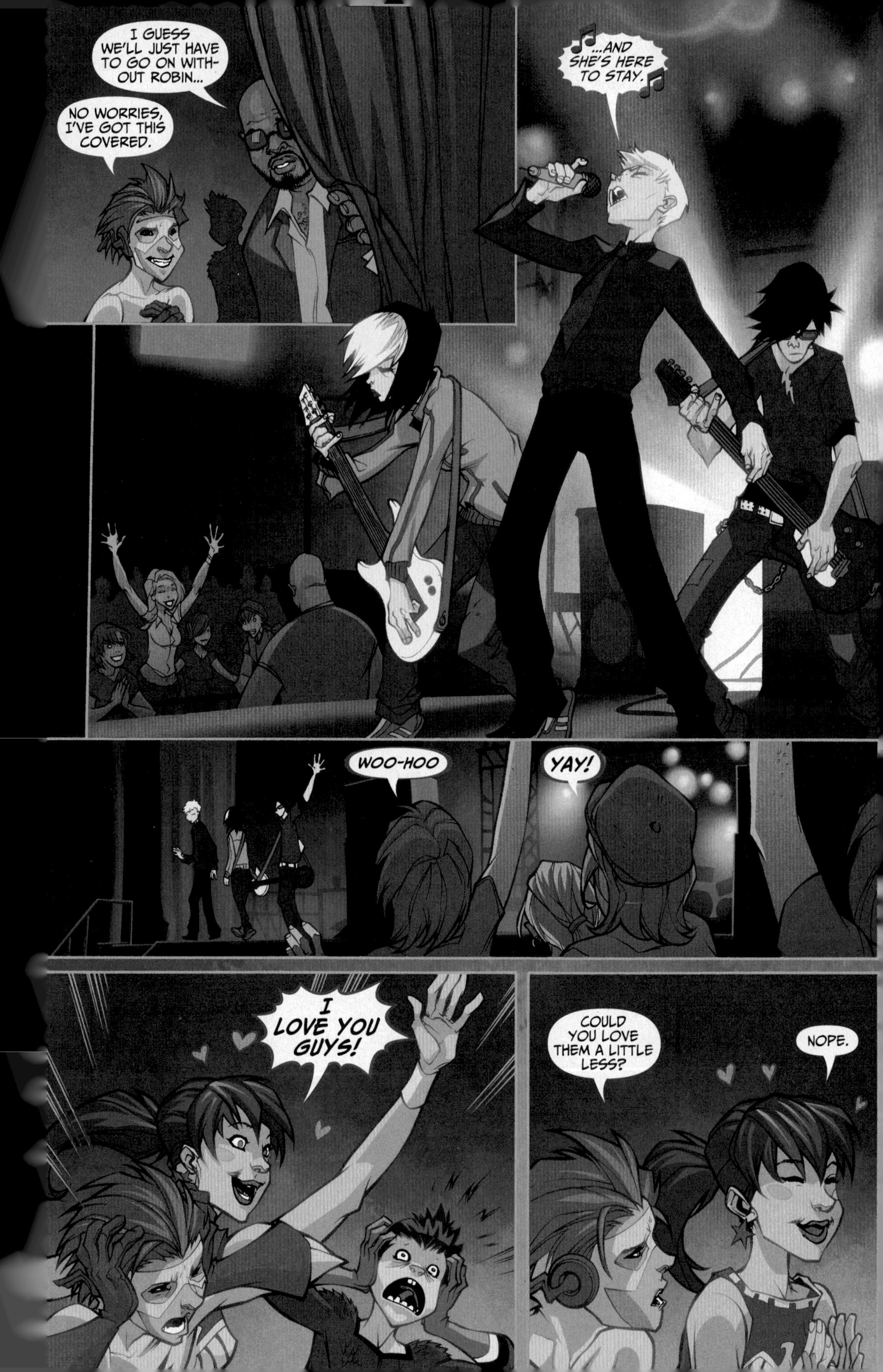
I GUESS WE'LL JUST HAVE TO GO ON WITH-OUT ROBIN...
NO WORRIES, I'VE GOT THIS COVERED.
...AND SHE'S HERE TO STAY.
WOO-HOO
YAY!
I LOVE YOU GUYS!
COULD YOU LOVE THEM A LITTLE LESS?
NOPE.

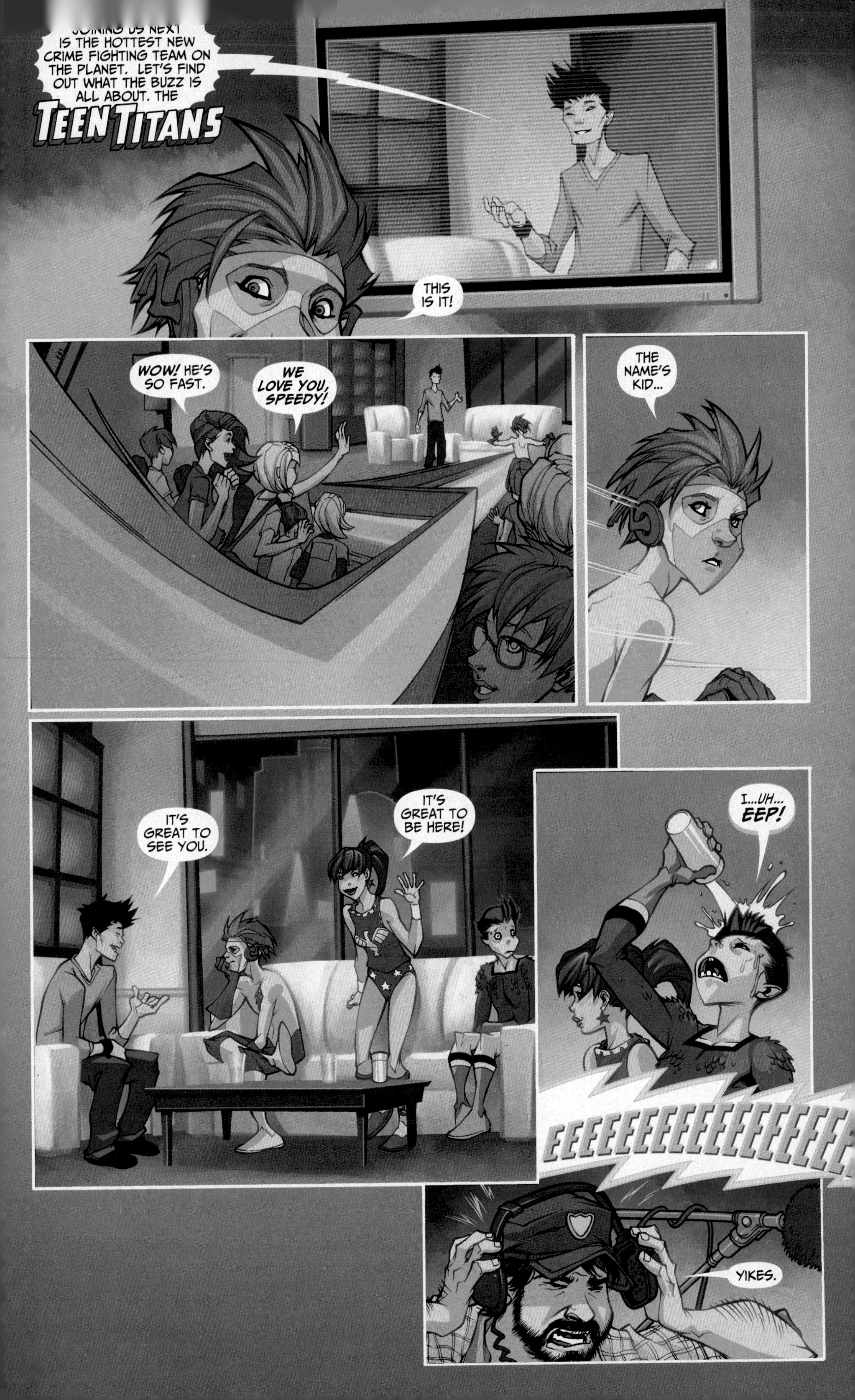
JOINING US NEXT IS THE HOTTEST NEW CRIME FIGHTING TEAM ON THE PLANET. LET'S FIND OUT WHAT THE BUZZ IS ALL ABOUT. THE
TEEN TITANS
THIS IS IT!
WOW! HE'S SO FAST.
WE LOVE YOU, SPEEDY!
THE NAME'S KID...
IT'S GREAT TO SEE YOU.
IT'S GREAT TO BE HERE!
I...UH... EEP!
EEEEEEEEEEEEEEEE
YIKES.

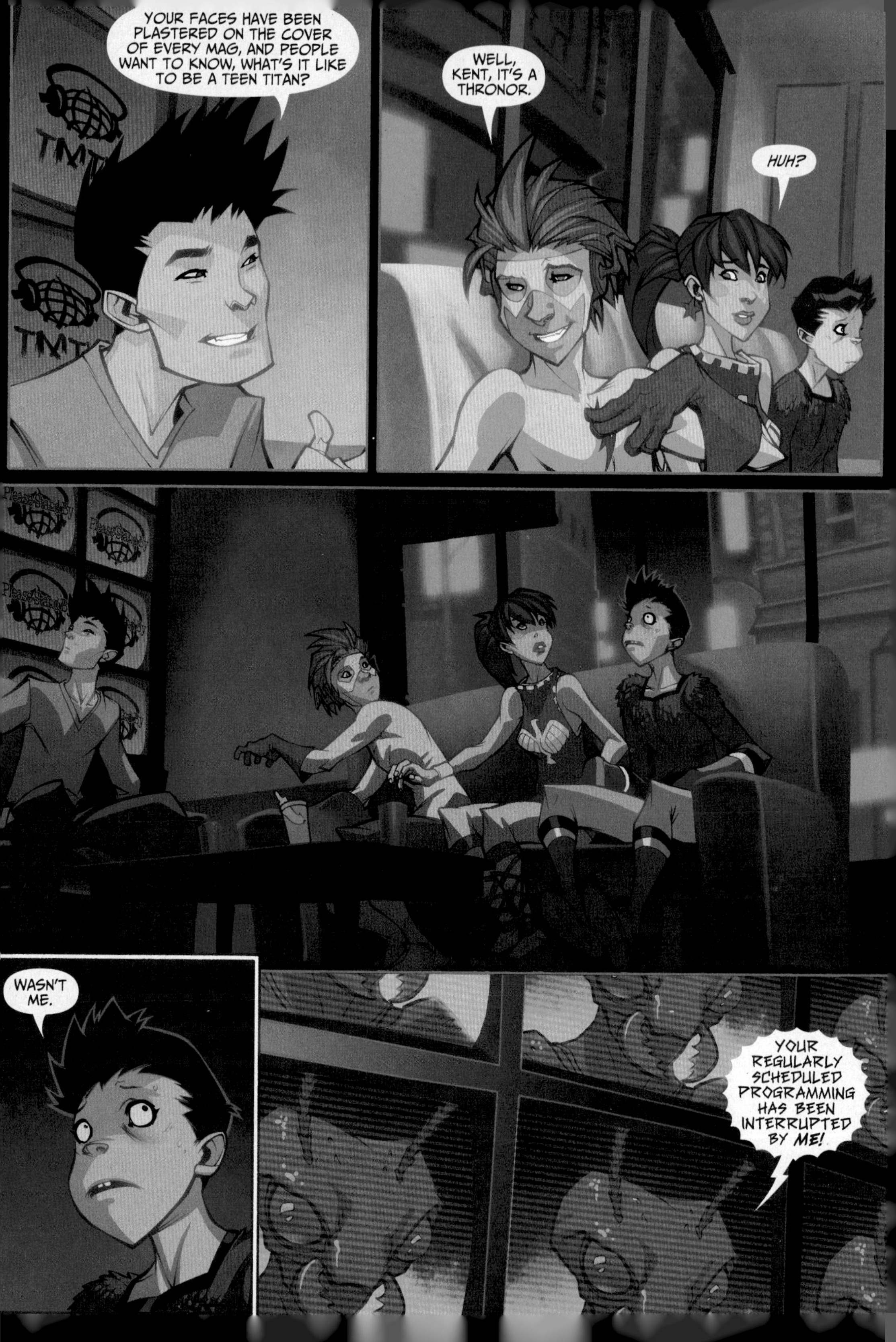
YOUR FACES HAVE BEEN PLASTERED ON THE COVER OF EVERY MAG, AND PEOPLE WANT TO KNOW, WHAT'S IT LIKE TO BE A TEEN TITAN?
WELL, KENT, IT'S A THRONOR.
HUH?
WASN'T ME.
YOUR REGULARLY SCHEDULED PROGRAMMING HAS BEEN INTERRUPTED BY ME!

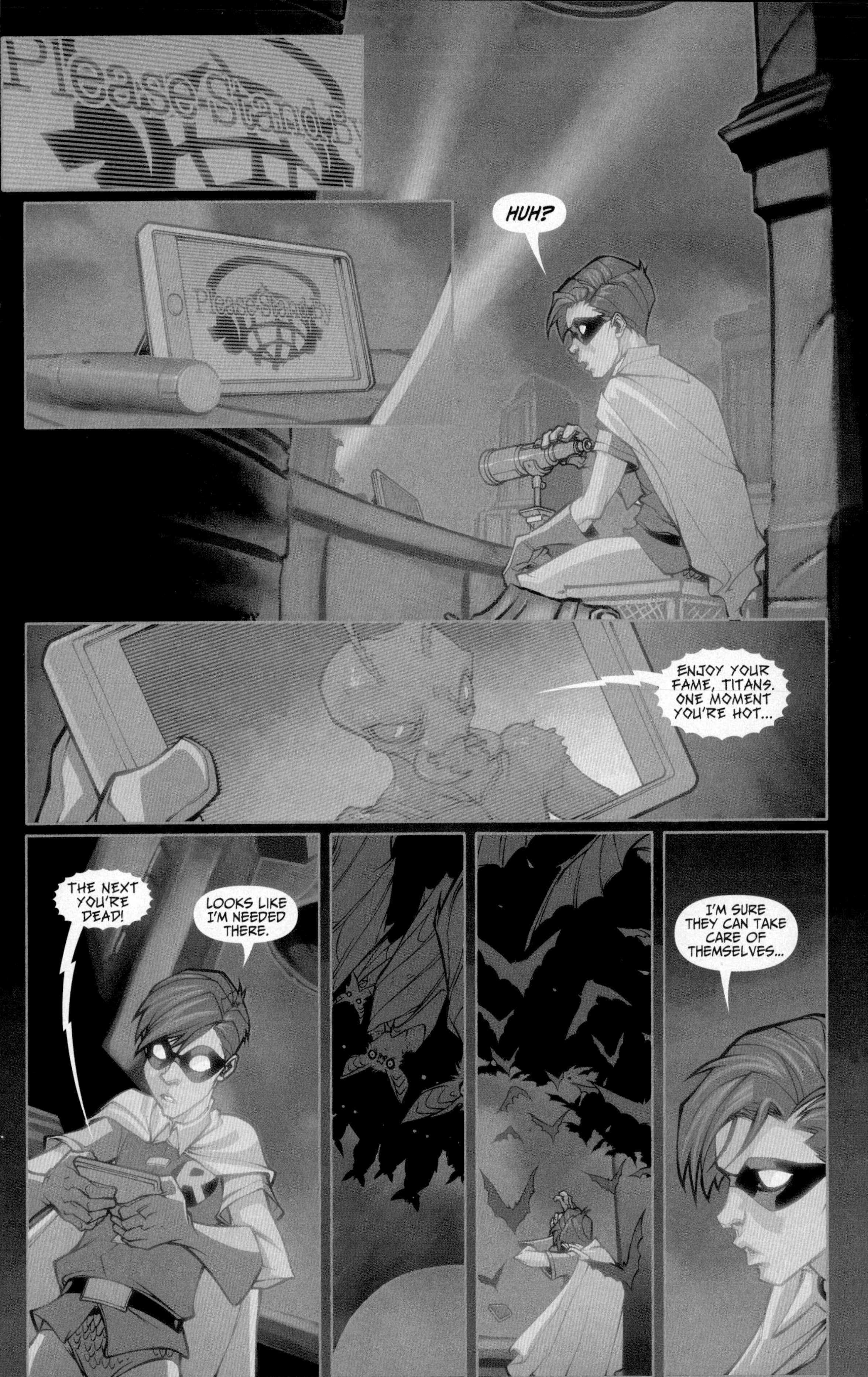
Please Stand By
HUH?
Please Stand By
ENJOY YOUR FAME, TITANS. ONE MOMENT YOU'RE HOT...
THE NEXT YOU'RE DEAD!
LOOKS LIKE I'M NEEDED THERE.
I'M SURE THEY CAN TAKE CARE OF THEMSELVES...

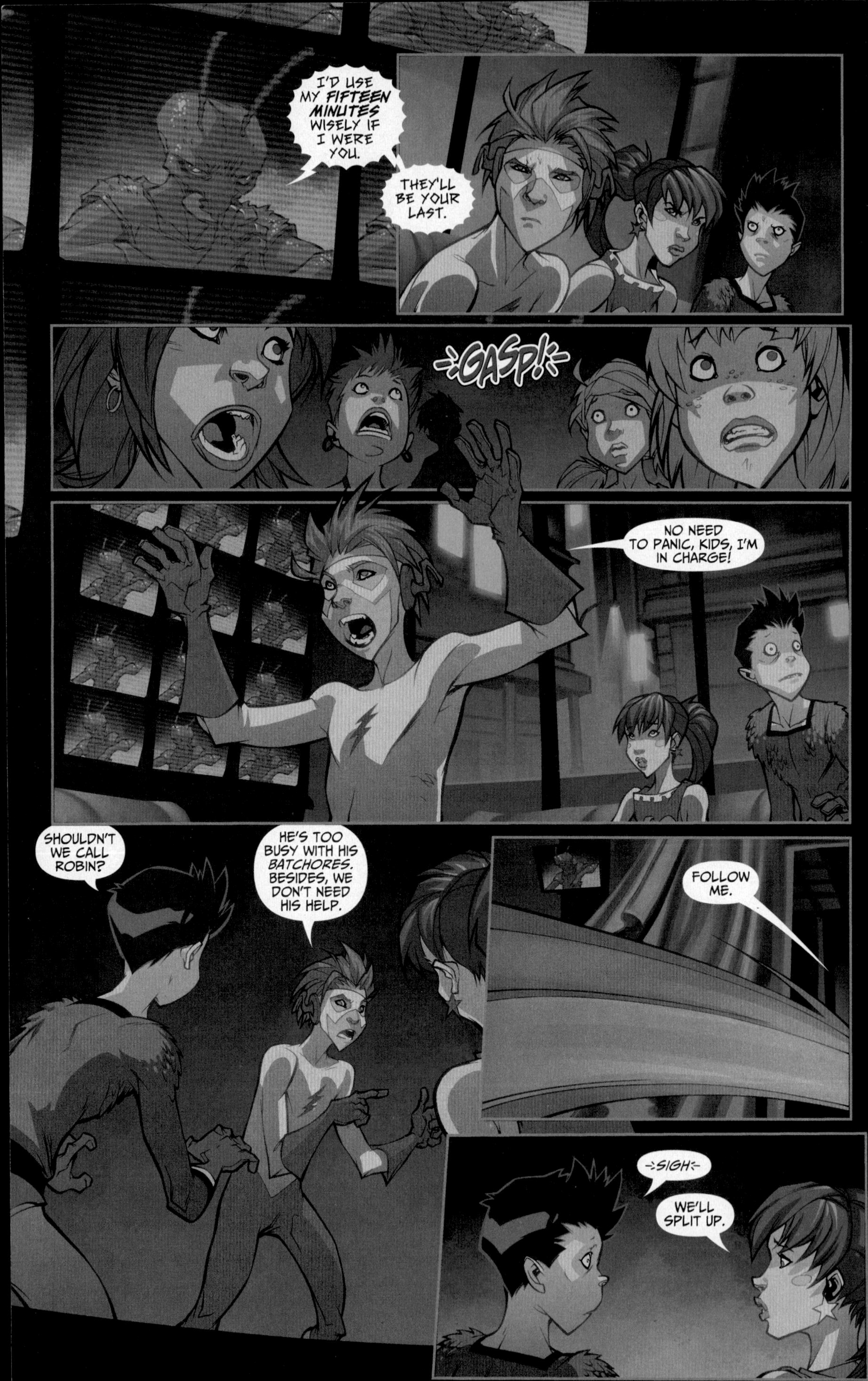

I'D USE MY **FIFTEEN MINUTES** WISELY IF I WERE YOU.
THEY'LL BE YOUR LAST.
GASP!
NO NEED TO PANIC, KIDS, I'M IN CHARGE!
SHOULDN'T WE CALL ROBIN?
HE'S TOO BUSY WITH HIS *BATCHORES*. BESIDES, WE DON'T NEED HIS HELP.
FOLLOW ME.
SIGH
WE'LL SPLIT UP.

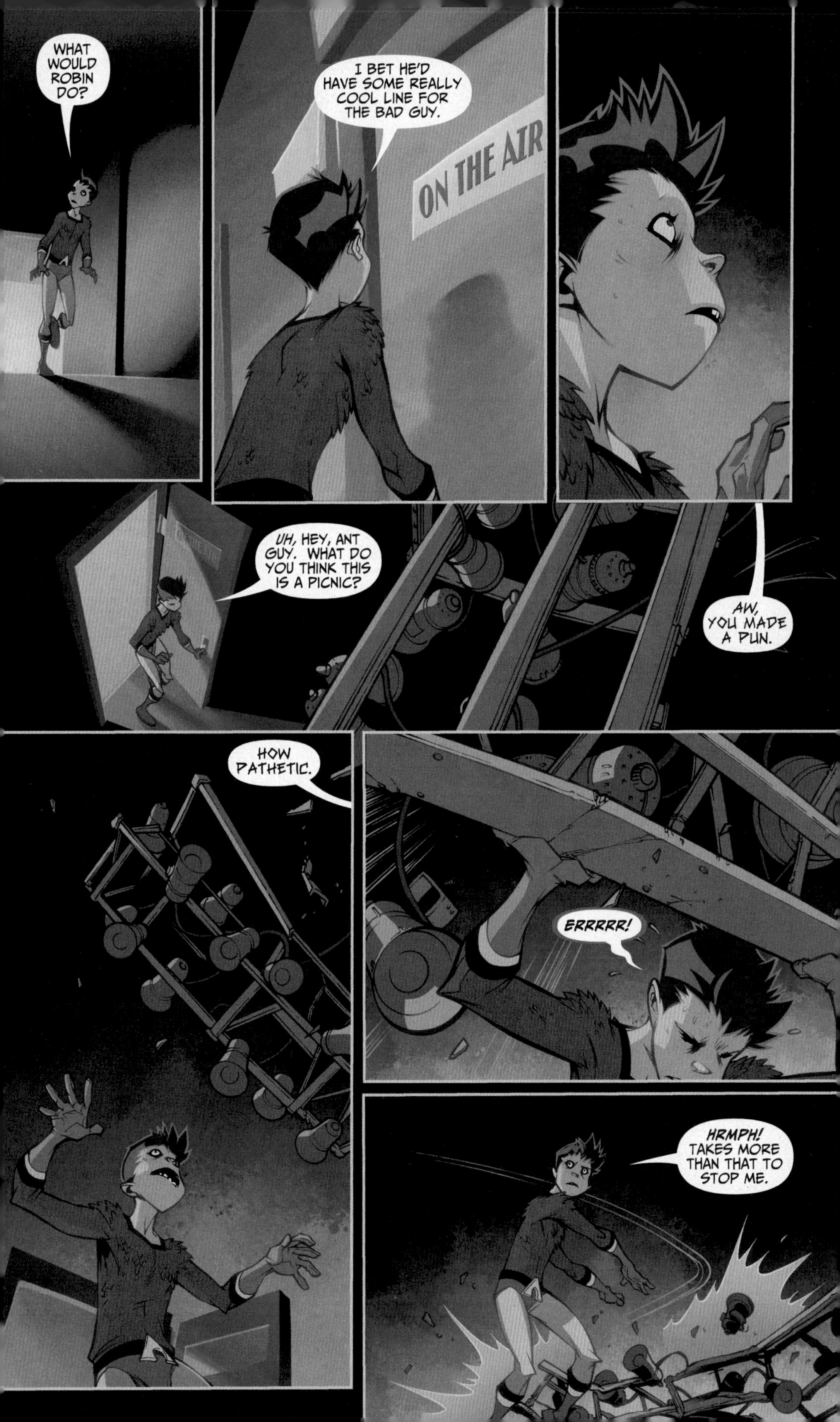
WHAT WOULD ROBIN DO?
I BET HE'D HAVE SOME REALLY COOL LINE FOR THE BAD GUY.
ON THE AIR
UH, HEY, ANT GUY. WHAT DO YOU THINK THIS IS A PICNIC?
AW, YOU MADE A PUN.
HOW PATHETIC.
ERRRRR!
HRMPH! TAKES MORE THAN THAT TO STOP ME.

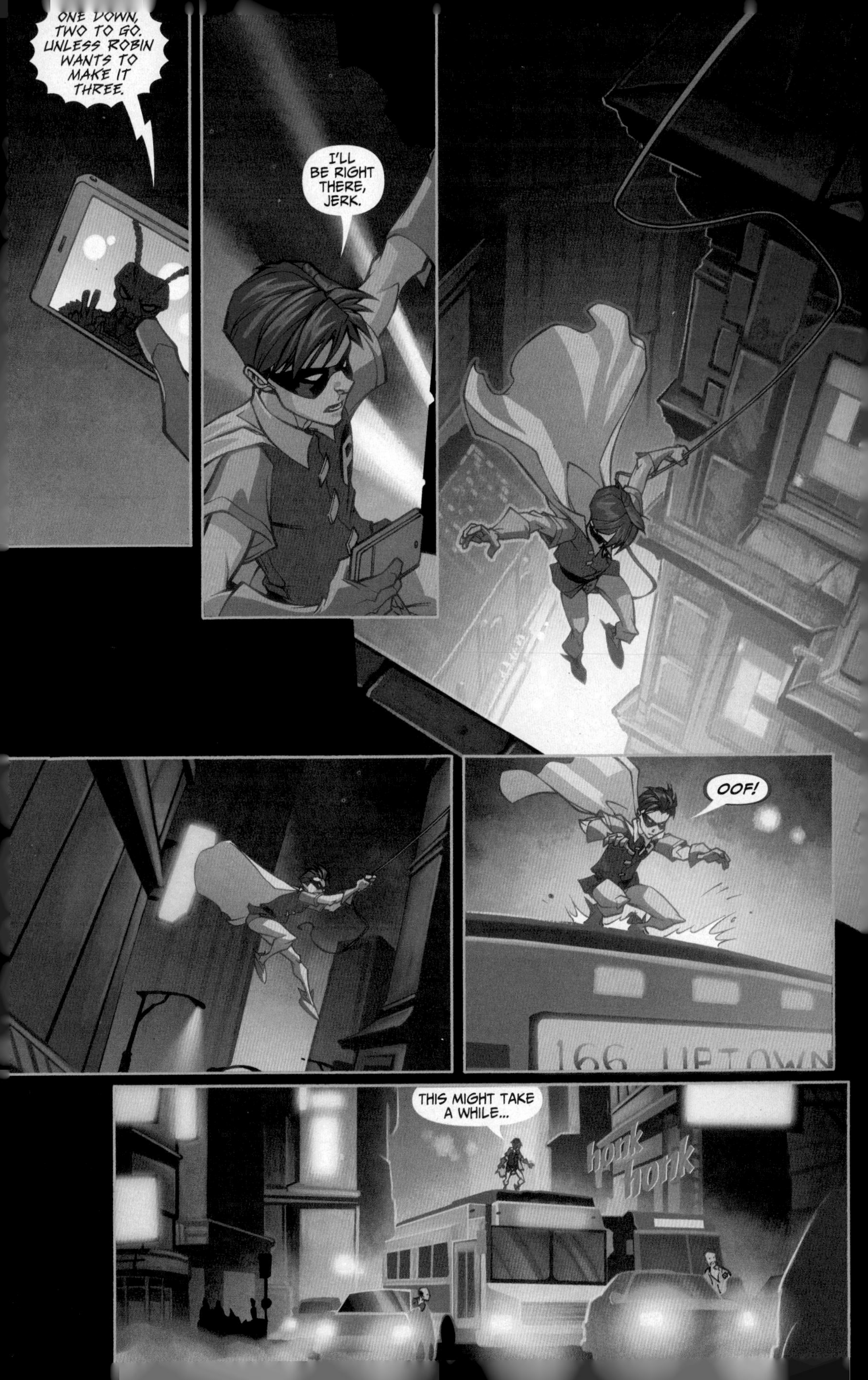

ONE DOWN, TWO TO GO. UNLESS ROBIN WANTS TO MAKE IT THREE.
I'LL BE RIGHT THERE, JERK.
OOF!
166 UPTOWN
THIS MIGHT TAKE A WHILE...
honk
honk

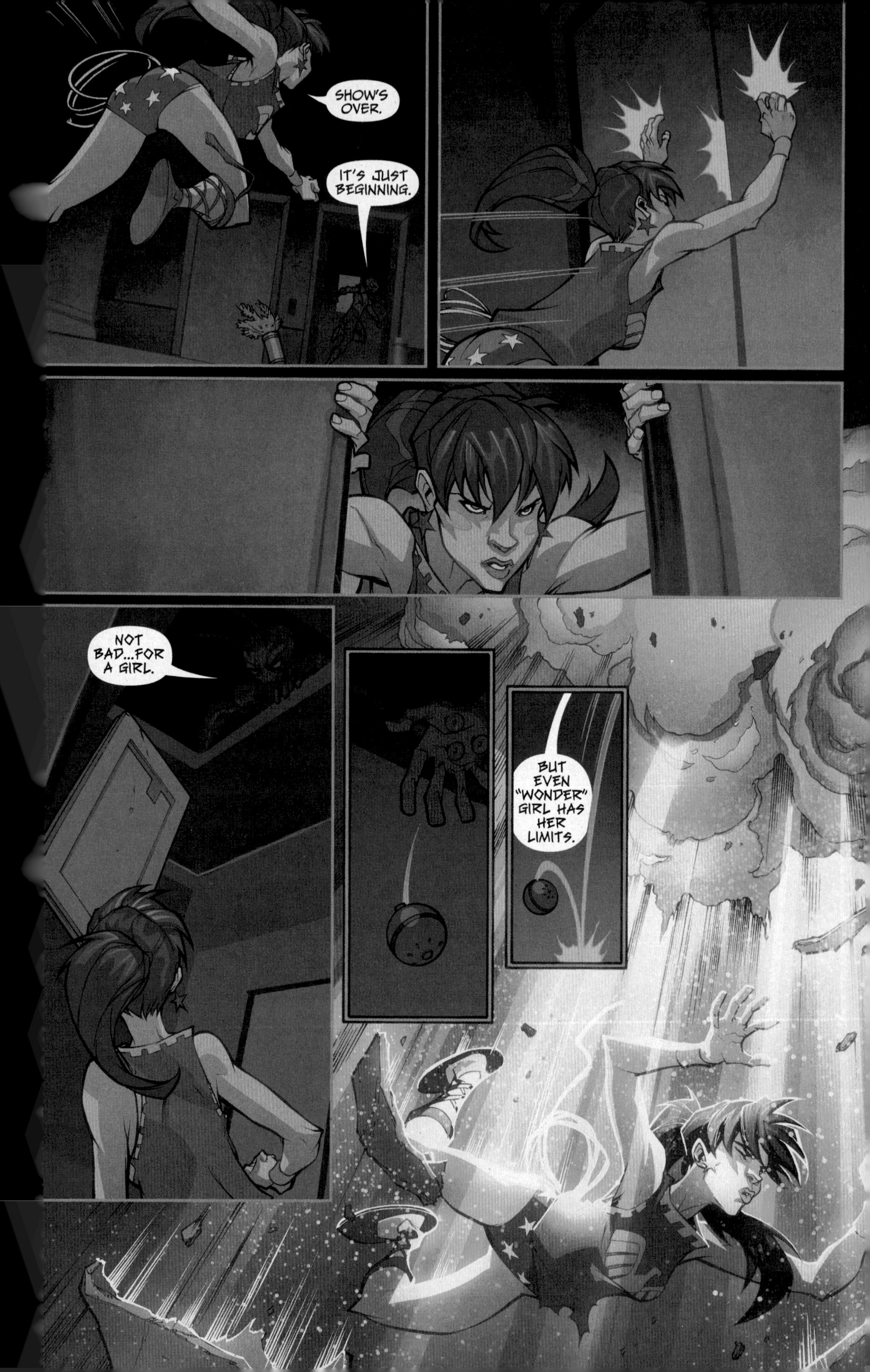
SHOW'S OVER.
IT'S JUST BEGINNING.
NOT BAD...FOR A GIRL.
BUT EVEN "WONDER" GIRL HAS HER LIMITS.

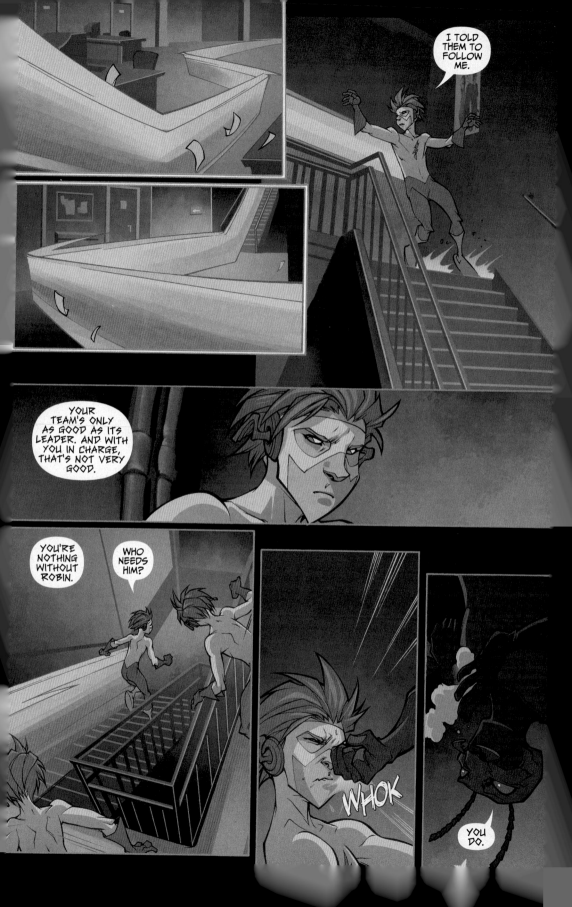

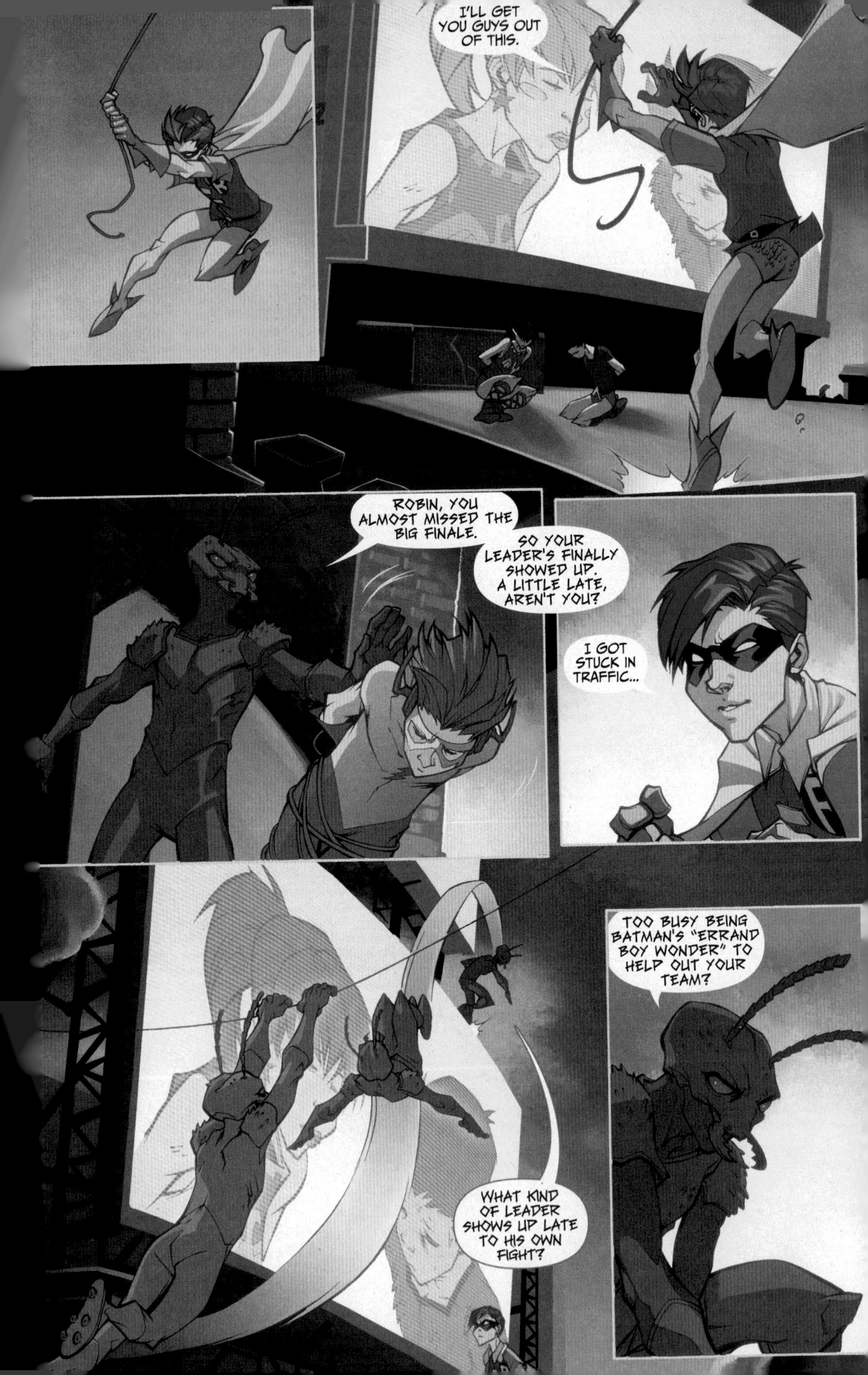
I'LL GET YOU GUYS OUT OF THIS.
ROBIN, YOU ALMOST MISSED THE BIG FINALE.
SO YOUR LEADER'S FINALLY SHOWED UP. A LITTLE LATE, AREN'T YOU?
I GOT STUCK IN TRAFFIC...
WHAT KIND OF LEADER SHOWS UP LATE TO HIS OWN FIGHT?
TOO BUSY BEING BATMAN'S "ERRAND BOY WONDER" TO HELP OUT YOUR TEAM?

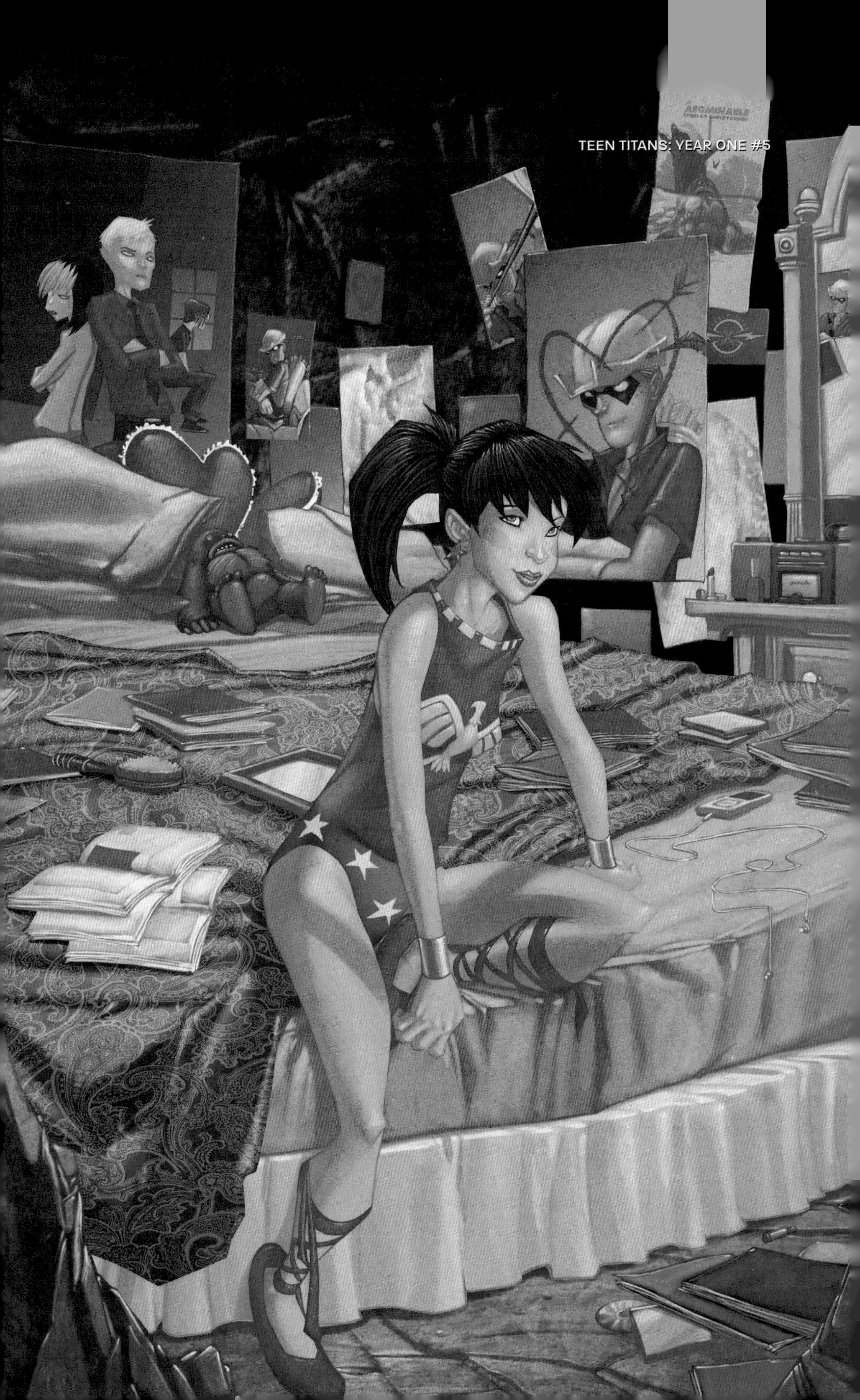
TEEN TITANS: YEAR ONE #5
ABOMINABLE
CHARLES CHRISTOPHER

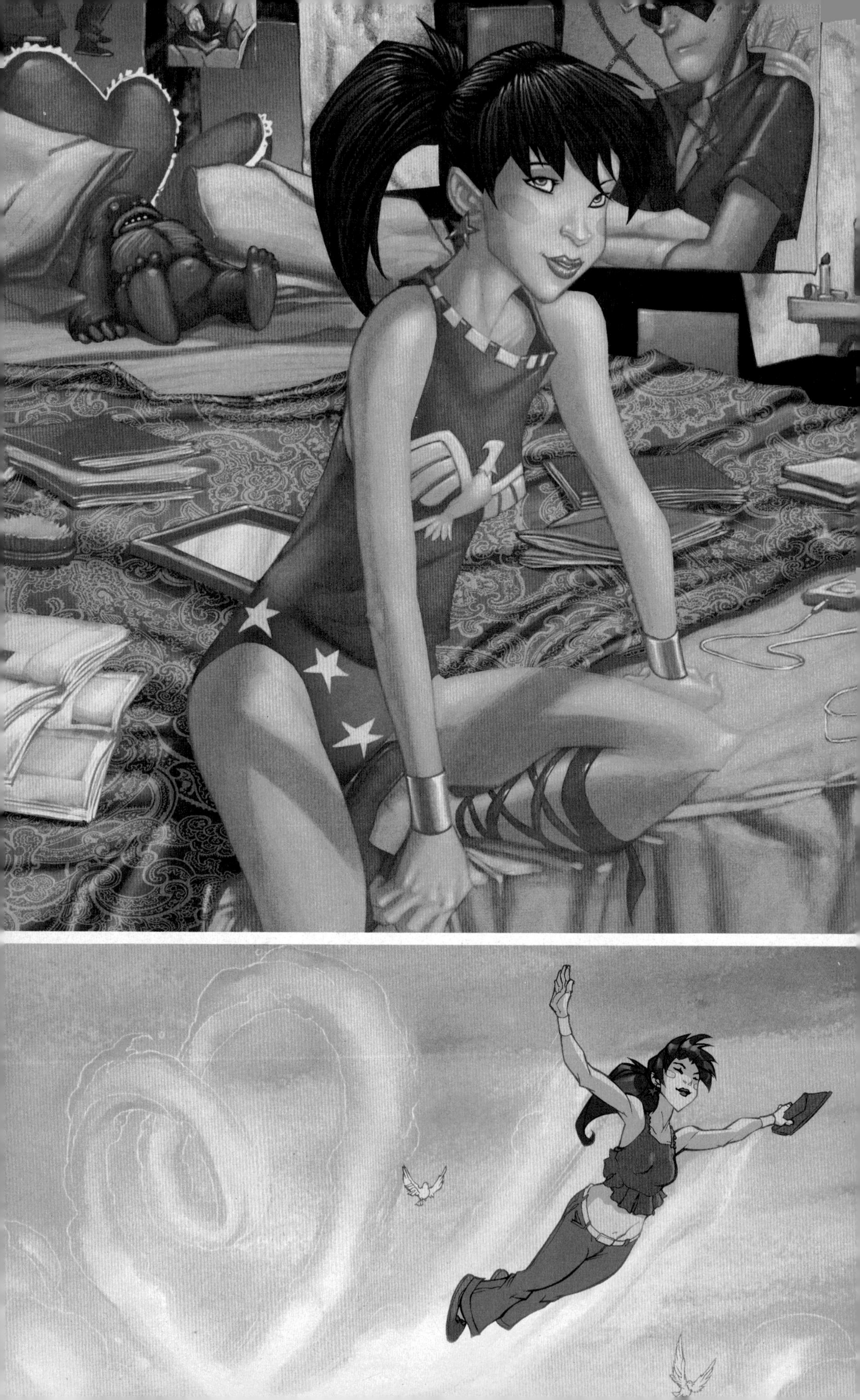

97

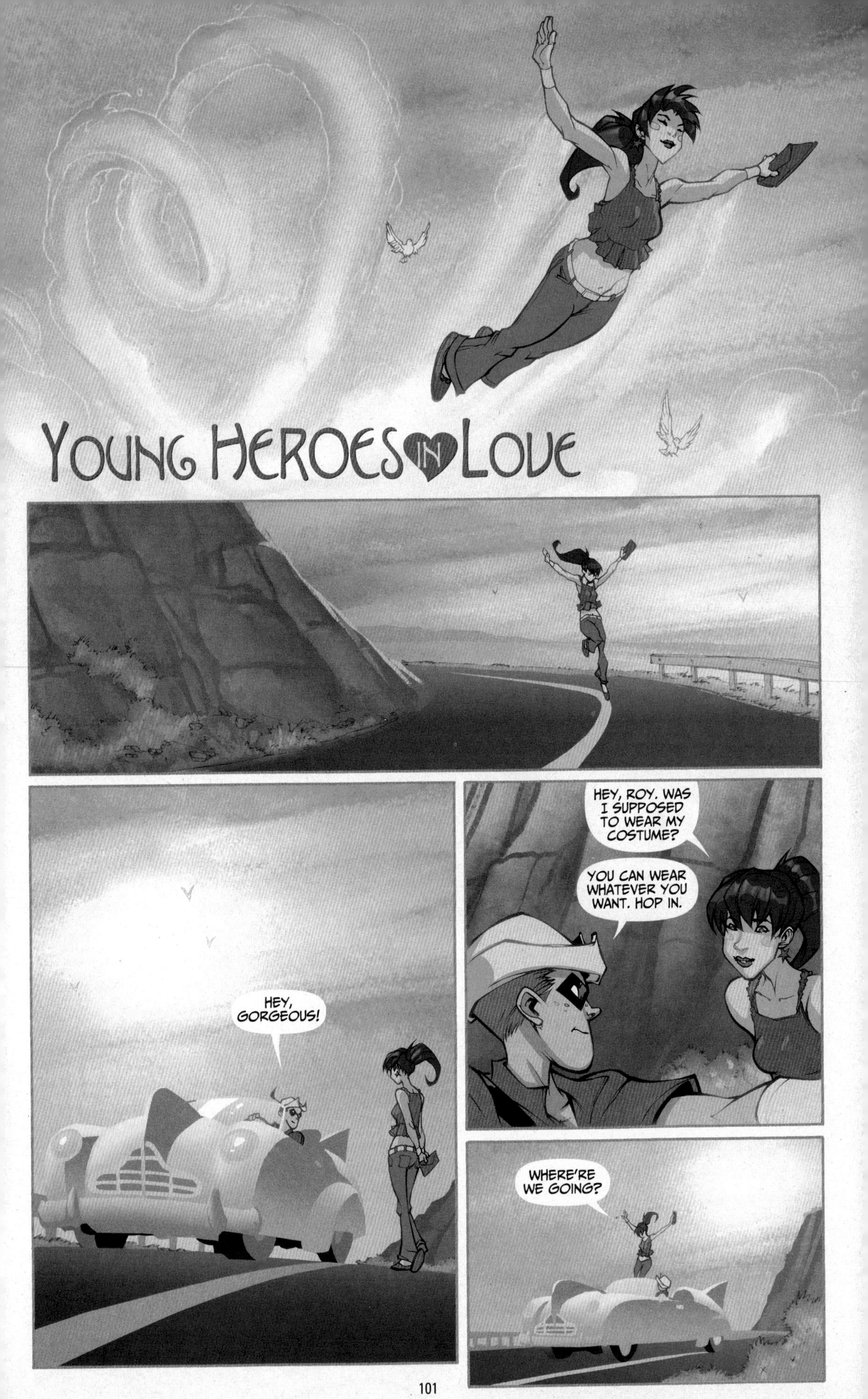
YOUNG HEROES IN LOVE
HEY, GORGEOUS!
HEY, ROY. WAS I SUPPOSED TO WEAR MY COSTUME?
YOU CAN WEAR WHATEVER YOU WANT. HOP IN.
WHERE'RE WE GOING?

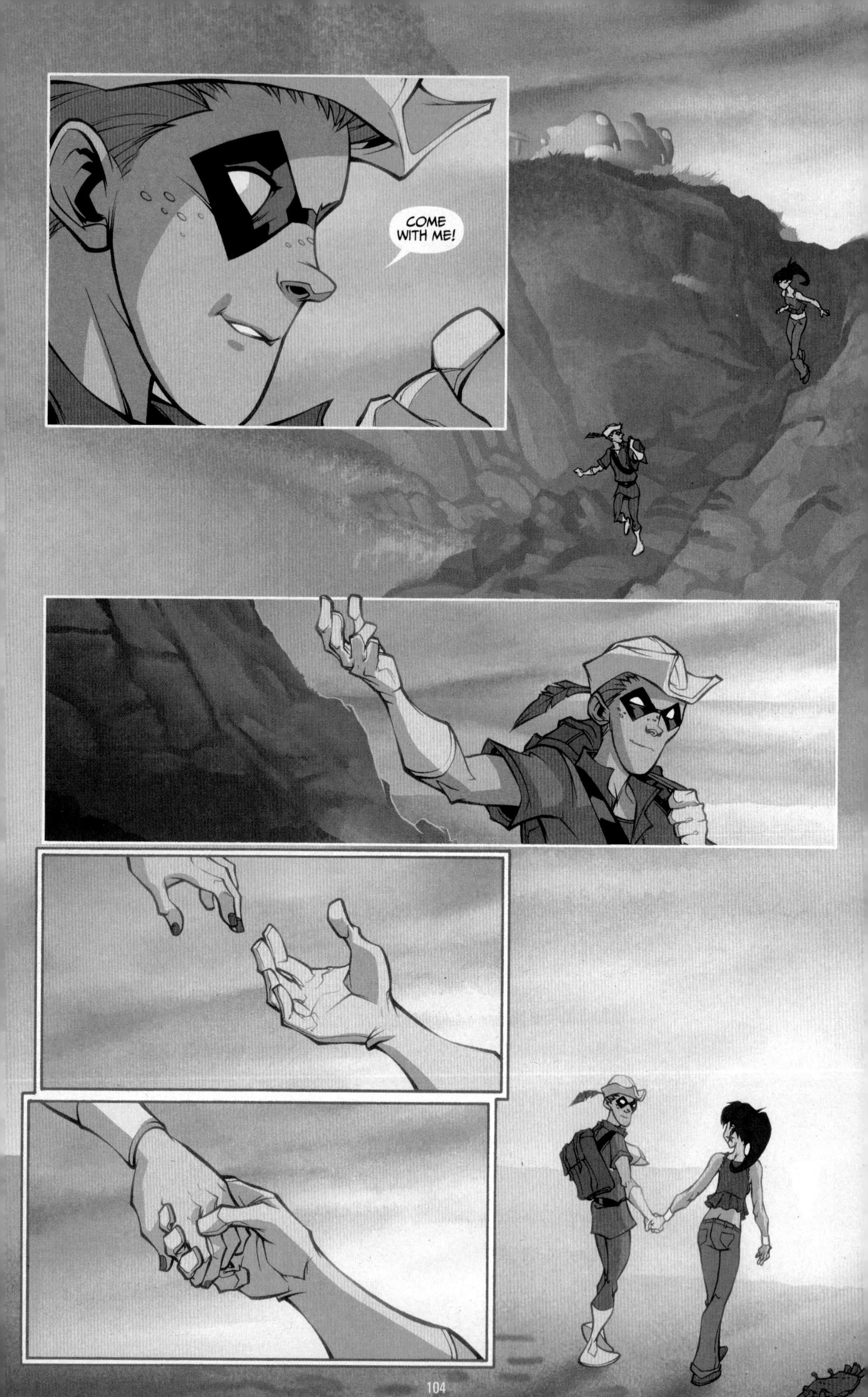
COME WITH ME!

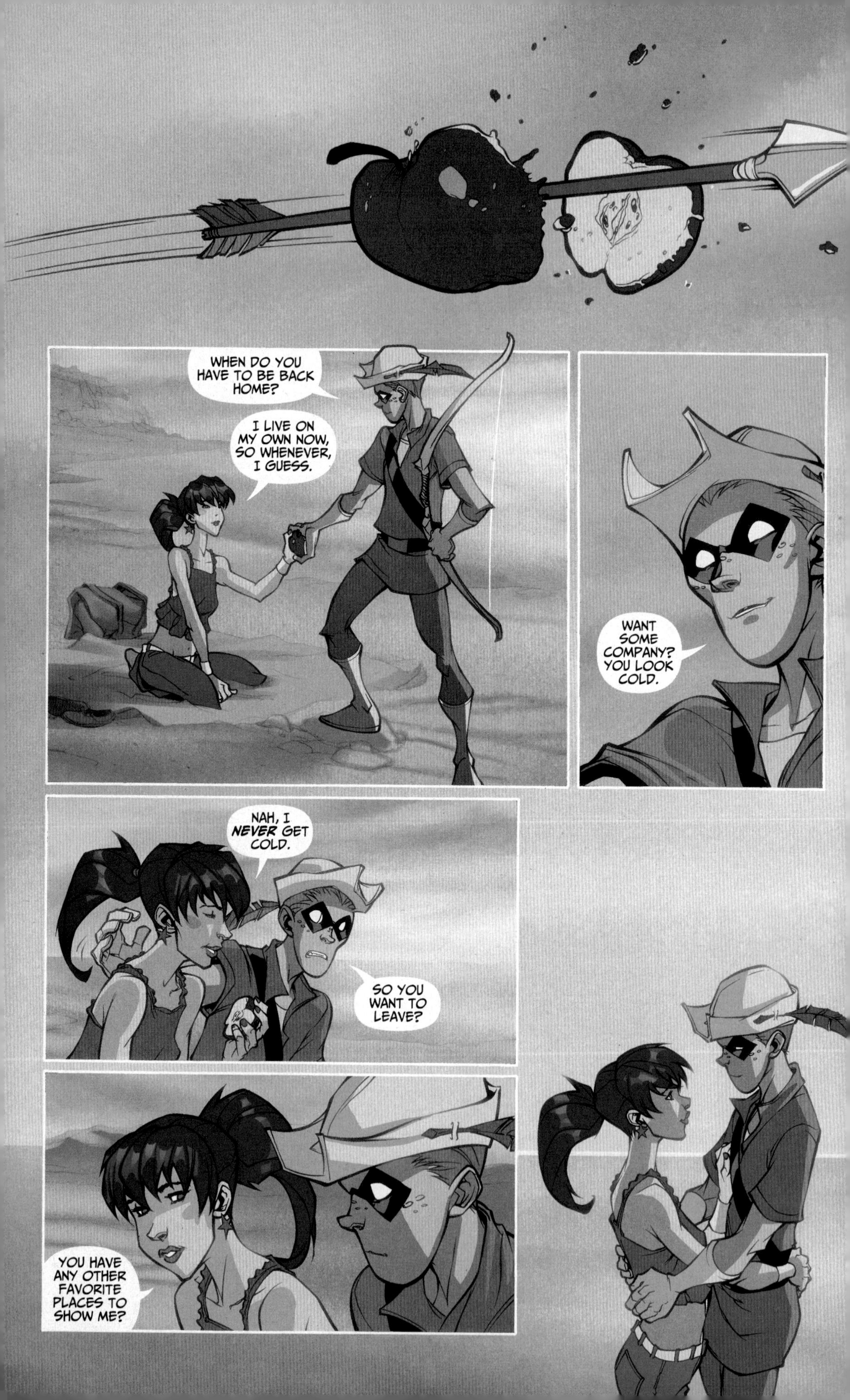
WHEN DO YOU HAVE TO BE BACK HOME?
I LIVE ON MY OWN NOW, SO WHENEVER, I GUESS.
WANT SOME COMPANY? YOU LOOK COLD.
NAH, I NEVER GET COLD.
SO YOU WANT TO LEAVE?
YOU HAVE ANY OTHER FAVORITE PLACES TO SHOW ME?

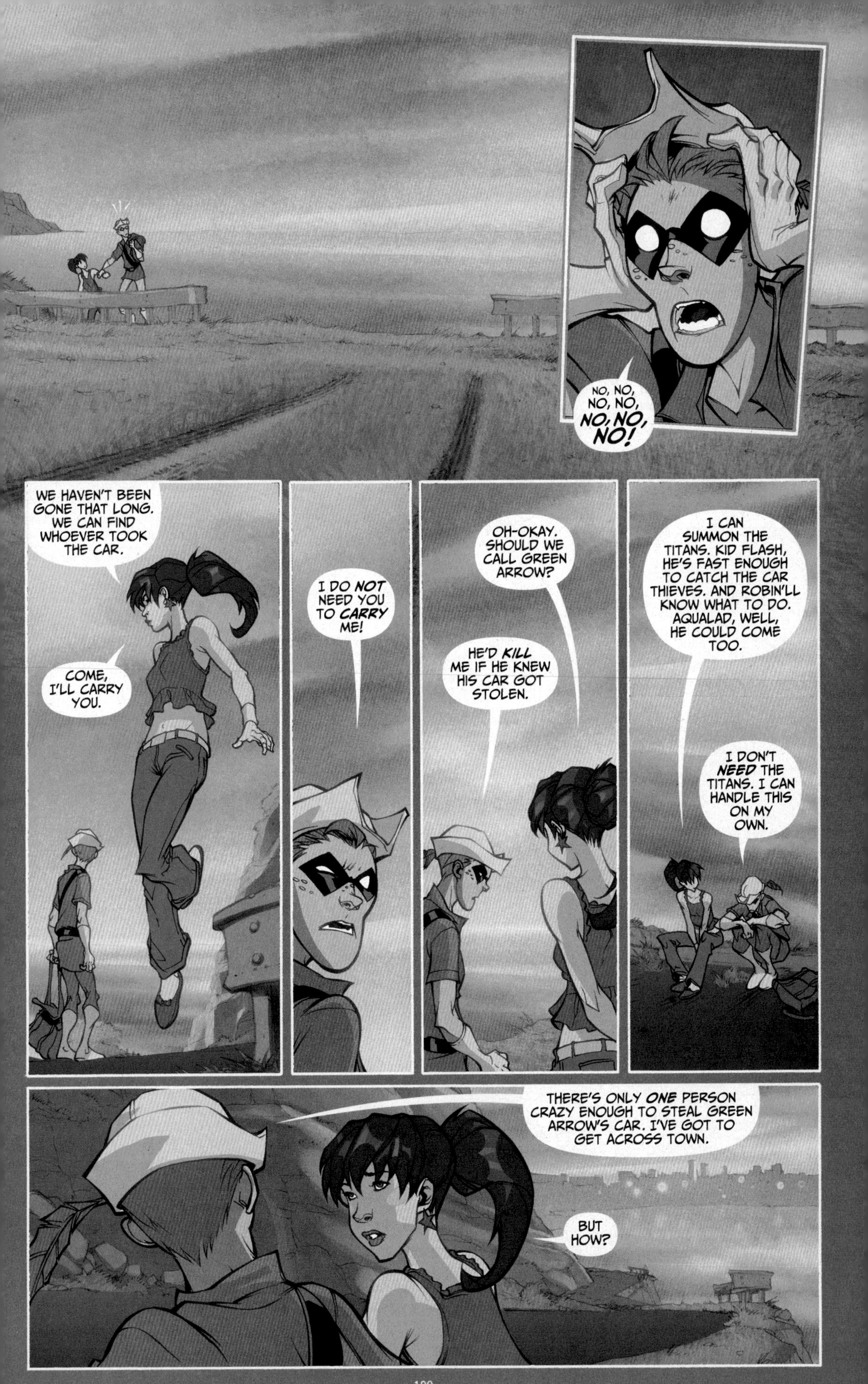
NO, NO, NO, NO, NO, NO, NO!
WE HAVEN'T BEEN GONE THAT LONG. WE CAN FIND WHOEVER TOOK THE CAR.
COME, I'LL CARRY YOU.
I DO NOT NEED YOU TO CARRY ME!
OH-OKAY. SHOULD WE CALL GREEN ARROW?
HE'D KILL ME IF HE KNEW HIS CAR GOT STOLEN.
I CAN SUMMON THE TITANS. KID FLASH, HE'S FAST ENOUGH TO CATCH THE CAR THIEVES. AND ROBIN'LL KNOW WHAT TO DO. AQUALAD, WELL, HE COULD COME TOO.
I DON'T NEED THE TITANS. I CAN HANDLE THIS ON MY OWN.
THERE'S ONLY ONE PERSON CRAZY ENOUGH TO STEAL GREEN ARROW'S CAR. I'VE GOT TO GET ACROSS TOWN.
BUT HOW?

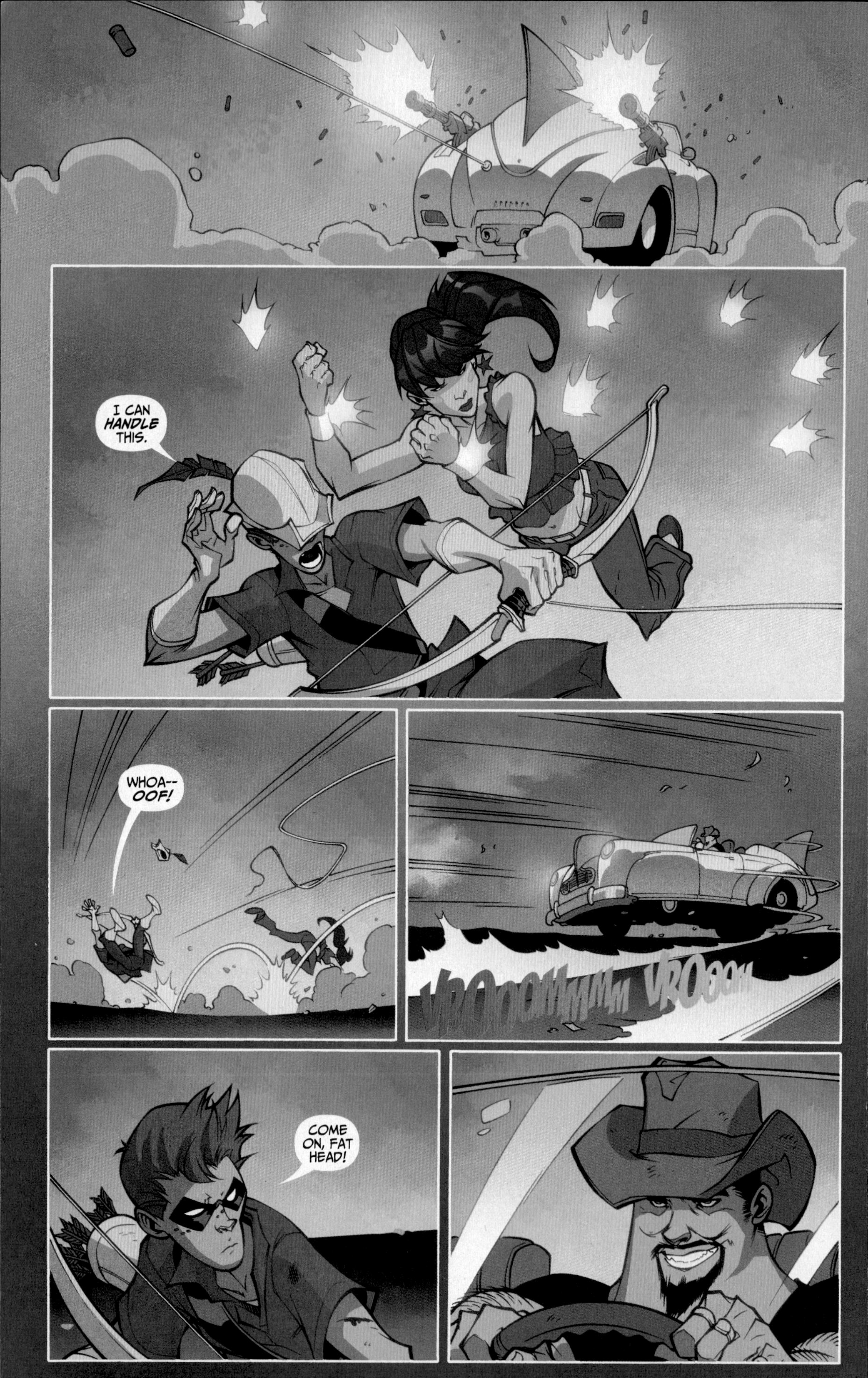

I CAN *HANDLE* THIS.
WHOA-- *OOF!*
VROOOMMMMM VROOOM
COME ON, FAT HEAD!

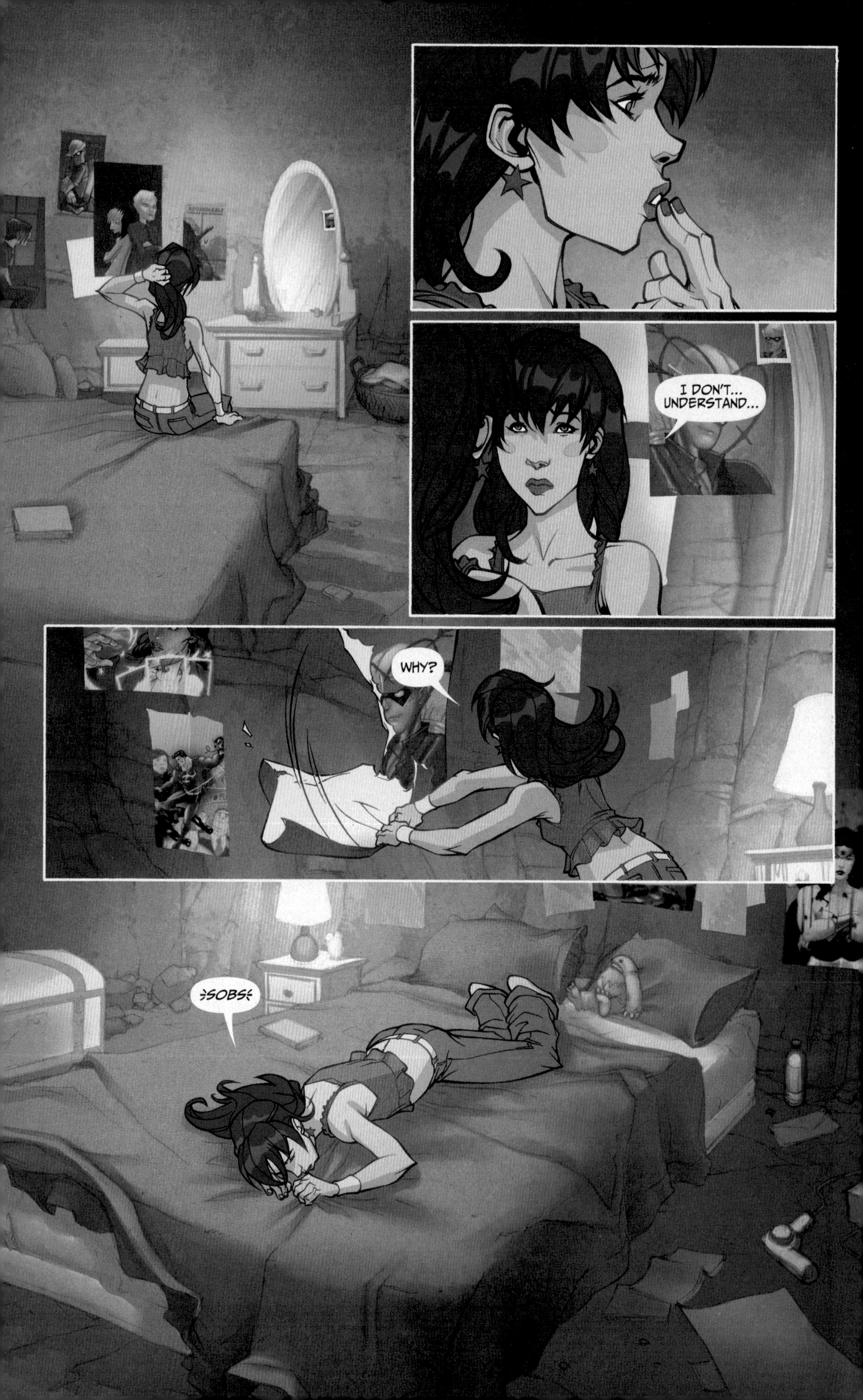
I DON'T... UNDERSTAND...
WHY?
≠SOBS≠

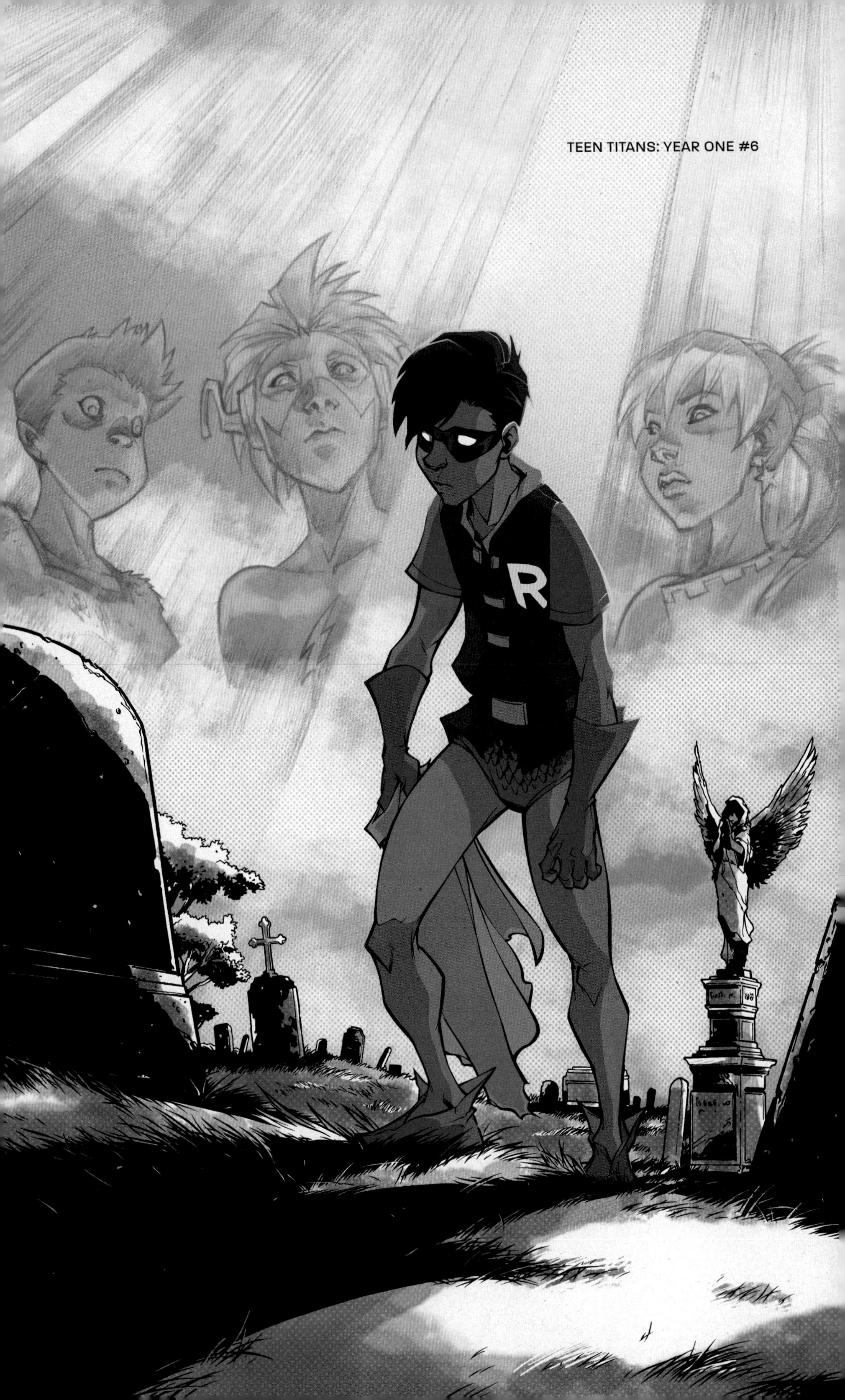
TEEN TITANS: YEAR ONE #6

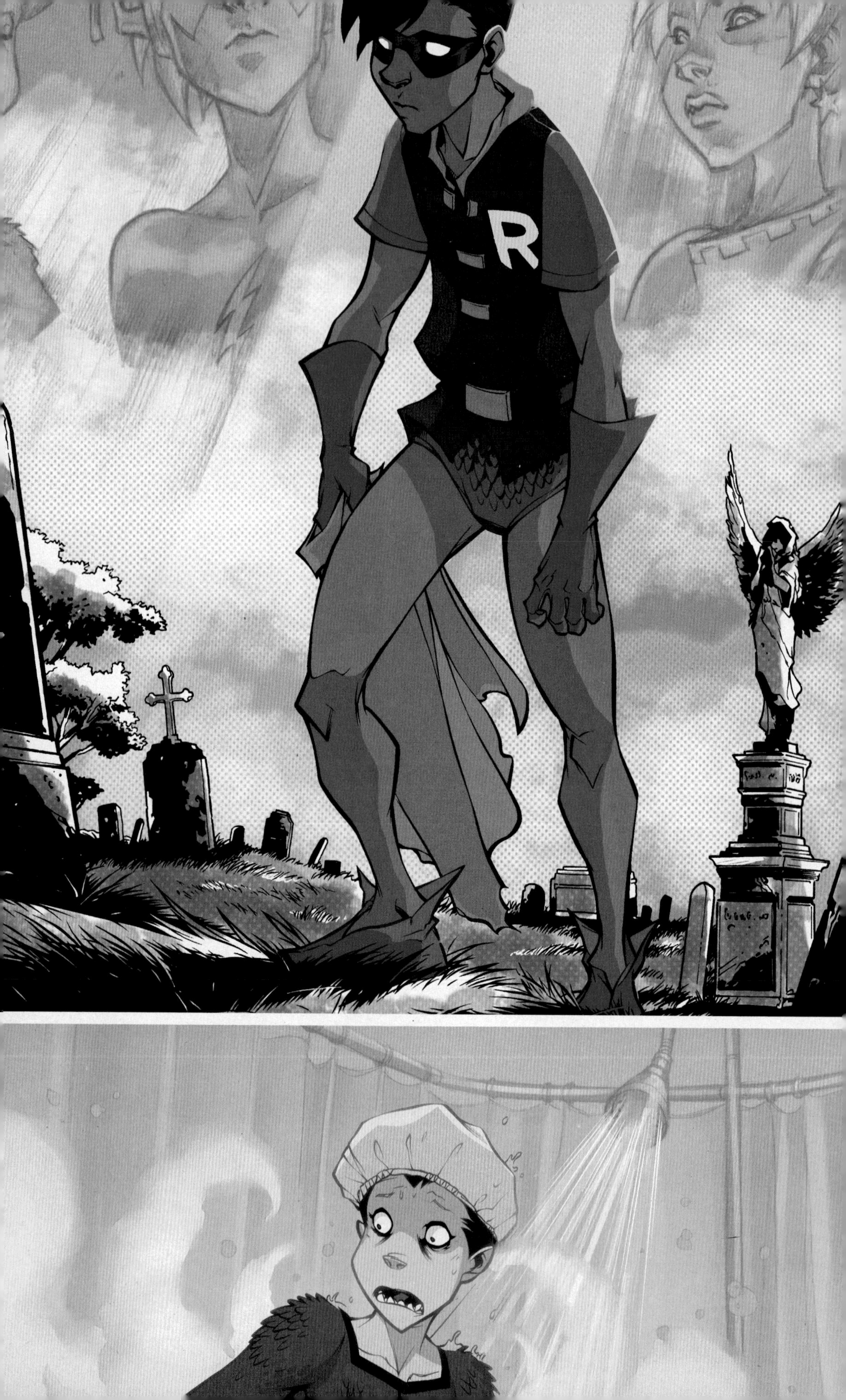

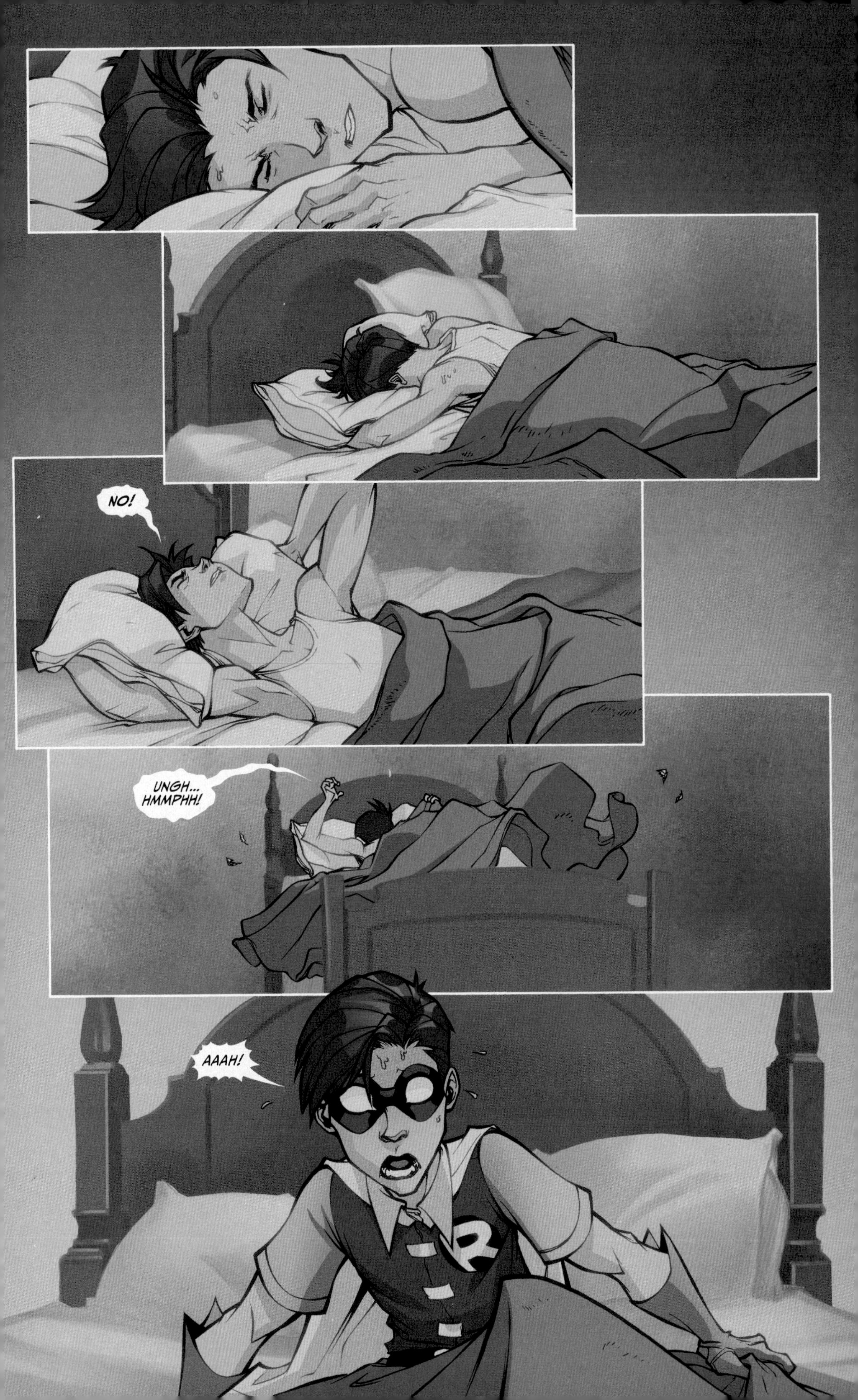
NO!
UNGH... HMMPHH!
AAAH!

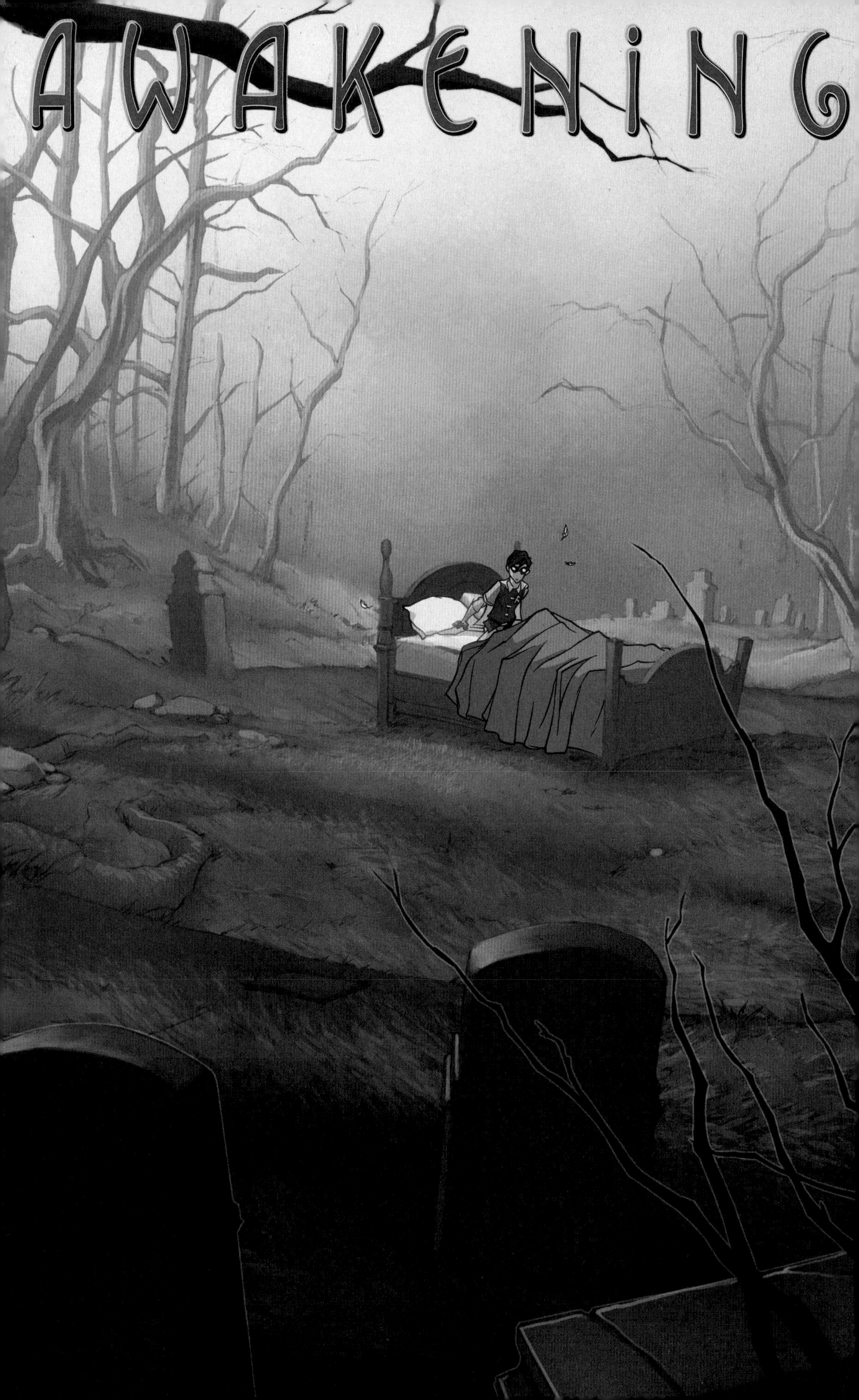
AWAKENING

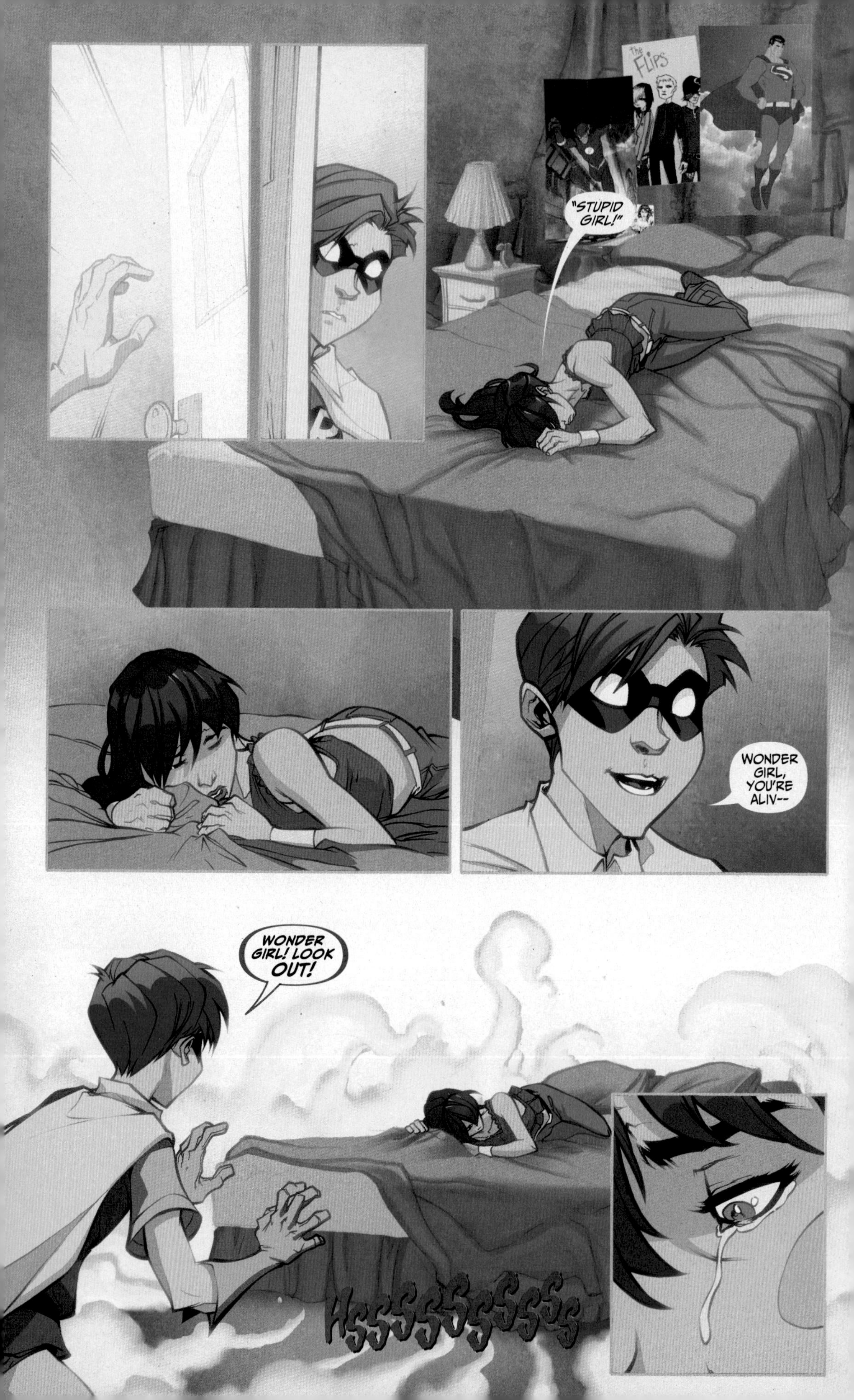
"STUPID GIRL!"
WONDER GIRL, YOU'RE ALIV--
WONDER GIRL! LOOK OUT!
HSSSSSSSSSS

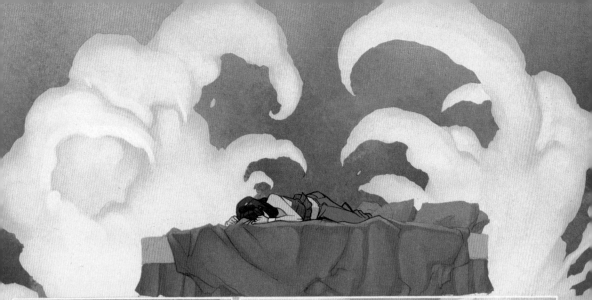

≩GASP≩

≩MMPH≩

WONDER GIRL!

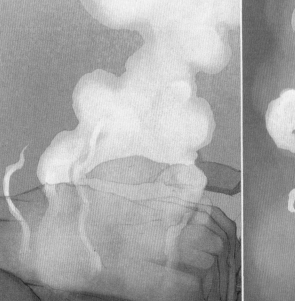

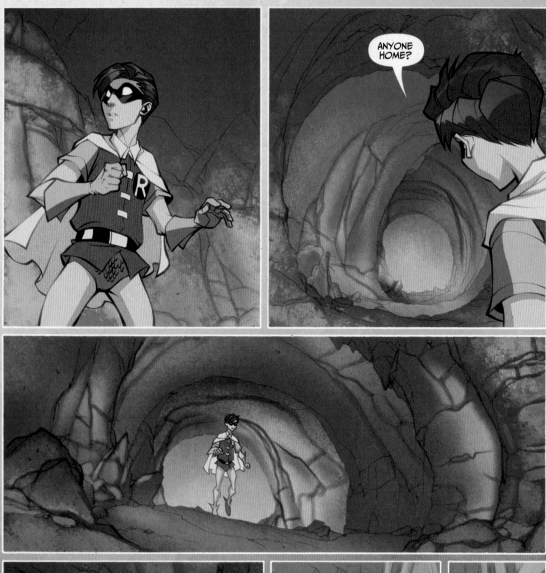

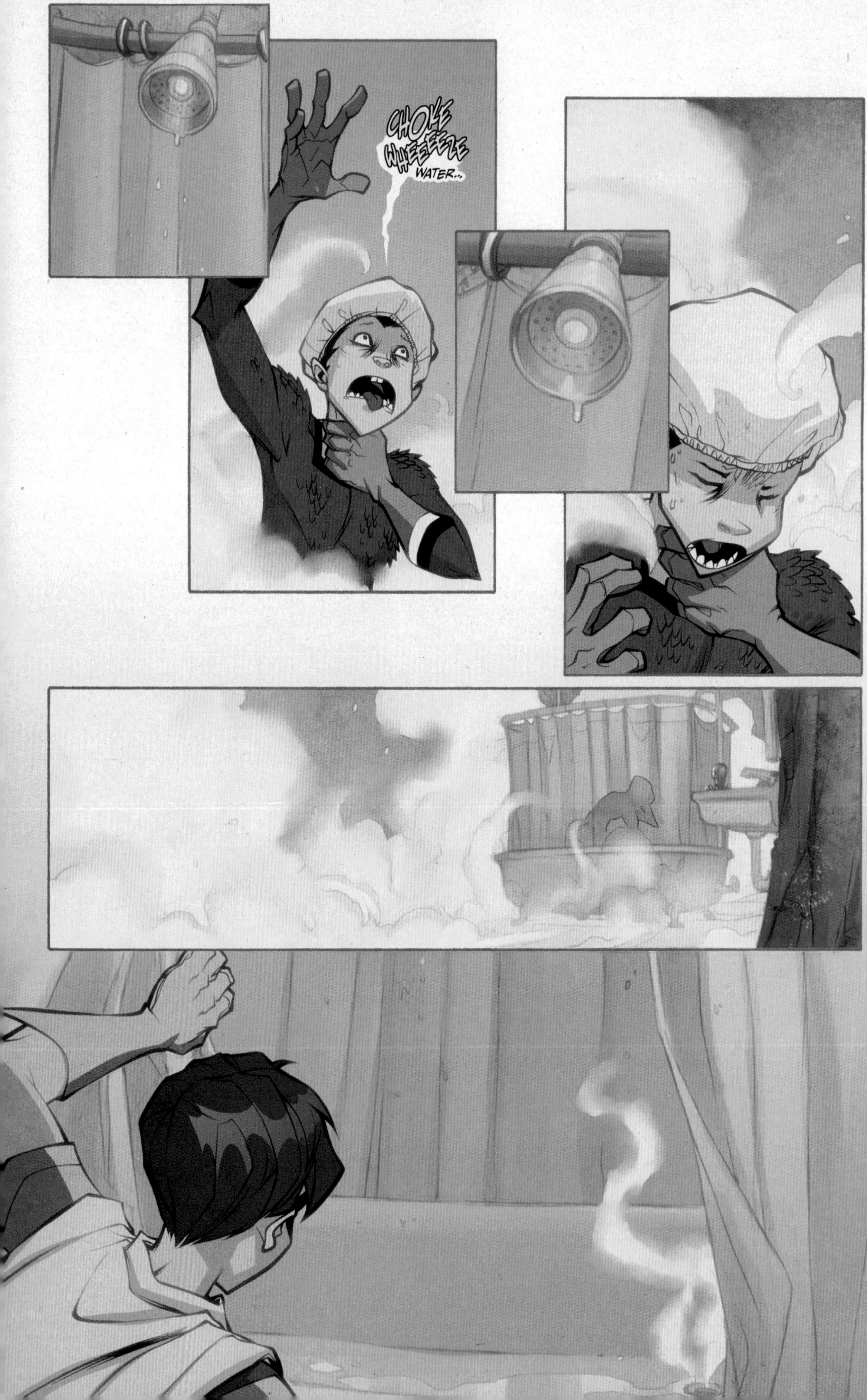
CHOKE
WHEEEEEZE
WATER...

"NO NEED TO PANIC, KIDS, I'M IN CHARGE!"

WRRRPPP

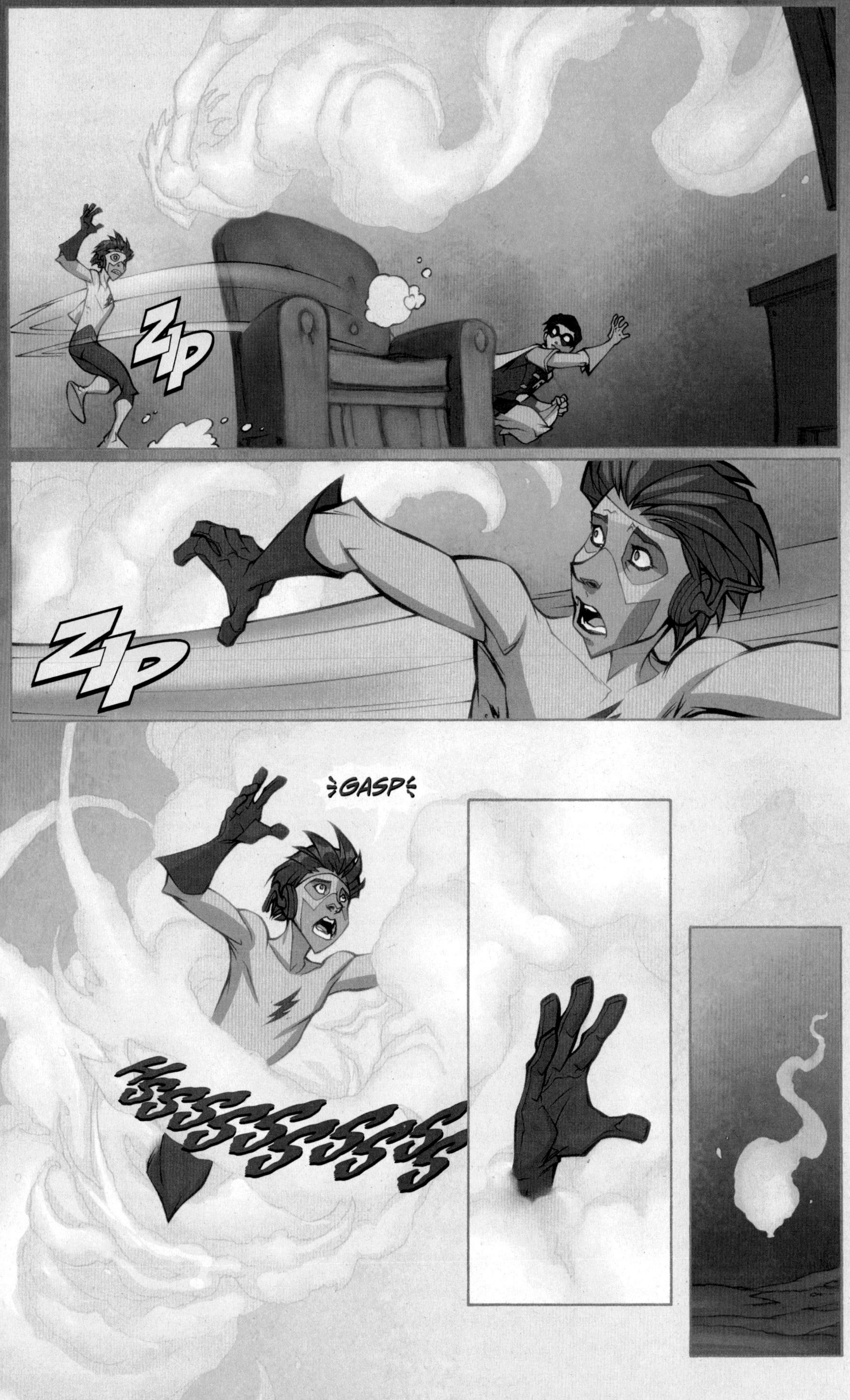
ZIP
ZIP
GASP
HSSSSSSSSS

135

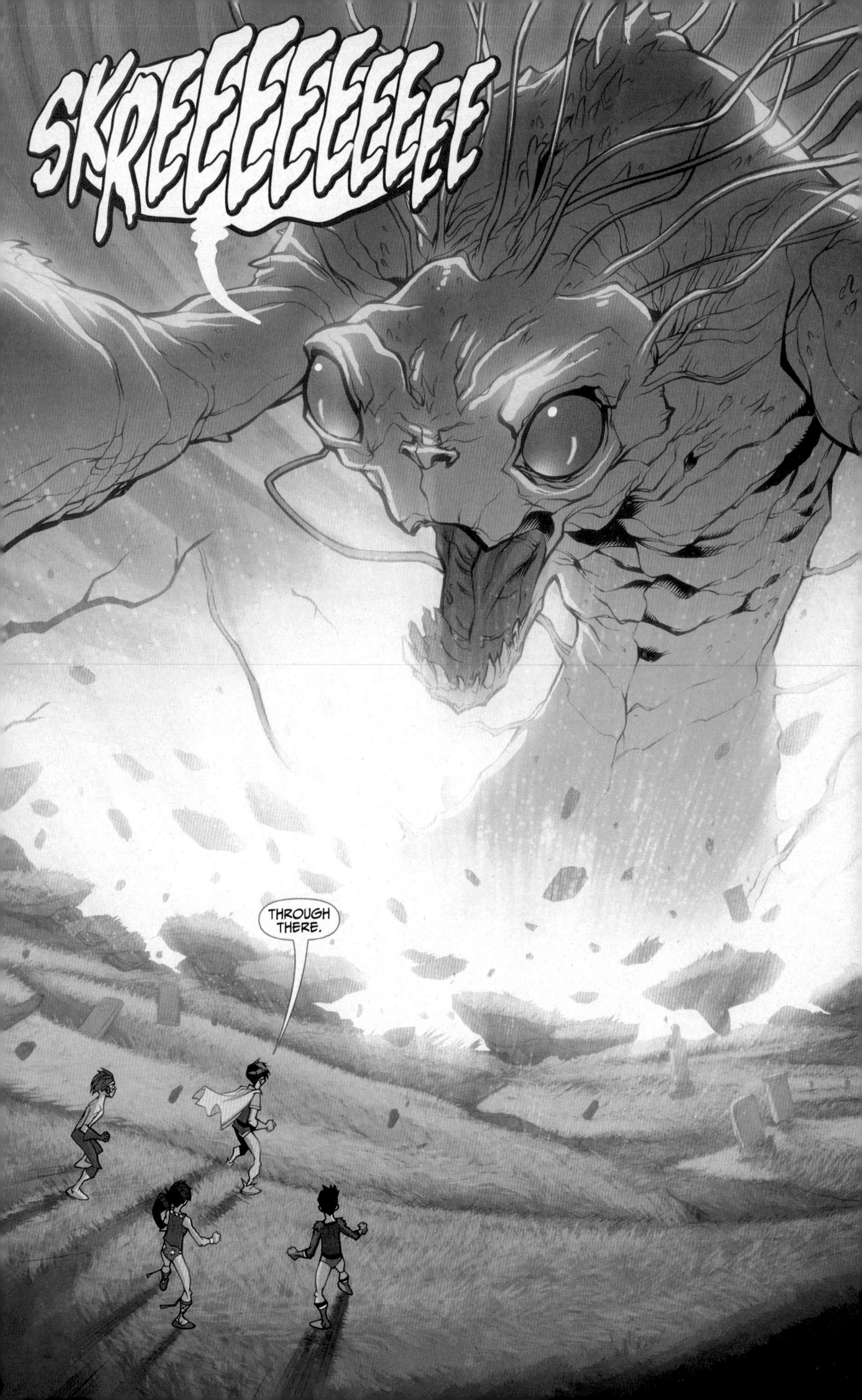
SKREEEEEEEEEE
THROUGH THERE.

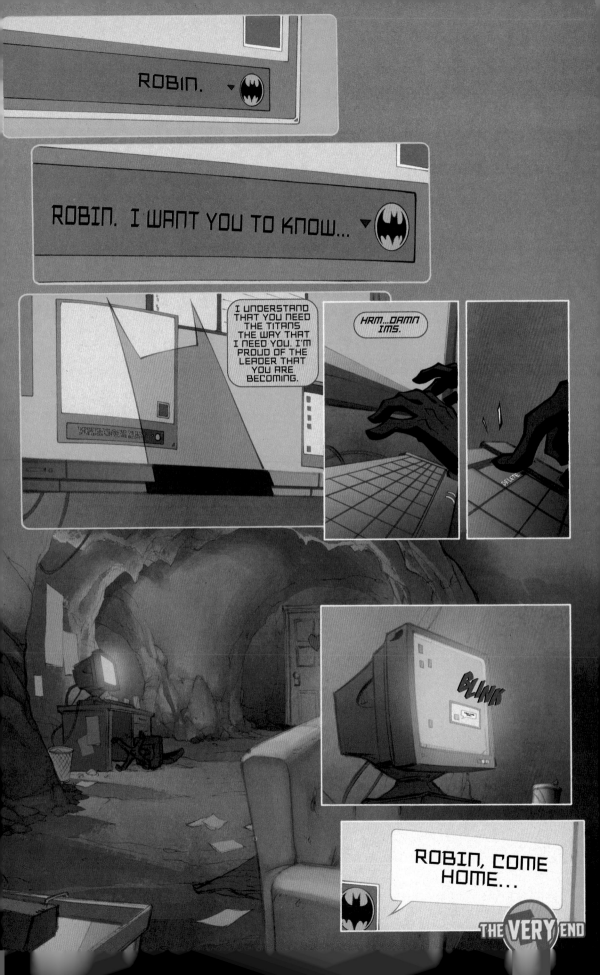

BONUS PINUP!

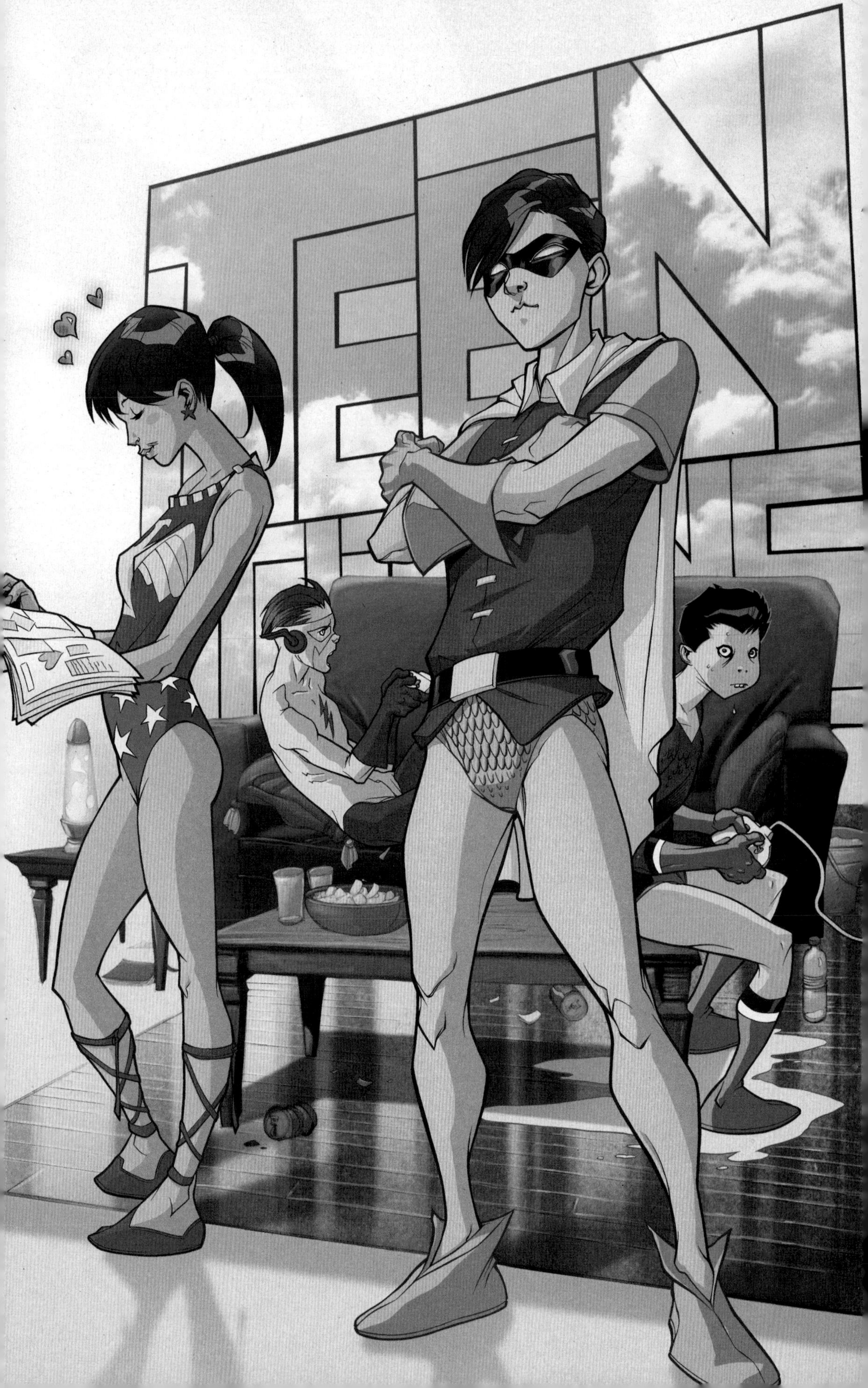